LATINOS AND NATIONHOOD

NICOLÁS KANELLOS

LATINOS AND NATIONHOOD

TWO CENTURIES OF INTELLECTUAL THOUGHT

THE UNIVERSITY OF
ARIZONA PRESS
TUCSON

The University of Arizona Press
www.uapress.arizona.edu

We respectfully acknowledge the University of Arizona is on the land and territories of Indigenous peoples. Today, Arizona is home to twenty-two federally recognized tribes, with Tucson being home to the O'odham and the Yaqui. Committed to diversity and inclusion, the University strives to build sustainable relationships with sovereign Native Nations and Indigenous communities through education offerings, partnerships, and community service.

ISBN-13: 978-0-8165-5185-9 (hardcover)
ISBN-13: 978-0-8165-5184-2 (paperback)
ISBN-13: 978-0-8165-5186-6 (ebook)

Cover design by Leigh McDonald
Typeset by Sara Thaxton in 10/14 Warnock Pro with Acumin Variable Concept

Publication of this book is made possible in part by the proceeds of a permanent endowment created with the assistance of a Challenge Grant from the National Endowment for the Humanities, a federal agency.

Library of Congress Cataloging-in-Publication Data
Names: Kanellos, Nicolás, author.
Title: Latinos and nationhood : two centuries of intellectual thought / Nicolás Kanellos.
Description: Tucson : The University of Arizona Press, 2023. | Includes bibliographical references and index.
Identifiers: LCCN 2022052450 (print) | LCCN 2022052451 (ebook) | ISBN 9780816551859 (hardcover) | ISBN 9780816551842 (paperback) | ISBN 9780816551866 (ebook)
Subjects: LCSH: Hispanic Americans—Intellectual life. | Hispanic Americans—Ethnic identity.
Classification: LCC E184.S75 K368 2023 (print) | LCC E184.S75 (ebook) | DDC 305.868/073—dc23/eng/20221130
LC record available at https://lccn.loc.gov/2022052450
LC ebook record available at https://lccn.loc.gov/2022052451

Printed in the United States of America
♾ This paper meets the requirements of ANSI/NISO Z39.48-1992 (Permanence of Paper).

As always, to the love of my life, Cristelia Pérez,
and my wonderful son, Miguel José Pérez Kanellos

CONTENTS

LATINOS AND NATIONHOOD

Introduction

Two Centuries of Latinos Pursuing and Transcending Nationhood

Latinos have resided in North America since before the arrival of the English at Jamestown and Plymouth.[1] They already lived in lands that became English colonies and later the states of the early American republic; of course, their largest populations dwelled in what became the southern and western United States, Mexico, and the Caribbean, most of which would be conquered or bought by the expanding United States during the nineteenth century. Whether before or after their incorporation into U.S. territory, the people that would in the future be called "Latinos" or "Hispanics" had a rich intellectual history, having introduced the first written European language, book culture, and universities to the hemisphere. They pondered and wrote about all the cultural and scientific themes that we think of as part of the Western tradition. They continued this rich intellectual activity in the lands that became part of the United States.

Over the course of U.S. history, Latinos thought about, struggled with, and wrote about the major philosophical and political themes of the nineteenth and twentieth centuries, including: (1) the meaning and implementation of democracy, especially through establishment of a liberal republic; (2) their democratic and cultural rights under U.S. dominion; (3) their growing sense of nationhood; and (4) the particular challenges of slavery and disenfranchisement of women in a democratic republic that had yet to realize its ideals.

From the very outset, Latinos thought about and expressed their opinions, and they penned and published philosophical, humanistic, scientific, and political discussions on all the major topics that today we consider as part of the national intellectual heritage of the United States. They did so through public speeches, books, periodicals, and classrooms; in fact, the earliest schools on the continent were missionary schools run by the Spanish friars, and the earliest imprints and newspapers in the West and Southwest were Spanish-language publications. What follows below and in the chapters of this book are stories about a few individuals who made an impact on the spread of intellectual thought, but these thinkers and activists were not alone in developing, articulating, and publishing important ideas; rather, they were members of communities of thinkers, writers, and political activists who helped them hone their ideas. Indeed, it would take volumes to adequately chart the full development of Latino thought; thus, this book is just an initial foray into a rich and complex intellectual history. In this foray, I have chosen *not* to review the thought about identity and nationhood of such giants of Latino thought as, for instance, José Martí, who was in the vanguard of so many ideas about democracy, race relations, and governance. Rather, the majority of this book is dedicated to presenting the work of lesser-known thinkers, most of whose works have been inaccessible until recently. The traditional Anglo- or Eurocentric history of the United States has consistently ignored Latino intellectual history, and especially is unaware of most intellectuals covered in this book. Today, this intellectual tradition, like that of other ethnic and minority groups, women, and the LGBTQ+ community, is key to achieving a fuller understanding of our development as a democratic nation striving for equity and the realization of ideals penned in the Constitution and its amendments. In the last three chapters of the book, I take the liberty of inserting my personal reading of three prominent literary figures from the Chicano Movement, a movement in which I have served as the most experienced editor/publisher.

The contributions of Latinos to the civilization of the Americas, including what later would become the United States, began during the period of exploration and colonization and include such legacies of American life as the technologies of farming, ranching, mining, and natural resource management. Most of these accomplishments can be attributed to mestizo culture (mixed European, African, and Native American), which arose not only south of today's border but also in the lands that would become the United States. However, the starting point for this book is properly the United States, shortly after it won independence from the British Empire and established a new form of government.

Since the days of the early American republic, Latino intellectuals have struggled to export to their countries of origin the democratic ideas learned from the U.S. Founding Fathers and the texts of the Declaration of Independence, the Federalist Papers, and the American Constitution. From the mid-nineteenth century on, under U.S. dominion, they have gone so far as to demand the implementation of these lofty concepts among minorities and the disenfranchised within the boundaries of the American republic, even as Latinos have struggled to define themselves within the American republic and to understand their relationship with the Hispanic world writ large. At first, these intellectuals from throughout the Americas, from as far away as Argentina and Peru, idealistically flocked to Philadelphia, Baltimore, and Boston to acquire this knowledge, translate it, and smuggle it to the various regions of New Spain; they did so in order to prepare for their independent nationhood, as separate from "the mother country" of Spain, and to create an ideological foundation on which to establish their own republics. As documented in chapters 1 and 2, most political thinkers were drawn to Philadelphia at the end of the eighteenth and beginning of the nineteenth centuries, not only because it was the cradle of American independence and at that time the capital of the United States, but also because it was home to numerous printers. For competitive fees, these printers made "freedom of the press" a reality for the Spaniards and Spanish American Creoles (*criollos*) whose mission it was to adapt U.S. democratic and republican principles in the political texts they would smuggle into the Caribbean and as far south as Argentina.

The Struggle to Establish Independent Nations

As Martin Luther King Jr. stated, "The arc of the moral universe is long, but it bends towards justice." The arc of Hispanic pursuit of nationhood is, indeed, long, extending from the early days of the American republic to the present. The first Spanish colony to proclaim (1810) and later gain (1821) its independence was Mexico, and numerous Mexican founding revolutionaries studied the ideas emanating from the young United States. More importantly for our book, the seeds of an independent Texas and first cradle of a "Latino" culture were broadcast from Philadelphia and sown in Texas soil precisely by one of those translators and disseminators of liberal democratic ideals: José Alvarez de Toledo (1779–1858), the focus of chapter 1, was one of the first intellectual activists to call for Cuban, Mexican, and Spanish American nationhood from the United States. A Creole born in Cuba and educated for a career as an officer in the Spanish Navy, Alvarez de Toledo was appointed to the Spanish Congress (Cortes) in exile to represent Santo Domingo during the Napoleonic occupation of Spain. Associating with the other liberal representatives from the Americas and participating in underground societies that discussed the new ideas and forms of government emanating from the United States, Alvarez de Toledo conspired with revolutionaries and went into exile in Philadelphia, where he plotted with many other such coconspirators who had migrated there from throughout the Americas. In his newspaper articles, political pamphlets, and fiery speeches, Alvarez de Toledo voiced such ideas as: "Sixteen million inhabitants occupying this delicious Continent are never represented in the eyes of the Government and Rulers in Europe, except as a horde of miserable slaves who must blindly obey whatever they are ordered to, and in profound silence kiss those same chains that they have dragged since the time of Cortez and Pizarro" (*Manifiesto* 49).[2]

As further elaborated in chapter 1, Alvarez de Toledo's particular contribution to the liberation of the Americas was to help organize an invasion of Texas and undergird it with the ideology of liberal democracy. It may seem unlikely that Alvarez de Toledo—or anyone else, for that matter—would be issuing manifestos to Mexicans from as far away as Philadelphia on the rights of the governed to select their governors and the need to establish an identity as "Mexican." However, Alvarez de Toledo conspired with José Bernardo Gutiérrez de Lara (1774–1841), a blacksmith from Revilla on the Rio Grande, to get support from the American government and business interests for the Texas Revolution, whose success was only temporary.[3]

Texican (Anglo-Texan) and Tejano (Mexican Texan) citizens finally won their independence in 1836, not from Spain, but from a newly independent Mexico. In fact, a Mexican intellectual who had participated earlier in writing Mexico's constitution and served in its Congress became the lead writer of the constitution and first laws of the Republic of Texas: Lorenzo de Zavala (1788–1836), the first vice president of Texas. Years of turmoil between liberals and conservatives followed Mexican independence, and the liberal Zavala was forced into exile in 1830. He subsequently took the opportunity to travel throughout the American republic, examining U.S. life, laws, and culture. In 1834, he published his book *Viaje a los Estados Unidos del Norte América* (Journey to the United States of North America), not only preceding Alexis de Tocqueville's celebrated *Democracy in America* (1835), but also offering a unique and often more insightful view of American democracy. Zavala was ambivalent, nevertheless, about what he saw and how it applied to the making of a Mexican nation; he wrote that the Mexicans had followed too closely the U.S. example. He was also critical of slavery in the United States (Mexico had abolished the inhuman institution shortly after its independence). In essence, Zavala, as an early transnational figure, had a vantage point to compare the American and Mexican cultures and systems of laws and governance as part of his mission to promote Mexican nationhood. He wanted to bring to the fore the best of both worlds; at the end of his book, he exhorts Mexicans to create their own nationhood precisely by choosing from both traditions. Zavala would play out this particular role in his contribution to the Texas Constitution. Further, this incipient biculturalism—after all, the Texas Constitution was bilingual—was of particular benefit to the life and culture not only of Texas but, eventually, of the United States as a whole. Bilingualism was instituted in the Southwest by the Treaty of Guadalupe Hidalgo (1848) and the subsequent state constitutions; it has not only been a basis for Latinos fending off such discriminatory actions as the English-only movement but can also be seen as a legalistic and even philosophical basis for today's bilingualism/biculturalism in education and government and the struggle for equity and acceptance of diversity as a natural right in democracies.

In writing the Mexican Constitution, Zavala had advocated a liberal, federalist government as opposed to a centralist government, one of the main issues that would later drive the Tejanos and Texicans to rebel against Santa Anna's centralized, despotic rule. He also not only advocated for property rights for Indigenous peoples and for the rights of mestizos in Mexico, but also led the effort to abolish slavery (Cleaves 32–69). Zavala moved to the northern Mexican province of Texas in hopes of fashioning a utopia (J. M. Rivera xxvii), one where biculturation (a twenty-first-century term) would help mediate the culture and politics of both Mexico and the United States. What Zavala and his fellow drafters of the Texas Constitution did, in fact, was select what was most convenient and comfortable for them from the laws of both Mexico and the United States. In Zavala's example can be seen the deep roots that bilingualism, biculturalism, and miscegenation (*mestizaje*) have in Latinos' pursuit of nationhood, so much so that the discussion of hybridity has been consistent even among today's thinkers, such as Rolando Hinojosa-Smith and Gloria Anzaldúa, who are represented in the last chapters of this book.

Latino Contributions to American Law

Spanish/Mexican laws, thus, passed into the Republic of Texas and, subsequently, into the state of Texas in 1850. They include many laws dealing with water usage, protection of the homestead, a single court system, and the definition of families and their members' rights—specific areas where Anglo-American law was seen as deficient. Aside from the many laws that govern property and water rights, the most taken for granted but far reaching are the laws regarding families. In contrast with Anglo-American law (according to which property belonged exclusively to the husband, with the wife, upon his death, receiving only life interest in one-third of his property), the Spanish legal concept of community property was codified in Texas law and eventually came to be a basic tenet for all the United States. Some scholars believe that even the right to file a joint tax return derives from the community property concept (Chipman 253; McKnight).

Numerous other concepts of Spanish/Mexican family law were incorporated into the legal code of Texas, eventually making their way into the laws of other states. Among these were the concept of common-law marriage. Children issuing from common-law marriage had to be treated as legitimate and could inherit the property of either or both parents. Adopted children, likewise, would have all the rights of biological children with regard to their adopted parents, but they could still claim rights from their biological parents. Entire books have now been written on the Hispanic legal concepts that today inform U.S. law, but few treatises have recognized the intellectuals like Zavala who foresaw and pioneered the concept of a bicultural American nation that would facilitate this type of legal *mestizaje*. Ironically, while Latinos are still struggling to establish their rights within the "American" nation, the nation itself has incorporated significant portions of their thought, if not their bodies—with full voting rights, equal treatment under the law, and recognition of refugee status, as children arriving with undocumented parents and growing up here, in popular culture representations, and more.

Latino-Led Caribbean Independence Movements from U.S. Shores

While Zavala was working on a constitution for a newly independent Mexico, in the northeast United States, Latinos from the Caribbean were still struggling for their independence from Spain. The longest lasting independence movement in the hemisphere was that of Spain's Caribbean colonies, Cuba and Puerto Rico, and much of their independence struggle and nation-building was to be plotted, funded, and written about from U.S. shores. Like their Spanish American predecessors in Philadelphia, Cubans and Puerto Ricans were learning all they could from their American hosts while also, like Gutiérrez de Lara and Alvarez de Toledo before them, seeking the sponsorship of American government officials and commercial backers.

Chapter 2 studies the intellectual contributions of one of Cuba's first and most illustrious exiles: the philosopher-priest Félix Varela (1788–1853), who founded the newspaper *El Habanero* in Philadelphia in 1824 and moved it to New York in 1825. Subtitled "political, scientific and literary paper," *El Habanero* openly militated for Cuban independence from Spain. Varela set the precedent for Cubans and Puerto Ricans of printing and publishing in exile and having their works circulate in their home islands. Varela was also among the expatriates who were actively translating American liberalism and government organization in an effort to construct the Cuban nation after independence. Despite his revolutionary writing, plotting with filibusters, and political organizing, Varela never lived to see Cuba liberated and independent; however, he did establish a solid base for the U.S. growth of Catholicism, a religion that was often scorned by mainstream thinkers and politicians in the nineteenth century.

The Struggle for Human and Civil Rights

Varela's midcentury death coincides more or less with the waning of Latin American idealism regarding the practice of liberal democracy in the United States. From the beginning of the nineteenth century, the young American republic had engaged in an expansionist program that resulted in the often-forced incorporation of formerly Hispanic lands into what was obviously becoming an American empire. From Florida to Louisiana to Texas—and culminating with the Mexican War, which wrenched away and incorporated into the United States the northern half of Mexico's sovereign territory—American expansionism was undergirded by the colonialist superiority of the Monroe Doctrine and the messianic racism of Manifest Destiny. Now, Latinos both inside and outside the United States feared for their rights and sovereignty while still struggling to make democracy a reality for themselves as newly declared American citizens in the South and Southwest, and as newly independent republics south of the border. Over time, both efforts would be connected intimately, as American neocolonialism in the twentieth century would dislodge citizens south of the border to find political and economic refuge in the United States, thus adding greatly to the country's Latino resident population and further confounding the struggle for nationhood.

Spanish-language newspapers from New York to Los Angeles became the sounding board for grievances about racial and religious discrimination against Latinos, who were often American citizens, while at the same time railing against the filibustering and imperialistic gaze that Uncle Sam was focusing on Mexico and Central America. That gaze would eventually lead to the incorporation of Cuba, Panama, Puerto Rico, and the Virgin Islands as American colonies and repeated military intervention in the Dominican Republic and elsewhere throughout the Americas. American economic expansion and foreign policy continuously produced the migration of more and more people from these areas to work in the fields and factories of the United States. Latino labor was to become just another commodity imported, like the agricultural products and raw materials imported by American companies. After the Civil War and the abolition of slavery in the United States, American agribusiness and railroad construction firms intensified their importation of cheap labor while at the same time converting the resident Mexican population of the Southwest into a proletariat.

Chapter 3 focuses on one of the first Latino intellectuals to link the internal and external effects of American expansionism and ideologies of racial superiority: Francisco Ramírez (1837–1908), who was born in Los Angeles when it was still part of Mexico. Like many other Latinos on the East Coast and in the Southwest, he was proud to become an American and looked forward to the blessings bestowed by the Constitution and the Bill of Rights. In 1855, when he was still a teenager, he founded *El Clamor Público* (Public Outcry). As the editorialist for the newspaper, he encouraged Spanish speakers to learn English, study the American Constitution, and exercise their franchise. He repeatedly demanded that the authorities honor the Bill of Rights, as well as the safeguards for property and cultural rights codified in the 1848 peace treaty with Mexico, but his indignation grew because of the disregard for the civil and property rights of Californios. He subsequently used his editorials to challenge the ideology of Manifest Destiny and its link to American imperialism, with its genocidal tendencies. He became one of the first Latinos in history to analyze U.S. imperial expansion and the threat it represented to all of Latin America—and he linked this external threat to Latin America to the oppression he and his people faced as a new minority within the United States. When Ramírez and his followers could not successfully insert themselves within U.S. nationhood, they abandoned California and crossed the southern border to create what turned out to be a failed colony.

Similar sentiments to those of Ramírez's print journalism were consistently expressed in the fiction written by the first Mexican American to write novels in the English language, María Amparo Ruiz de Burton (1832–95). A well-to-do Southern California landholder, married to a U.S. Army officer, Ruiz de Burton wrote under the pseudonym C. Loyal, which revealed neither her ethnicity nor her gender. Her correspondence evinces her lifelong opprobrium of societal limits on women, a position that has been voiced consistently by Latinas to the present. Her romance *Who Would Have Thought It?* (1872) deconstructed racial and gender relations in the northeast United States during the era of the Civil War, and her novel *The Squatter and the Don* (1885) documented how the railroad monopolies and the banks colluded to deprive Californios of their lands. Like Ramírez, she related the United States' westward expansion to its imperialist designs on Latin America. As Rosaura Sánchez states, "the space of fiction allowed the writer to address the rhetoric of liberal democracy and denounce not only imperialist practices abroad but colonialist, classist, racist and nativist policies at home" (117).

In a move that seems contemporary to us today, Ruiz de Burton indicted monopolies and corporations for the power they held over legislatures and Congress. She also criticized racial and cultural discrimination, even among the abolitionists of the North. In *Who Would Have Thought It?*, Ruiz de Burton subtly allegorized "the fall of a romantic conception of politics and the unmasking of liberal/democratic ideologies" (Sánchez 123). Thus, while attacking the real-life perversion of the nation's democratic ideals, Ruiz de Burton was already reflecting the disenchantment that was becoming widespread among Latino intellectuals, who had at first wholeheartedly embraced the exceptionalism and leadership of the United States as a true liberal democracy.

Obviously, Ramírez and Ruiz de Burton were able to achieve a bicultural perspective not only because of their bilingualism and subjugation as a conquered people, but also because they were living on the frontier, where two worldviews were clashing, revealing to them the betrayal of the "American" ideals and protections written into the nation's founding documents.

Similar clashes of the two worlds occurred throughout what would become the Southwest of the United States. Whereas writers and intellectuals such as Ruiz de Burton and Ramírez left individual written records of their struggles, in New Mexico the pursuit of nationhood was very much a collective struggle. After the printing press became accessible to many Spanish speakers with the arrival of the railroad in 1879, the territory of New Mexico experienced an explosion in the growth of print journalism in towns and small cities populated predominantly by Hispanos (their preferred identifier), even to the extent that a newspaper association was founded: La Prensa Asociada Hispano-Americana. Over the course of the next twenty years or so, beginning in the early 1890s, according to Gabriel Meléndez, the editors set about developing and popularizing a *nuevomexicano* "national" culture, which consisted of preserving the Spanish language and writing their own version of history and creative literature (58). Creating and fortifying their national identity was a positive effort to enter the union as a proud people, as well as a contestation to the aggressive racism and dispossession promoted by the doctrine of Manifest Destiny, which cast Hispanos as half-breed barbarians bereft of civilization. As Doris Meyer has stated, the Spanish-language press in New Mexico "served as a counter discourse contesting the Anglo myth of the frontier and claiming a space for otherness in American society" (110). In defense of their people, as well as property and civil rights, the Hispano editors constructed a myth that asserted that they were the original introducers of civilization to the Southwest. They chose to deemphasize Indigenous genes and cultural contributions in favor of Spanish conquistador origins (Meléndez 108–9), even reflexively looking on the Anglo adventurers coming into the territory as barbarians. Thus, like Ruiz de Burton, they too devalued their Indigenous and mestizo past, instead promoting their own "pure Spanish" origins.

Another longtime resident who was confronted with the clash of the Hispanic and Anglo worlds and was actively fighting for Cuban nationhood as well as Hispanic American solidarity was José Martí (1853–95). Unlike Ramírez, Ruiz de Burton, and the *nuevomexicanos* who were already living in colonial conditions within the United States, Martí used the United States as a base from which to fight for Cuba's independence from Spain. He benefited from the perspectives gained from living inside and outside of the

American republic and in the process came to be one of the most revered thinkers in the Spanish-speaking world. Through tireless organizational efforts in New York, Tampa, Key West, and New Orleans; through fundraising and lobbying among tobacco workers; and through penning and delivering eloquent political speeches and publishing a variety of essays in Spanish and English, José Martí was the Latin American quintessential intellectual "man of action," becoming simultaneously a leading figure in Spanish American literary modernism and a soldier fighting on the battlefields of Cuba for the island's independence.

Martí, who was born in Havana and inherited the example of Varela, lived for more than fourteen years in exile in the United States and invested his life in the cause of Cuban independence from Spain; he also attempted to create a basis for Spanish American solidarity and identity so as to present a united front against the threat of the United States. This was most eloquently represented in his essay "Nuestra América" (Our America). In New York, Martí published a newspaper, *Patria* (Fatherland), as a forum for the Cuban revolutionary movement and for his warnings against American expansionism, unmasking monopoly capitalism and demystifying liberal democracy, among many other topics. "Far from the melting pot," he explains, "the United States is a divided nation, a place of conflict and hatred on the basis of region, class and race/ethnicity; here freedom is not equally shared," and democracy is corrupted and weakened (2: 118).

Martí's extensive travels throughout the United States, observing its inner dynamics and its Native American and Afro-American minority cultures, as well as his trips through the southern hemisphere, led him to create an overall vision of life in the New World. He pressed the need for Latinos both within and outside "the belly of the beast" (by which he meant the U.S. empire) to stand firm and preserve their continental identity and sovereignty. Like all his predecessors, Martí was incensed by racism both in Latin America and in the United States. He traveled extensively in the Jim Crow South and reported on segregation and the lynching of Black people. His influential essays "Mi Raza" (My People) and "Nuestra América" envision a future without the separation of races and the vestiges of slavery (Martí 2: 298).

But, as studied in chapter 4, it was Martí's close associate the Afro–Puerto Rican Arturo Alfonso Schomburg (1874–1938) who contributed the most depth and understanding of the African racial heritage, not only in the Americas, but across the world. With only a high school education, obtained after moving to New York in 1891, Schomburg became the secretary of the Cuban and Puerto Rican revolutionary organization Las Dos Antillas (Two Antilles); he was also the secretary for Latino Masonic lodges. After the war with Spain, he became heavily involved in the African American community of New York. Schomburg soon became the greatest bibliographer of the African diaspora to that point, wrote essays, and amassed the world's largest multilingual library dealing with African culture in the United States, the hemisphere, and the world. The knowledge he collected, analyzed, and disseminated helped catalyze the Harlem Renaissance cultural movement of the 1920s and 1930s. Many Afro-Caribbeans were stigmatized because of race on the islands and on U.S. soil, but Schomburg proudly identified himself as a "Negro" and was accepted as a leader among African American artists and intellectuals. Chapter 4 also studies a number of his ideas that were originally developed and shared by a compatriot in exile and in Afro-Caribbean culture, Sotero Figueroa (1851–1923). Like Schomburg, he was an Afro–Puerto Rican whose exposure to liberal intellectual thought was as a typesetter; and like Schomburg, he wrote some of the first biographies of unheralded but distinguished Afro–Puerto Rican thinkers, activists, and teachers.

No discussion of Cuban or Puerto Rican revolutionaries or their sojourn in and contributions to Latino thought would be complete without mention of the poet, essayist, and revolutionary Lola Rodríguez de Tió (1843–1924). From an early age, Rodríguez de Tió was an activist in favor of Puerto Rican independence. She was also an abolitionist—Spain permitted slavery in Puerto Rico until 1873—as well as a promoter of women's rights. As an early feminist, she challenged the fashion of the times by wearing her hair short, like a man, and sporting high-collar blouses with a type of bow tie. More importantly, she related the education and liberation of women to the creation of nationhood (Pineda-Madrid). In response to her organizing for independence from Spain, Rodríguez de Tió was exiled three times, and she spent a long sojourn in the United States, where she collaborated with José Martí and hosted meetings of the revolutionary conspirators. In New York, Rodríguez de Tió was elected president of the Rius Rivera revolutionary club in 1896 and secretary of another activist club, Caridad, in 1897. When in 1898 the United States intervened in Cuba and Puerto Rico's war of independence, shunting aside the revolutionary leaders of both islands, Puerto Rico passed from being a colony of Spain to a colony of the United States. Refusing to return to her homeland under such conditions, she left the following year from New York for Cuba, which was afforded a greater degree of independence as a so-called republic under the U.S. right of intervention at any time. She would live as a celebrated poet and intellectual in Cuba in self-exile for the rest of her life.

Radical Organizing and Conservative Values

Once Cuba and Puerto Rico became colonies of the United States, the struggle for democratic rights by Cubans and Puerto Ricans both on the islands and on the continent continued, now focused against racial oppression on the continent and in favor of freedom and independence for the islands. In the twentieth century, an Afro–Puerto Rican brought the nationalist struggle to the forefront of the American consciousness: Pedro Albizu Campos (1891–1965). In the tradition of passionate and eloquent orators such as Martí, Albizu Campos became one of the most influential Puerto Rican political figures in the twentieth century ("Free Pedro Albizu Campos!"). He reinvigorated the independence movement through his speeches, writings, and organizational leadership and also became an outspoken critic of racial discrimination in both Puerto Rico and the continental United States. A Harvard-educated lawyer who had served in the U.S. Army during World War I, he became a member of the Nationalist Party in Puerto Rico and, in 1930, assumed its presidency. Under his direction, the party supported labor organizing and helped win several strikes, but official suppression intensified in 1936 with the killing of various leaders and the arrest of Albizu Campos for breaking U.S. sedition laws and in 1937 with a massacre of demonstrators by police. Albizu Campos was imprisoned at the federal penitentiary in Atlanta until 1943, and his U.S. citizenship was revoked. Nevertheless, when released he returned to leadership of the party. He was arrested once again, in 1950, when nationalists attacked the residence of President Harry S. Truman, but his sentence was suspended in 1953, only to be renewed in 1954, when nationalists shot up the House of Representatives. He remained a prisoner, although one who had suffered a massive stroke and was hospitalized, until his death in 1965.

In such essays and speeches as "Observations on the Brookings Institute Report," Albizu Campos indicted the despotism of the United States and its puppets within the colony's ruling class; he protested absentee landlords and the lack of self-determination of Puerto Ricans; he condemned the military presence on the island as well as the imposition of a foreign language and its exclusive use in public education; and he lambasted what he saw as a betrayal of American democratic ideals in the United States' imperial relationship with Puerto Rico. Albizu Campos equated the status of Puerto Rico to enslavement by the United States, echoing his personal heritage of being a descendant of enslaved people, which led to him being an outspoken enemy of racism. A speech that he delivered in September 1950 eloquently stated this concept:

> One cannot give a speech while the newborn of our country are dying of hunger, while the adolescents of our country are being poisoned with the worst virus, slavery. While the adults of our homeland must leave Lares (their hometown) and don't even have exit to foreign countries different from the enemy power that binds us. They must go to the United States to be slaves of economic powers, of the tyrants of our country, they are the slaves who go to Michigan out of need, to be scorned and outraged and kicked. One cannot give a speech easily while this tyrant has the power to tear sons out of the hearts of Puerto Rican mothers to go to Korea, into hell to be killed, to be the murderers of innocent Koreans. ("Pedro Albizu Campos Speech in Lares")

In "Concept of Race," Albizu Campos negated the biological and phenotypic definition of race to embrace the Spanish meaning of the term *raza* as a cultural uniting of the peoples of the world, as when through the discovery of America the bloodlines of the peoples of Europe, Africa, and the western hemisphere were blended into a cultural unity. This represented his hope that Latinos would be the example and harbinger of the elimination of racial distinctions and superiority—a sentiment foreshadowing the promise of *mestizaje*, which Gloria Anzaldúa would further half a century later. Albizu Campos added an extra step in the evolution of Martí's dream of racial understanding and integration.

The vast majority of migrants from the Caribbean (displaced by U.S. colonialism) and immigrants from Mexico and elsewhere in the Hispanic world were often recruited when manpower was needed during wars and economic expansion. They were economic refugees who brought with them their Catholic faith, traditional family values and gender roles, and a predominantly working-class motivation for improving economic and social status. This sometimes-conflictive dynamic added to and reinforced the proletarization that took place in the Southwest as former Mexican residents lost their lands and entered the agricultural, mining, and railroad construction labor force. The dynamic tension between the need to preserve family, religion, and national identities and the need to resist rampant capitalist abuse of labor was expressed wholesale by thinkers on one extreme or the other. There were those who advocated socialist and anarchist reforms, even the overthrow of the state, capital, and organized religion. Others strove to make religion and allegiance to a fondly recalled homeland the basis for preserving gender roles and the social class structures brought by Latinos into the United States. Anarchists sought to erase national allegiances, while nationalists sought to extend the homeland identity into their U.S. communities, that is, create a Mexican or Cuban or Puerto Rican nation within the United States.

Many influential Latino activists on this side foreswore national/ethnic identities in favor of uniting all working-class peoples in the world and abolishing political borders, social classes, and even government. By far, the most productive anarchist writer was not a university graduate, nor a political exile, nor someone involved in armed insurrection. Rather, this writer was a transmigrant who worked as a labor organizer in the Caribbean, Tampa, and Long Island: Puerto Rican Luisa Capetillo (1879–1922). Capetillo was largely self-educated and belonged to the working class, which women intellectuals aspired to liberate. Perhaps this partially explains her more radical embrace of anarchism's antinationalist program and its goal for a classless society in which there was absolute equality of the sexes. Born in Puerto Rico and raised by autodidactic, unwed, working-class parents, Capetillo was politicized from a young age, especially by her mother, who participated in literary and study groups often as the only woman in attendance (Valle-Ferrer 44–45). After Puerto Rico came under U.S. domination, Capetillo became active in the island's major labor union and began publishing articles in newspapers such as *Unión Obrera* (Worker Unity) (Matos xv). Capetillo became a purveyor of working-class ideologies when she joined the ranks of the most important institution for worker self-education as a *lectora*. An almost exclusively male profession in cigar factories on the island and the continent, the *lector* would read to the workers, spending half the day reading newspapers and the other half reading a variety of matter, including the works of Peter Kropotkin, Mikhail Bakunin, and other theorists of anarchism and socialism.

Capetillo's mission to educate workers as to their human rights and as to participation in the social revolution that would remake world culture was not limited to reading in factories but eventually extended to writing newspaper articles, plays, and books, including *Ensayos libertarios* (Libertarian Essays, 1909), *La humanidad en el futuro* (Humanity in the Future, 1910), *Mi opinión sobre las libertades, derechos y deberes de la mujer* (My Opinion on the Liberties, Rights, and Duties of Women, 1911) and *Influencia de las ideas modernas* (The Influence of Modern Ideas, 1916). She also founded and edited a magazine entitled *La Mujer* (Woman). In her personal life as in her writing, Capetillo was iconoclastic, refusing the authority of men, the church, and the state; deconstructing and criticizing patriotism; working for women's suffrage; and advocating free love.

Chapter 5 is an overview of the Hispanic anarchist movement in the United States, its leading thinkers, and its support of the Mexican Revolution, U.S. labor organizing, and women's politicization. This chapter also highlights the work and legacy of one woman who published newspapers, founded a center for the international worker, and penned important essays: the Colombian immigrant Blanca de Moncaleano (dates unk.), whose essay/speech "Manifiesto a la Mujer" (Manifesto to Women, 1915) encapsulated the idea that women had to take the leadership in remaking society worldwide. Chapter 6, on the other hand, reviews the persistent influence of religious institutions and conservative thinking in Latino communities. In particular, it examines the role of educated and wealthy immigrant leaders of influential print media and social organizations in promoting the ideology of *México de afuera* (a Mexican nation abroad), whose ubiquitous messages encouraged not only immigrants but also U.S. Latino citizens in the Southwest to identify with a Mexican homeland that some of them never had experienced; to protect Catholicism from what was seen as an unholy Protestant environment; and to maintain traditional gender roles so that the national identity would be socially inherited at home and uninfluenced by the liberation of women in the larger U.S. social context. Under this ideology, purity of thought and of genes was valued, while all hybridity in behavior or exogamous coupling was abhorred. There was no greater advocate for the *México de afuera* doctrine than the famed writer, editor, and orator Nemesio García Naranjo (1883–1962), although he lived somewhat of a hybrid life himself.

Perhaps a middle ground between the radicalism of a Blanca de Moncaleano and the ultraconservatism of a Nemesio García Naranjo was exemplified by intellectuals such as Clotilde Betances Jaeger (1889–c. 1970), who, out of religious practice, sought to reform the structures oppressing Latinos and women. A Puerto Rican writer, Betances Jaeger enjoyed a middle-class upbringing with enough family resources to pay for an education at Cornell University, receiving her degree in natural sciences in 1916 and later going on to earn a master's degree in religious studies at Butler University in Indianapolis in 1949. After receiving her BS and returning to Puerto Rico, Betances Jaeger began her career as a schoolteacher and columnist for periodicals in San Juan. In 1923 she moved to New York City, where she wrote for Spanish-language newspapers and magazines in the city. She would spend the rest of her life in New York, teaching and producing an important body of feminist thought, as well as religious writing, in a broad range of periodicals published not only in the city but also in Spanish America and Spain.

Betances Jaeger took the women's fashion and beauty beat as a foothold into the male-dominated media, a foothold that she subsequently transformed into a space for the exploration of feminist issues. In *Gráfico*, for which she penned more than fifty columns in 1929 and 1930, she took on issues relating to women's new role in society, especially the implications of the right to vote; the growing numbers and importance of women in the workplace; the importance of women receiving professional training; the need to free women from the bonds of marriage and move toward economic independence and even free love; a woman's control over her body, even to the extent of family planning, using contraceptives and abortion; and such political topics as the poor quality of the schools, racism in the United States and Puerto Rico, the church, American imperialism, and the colonial status of Puerto Rico and other Latin American countries (Vera-Rojas).

In her construction of a *mujer nueva* (new woman), Betances Jaeger encouraged women to participate in the economy and in politics both nationally and internationally. In her columns, she commented on city and national politics, presidential campaigns, international affairs, and war (this last of which she denounced repeatedly). She consistently advocated for women to participate in the development of the American nation, not only as voters, but as leaders. In her June 15, 1929, column, for example, she analyzed how women's liberation was intimately linked to the economy and said that in a time of crisis, like the onset of the Great Depression, it was incumbent on women to educate themselves and become consciously involved in the economy: "Woman of the heart, woman of the mind, new woman, the economy is your imminent problem, and you have to solve it. The economy of the home is part of your jurisdiction; the economy of the world is your heritage."[4]

Rather than look for foremothers in the past, as other Latina feminists had in seventeenth-century writer Sor Juana Inés de la Cruz, Betances Jaeger sought out contemporary role models of women who were seeking to free their sisters from economic subjugation and the fiction of the nation. She wrote about Spanish, Cuban, Puerto Rican authors, among others, and reviewed their books as points of departure for her own essays. While she advocated Puerto Rican independence from the United States, in the main she considered the question of women beyond the constraints of national projects and, thus, chose her models from throughout the Spanish-speaking world.

Latinos Fight for Their Country and on Their Return Home Demand Civil Rights

While Albizu Campos did everything possible to break away from the United States, another World War I veteran struggled for integration and the implementation of civil rights for his people: Alonso S. Perales (1898–1960). Across both world wars, proportionate to their population, Latinos in the U.S. armed forces received the most casualties and earned the most medals for valor. Returning home, they demanded the rights they were entitled to as American citizens, and several veterans founded civil rights organizations. It was their chance to obtain official and recognized membership in the American nation, after so many years of discrimination and the widespread perception that they were aliens. Perales (a grassroots activist and lawyer in San Antonio) and fellow veteran José de la Luz Sáenz cofounded in 1929 the League of United Latin American Citizens, a civil rights organization that is still active today and counts numerous chapters throughout the United States and Puerto Rico. An indefatigable orator and writer for more than fifty years, Perales wrote Spanish-language columns in San Antonio's *La Prensa* and other periodicals, had a radio broadcast, and published three volumes of essays and speeches, besides maintaining an active life as an unpaid lobbyist for the advancement of Mexican Americans, fighting for their constitutional rights and education. Perales insisted that Mexican Americans should retain their culture while maintaining their American citizenship (Rosales, *Dictionary* 347).[5] He led activists to participate in party politics and worked for the passage of bills in the Texas Legislature and Congress to outlaw discrimination based on race. In a plea that harked back almost a century to Francisco Ramírez, he wrote demanding respect for Mexican American civil rights and an end to segregation and such abuses as lynching:

> What we long for is the respect of our unalienable rights and privileges. We would like equality of opportunity in the various battlegrounds of life as well as before courts of justice. We would like for persons of Mexican descent in violation of the laws that govern the country to be tried before a competent Court of Justice and not to be lynched. . . . We would like to go to a theater, a restaurant, dance hall, or any other establishment whose doors are wide open to the general public, whenever we feel like it. We do not want to be ousted, as is frequently done, with the mere excuse of our racial origin. In one word, we ask for justice and the opportunity to prosper. (Perales 167)

Perales also influenced academic thought through his frequent correspondence with Carlos Castañeda, a historian credited with laying the groundwork for the recovery of Hispanic history, opening up educational opportunities for Latinos, and establishing an intellectual basis for the Chicano Movement of the 1960s. Many leaders of the movement, such as José Angel Gutiérrez, first encountered the research of Castañeda in their university classes. And, of the five most recognized movement leaders—Gutiérrez, Reies López Tijerina, Rodolfo "Corky" Gonzales, Dolores Huerta, and César Chávez—only Gutiérrez disseminated his thought on a wide scale through print, as did Castañeda.

The Legacy of the Chicano Movement

The most recent Chicano civil rights movement began in the mid-1960s, ignited by efforts to organize farmworkers in California. As intellectuals, writers, artists, and college students joined the movement over the next few years, it expanded beyond the agricultural fields to factories, schools, universities, government, and the media as an effort to define the Chicano people as a resident population that had historically and to the present suffered great racial and class discrimination. Chicanos, particularly the youth, not only took to the streets in marches and boycotts, but also sought structural reform by electing Mexican Americans to judgeships, city councils, and school boards, and even by founding a Chicano political party, La Raza Unida (United Race), spearheaded by José Angel Gutiérrez (1944–). Mexican American print journalism, magazines, and publishing houses participated in defining a cultural nationalism for Chicanos. The publishing house Editorial Quinto Sol, for example, issued journals and anthologies and even offered a national award for Chicano literature. What emerged in the intellectual sphere were university classes and ethnic studies departments, bilingual/bicultural education as a field of study and as an educational specialty, and an incipient literary canon that regarded the first three Quinto Sol prizewinning books as the models for subsequent literary and artistic development. The national Chicano imaginary that publishers and academics fostered in the late 1960s and early 1970s celebrated Indigenous Mesoamerican roots, masculinity, and a distinctive, autonomous Chicano culture in opposition to or in tension with Anglo-American as well as Mexican national culture.

The Chicano Movement leaders Reies López Tijerina (1926–2015), Rodolfo "Corky" Gonzales (1928–2005), and Gutiérrez were most influential in defining the Chicano nation. All three subscribed to and promoted the "lost land" legacy as central to Mexican American identity: the loss of ancestral lands was to define them as a people who had remained in a territory—spanning from Texas to California and as far north as Nevada and Utah—that was conquered by and incorporated into the United States. They pointed to the history of the resident Mexican population being pushed off the ancestral lands to become a proletariat in service to the new owners of ranches, farms, mines, and other producers of the wealth of today's Southwest, not to mention the subsoil wealth that was later discovered and exploited on those same lands. Tijerina, a Pentecostal minister and most radical of the three, led his followers to research and recover land grants in New Mexico and even to challenge the federal government by "taking back" portions of a national park that had been a land grant, setting up their own government there and later taking up arms and raiding the Rio Arriba County Courthouse to free their jailed members. Tijerina was apprehended and ultimately convicted of destruction of federal property and assault on a federal officer; he served a sentence of two years and left prison a much humbled and politically inactive man.

Rodolfo "Corky" Gonzales, while starting out as a Democratic political operative in Colorado, became disenchanted with the party and American government in general; largely self-educated, he researched the history of Mexican Americans and the oppression they faced as a national, colonized minority and wedded politics to culture in the movement he baptized as the Crusade for Justice. The crusade, which recruited largely among Chicano youths, promoted militant struggle but within the law and not to the extremes taken by Tijerina. Gonzales, who strongly believed in education and the power of art and literature to inspire change, was a poet and playwright himself, having penned the bilingual epic poem *I Am Joaquín / Yo soy Joaquín* (1967), which was reproduced in community and movement newspapers throughout the Southwest and was even dramatized and produced in a film version by playwright-director Luis Valdez. The poem represented Chicano identity as a composite or blending of the European and the Indigenous, the oppressor and the oppressed, and celebrated *mestizaje.*

But Gonzales went beyond poems and plays to establish Chicano Youth Liberation conferences in 1968 and 1969, the latter year producing a foundational document for the Chicano Movement: "El Plan Espiritual de Aztlán" (Spiritual Plan of Aztlán). The plan called for the youth to reject the values of the dominant Anglo-American society and its culture, and to study and forge their own culture as part of creating power in the Mexican American community, with the goal of achieving self-determination and creating their own political organizations and educational systems. The conferences and the plan—other conferences followed in subsequent years—inspired young people to return to their colleges and establish Movimiento Estudiantil Chicano de Aztlán (Chicano Student Movement of Aztlán) organizations. Importantly, the plan was one of the first documents to further the idea that the "lost land" was Aztlán, the mythical place of origin of the Aztecs, identified as the five southwestern states with the largest Mexican American population. Leading participants in these conferences were the poet Alurista (Alberto Baltasar Urista) and Luis Valdez, who in their poetry and plays became the leading advocates of the indigeneity of Chicano identity. However, the Aztec and Maya roots or inspiration for the Chicano cultural movement went far beyond the written word to populate the iconography of mural and easel art throughout the Southwest and even the music and dance of community *folklóricos*, ubiquitous to this day. This indigeneity-rooted understanding of Chicano identity has survived through the years, especially in the three decades of writing by foundational author Rudolfo Anaya, and ultimately was transformed into a new concept of *mestizaje* in the writing of Gloria

Anzaldúa. Whereas these writers and performers popularized the nationalist concept of Aztlán around the United States, Gonzales took a more separatist tack by founding in 1971 the Escuela Tlatelolco in Denver, which offered an alternative to Anglo-dominated public education. He also founded the short-lived political party Congreso de Aztlán, which influenced Gutiérrez's creation of La Raza Unida in Texas.

Gutiérrez, a well-educated Chicano with a middle-class background, was an activist from his high school and college days, being one the founders of the Mexican American Youth Organization in 1967. While allied with Tijerina and Gonzales, he nevertheless led the civil rights movement into established "American" pathways for reform rather than revolution. All the while inspiring crowds of students and demonstrators with fiery rhetoric and controversial separatist-type statements, Gutiérrez was unrelenting in his march toward the achievement of political power in order to make the Chicano nation a force to be contended with in the politics that he knew controlled education, the economy, and pretty much all aspects of life in the United States. In 1970, he founded La Raza Unida, the first viable third-party movement in American politics, and the first to be ethnically based. The party won local elections in South Texas and sporadically in other states where it spread. Gutiérrez himself was elected to the city council and later the school board of Crystal City, Texas, and served as a judge in Zavala County (1974–81). As late as 1993, Gutiérrez ran unsuccessfully for U.S. senator from Texas. Since the days of his civil rights leadership and authorship of such guides to political power as *A Gringo Manual on How to Handle Mexicans* (1974), Gutiérrez obtained a PhD and JD and has become a prolific chronicler of the civil rights and nationalist movement.[6]

As is evident from the foregoing conversation, men dominated the first phase of the Chicano Movement, even while women were actively organizing and spreading messages of national liberation. The Chicano Movement leader Enriqueta Vásquez (1930–), however, refused to subordinate women's liberation to nationalist ideology. Often unheralded because of the male-oriented politics of the movement, she was one of the first of a strong cohort of Latina feminists who for the next few decades would define and articulate women's rights as being just as important as the larger Latino community's overall struggle for legal, economic, educational, and cultural rights.

With the deep and varied experience of farmworker poverty, spousal abuse, and eventually a few community-college courses, Vásquez became one of the most influential voices to arise out of the Chicano Movement. A passion and clarity of thought characterized her weekly columns in the widely disseminated newspaper *El Grito del Norte* (Shout from the North), which was published in Española, New Mexico, from 1968 to 1973. The widely read Vásquez was in the vanguard of developing a Chicano cultural nationalism that sought to reclaim the Indigenous past while countering the overwhelming pressure for conformity exercised by the Anglo-American mainstream. She was a tireless enemy of discrimination, racism, and sexism, while seeking to mediate feminism within a nationalist ideology. "Vásquez . . . fundamentally accepted Chicano nationalism as a strategy of struggle for *raza* liberation and self-determination. She was convinced that cultural nationalism did not have to be a restrictive and constraining ideology for women. Rather, she criticized how the male construction of cultural nationalism equated tradition with women's subordination" (Espinoza 208).

Through denunciation and humor, Vásquez crafted what scholar Lorena Oropeza has called "a unique pedagogy of hope" (xxi). Vásquez's perspective, like those of Ramírez, Ruiz de Burton, Martí, and Albizu Campos before her, was international, linking the Chicano struggle to nationalist movements around the world and among ethnic groups in the United States, most importantly that of Native Americans. She directly promoted the myth of the Chicano homeland of Aztlán, which would later be taken up by Gloria Anzaldúa. Aztlán "brought us back to our beginnings. . . . It gave us a myth. . . . This made us a tribe," she has stated (qtd. in Oropeza xxxviii).

Vásquez's quest to accord women their due place in the Mexican American civil rights movement was not unique. The struggle to realize the promises of democracy and republican statehood was long and gave rise to much of the intellectual ferment of Latinos in the United States. The struggle for the rights of women was no less protracted or intense, although for most of Latino history the struggle for women's suffrage and, after the vote was won, for their equal enjoyment of *all* the fruits of citizenship was often treated as subordinate to achieving political and civil rights in the movements headed by men. Even in the nineteenth century, the strong women who helped organize the Cuban and Puerto Rican independence movements, such as Lola Rodríguez de Tió, had to devote most of their energies and writings to their countries' revolutions and nation-building, rather than their own desire for gender equity. This explains why Ruiz de Burton used a pseudonym and only openly addressed gender discrimination in her private correspondence.

In revolutionary Cuba, Lourdes Casal (1938–81) emerged as a writer and social scientist, but in her life and studies in the United States during the 1960s and 1970s, she experienced biculturation and developed approaches to the intersection of class, race, gender, sexuality, and language that only later in the twentieth and early twenty-first centuries would prevail among writers and academics (L. Lomas). She anticipated Kimberlé Crenshaw's concept of intersectionality, which views identity as the intersection of these aforementioned categories, as well as Gloria Anzaldúa's concepts of borders and *mestizaje*. In fact, Casal updated Martí's definition of "Nuestra América" by emphasizing that the true identity of the hemisphere derives from *mestizaje* and the oppressed working classes—the concept thus applied equally to racial minorities within the United States. As Laura Lomas has stated, Casal clarified that the culture of "Nuestra América" pertains to "the oppressed, in terms of class, and not in terms of geographic or national origin" (24). Casal, a respected academic who went beyond the ivy-covered walls to engage with politicians, writers, and working-class folk, wrote from her circumstance of being an Afro-Chinese Cuban lesbian in the diaspora who was an equally excellent writer in Spanish and English.

In 1974, Casal launched and edited the progressive Cuban diaspora magazine *Areíto*, which for the first time established a common ground between Cubans living outside and Cubans living on the island, conceptualizing interior and exterior colonialism and moving toward the concept of biculturalism. She was a leader in organizing the Antonio Maceo Brigade, which allowed young Cuban Americans to visit the island between December 1977 and January 1978, thus solidifying their binational identity.

A Personal Reading of Chicano Authors

At this point, I request forbearance from the reader in allowing me to insert my personal experience into this book. I was active in the Chicano and Latino civil rights movements of the late 1960s and 1970s, marching, boycotting, registering voters, training poll watchers, and acting and directing in agitprop theater groups. Given my childhood love of reading both English- and Spanish-language literature, I directly participated beginning in my twenties in the development of Latino literature and thought as co-founder and co-editor of *Revista Chicano-Riqueña*, which we published for some twenty-five years, and as editor and founder of Arte Público Press.

Founded in 1979, Arte Público Press is the oldest and largest publisher of Latino literature and culture in the United States. It has been my honor to have worked with most of the foundational figures in Chicano, Nuyorican, Cuban American, and Central American–American literature, and to have been among the earliest presenters of our literature in the major literary and academic venues. In 2019, Arte Público Press was awarded the Ivan Sandrof Lifetime Achievement Award by the National Book Critics Circle, making it one of only a few publishers to ever have received this honor. That was two years after author Rolando Hinojosa received a similar lifetime achievement award from the same association.

One might consider me the senior editor of Latino literature. I was an actor and director in the Chicano/Latino theater movement from 1969 and a historian of that movement. I have edited and published Latino authors since 1973 but have directed most of my scholarly work to recovering the Latino written legacy in documents dating back to the colonial period. I have published anthologies and reference works on that written legacy as well as two monographs on that historical literature and theater. I have witnessed the development of Latino literary criticism over the past fifty years and observed the application of various models and theories to understanding and making accessible that literature. From my vantage point as a cultural historian, I bemoan the fact that most scholars have limited their studies to the literature created from the 1970s to the present and not plumbed the depths of the two centuries of thought and expression that preceded these recent decades' work. And to my chagrin, they have at times tended to superimpose critical apparatuses and theories on these latter works, glossing over or ignoring what the writers have actually stated in their works. As an editor and publisher who is used to paying close attention to the actual words of the writers, I have been surprised at how far some interpretations range from actual author intentions and the meaning they hoped to convey in their works.

In the last three chapters of this book, as in the preceding six, I strive to understand what the writers have actually written and to believe what they say. I beg the reader's indulgence as I provide a reading of three foundational writers of Chicano literature and thought on the concept of nation. I choose these writers—Tomás Rivera and Rolando Hinojosa-Smith (both of whom I have had the privilege of publishing their entire oeuvre) and Gloria Anzaldúa—because they embody bilingualism and biculturalism as integral to their written expression and identities, and their novels and essays clearly address the question of national identity. I could have interpreted the works of Alurista, Sandra Cisneros, Tato Laviera, Alicia Gaspar de Alba, and any number of writers along these lines, but I confess a longer relationship and consequent reading experience with Rivera and Hinojosa, as well as an admiration for the absolutely original and groundbreaking thought of Anzaldúa.

Chapter 7 focuses on the thought represented in the works of Tomás Rivera (1935–84), an influential creative writer and academic whose novel *. . . y no se lo tragó la tierra / And the Earth Did Not Devour Him* (1971) was the first winner of the Quinto Sol award. It is not an exaggeration to state that this novel's publication initiated a three-decade-long pursuit by creative writers to define the Chicano nation. While this novel never employs the term "Chicano," academics and movement leaders embraced it as the primary example of defining their people by drawing from the internal strength, from the will to exist as a people, as a proclamation that working-class people have their own culture and, indeed, can write and create art. Rivera, in his essays and speeches, went on to define the Chicano nation as separate and apart from the U.S. and Mexican mainstreams, as an entity unto itself with its own language(s), folklore, spirituality, and working-class ideology.

Chapter 8 studies the thought elaborated in the works of one of the most prolific Chicano writers, Rolando Hinojosa-Smith (1929–2022), the winner of the third annual Quinto Sol award. It is with Hinojosa and his continuing novel the Klail City Death Trip, written in Spanish and English, that the theme of the U.S.-Mexican border becomes part of the discussion of nation. While many thinkers before him, such as Nemesio García Naranjo and even Tomás Rivera, did not value hybridity per se as part of identity—and of course anarchists such as Blanca de Moncaleano and Luisa Capetillo saw nationalism as divisive—Hinojosa built a system of thought based on the lived language, customs, and experiences of border residents, and in so doing rejected national constructs of any sort, refused to accept unitary definitions of ethnicity and culture, and embraced hybridity. The multiplicity of perspectives and subjectivities, nationality projects in conflict, canonizing institutions, and marginalized communities drove Hinojosa to develop a praxis of skepticism within the pursuit of ever-evasive ultimate truths.

Gloria Anzaldúa (1942–2004), another thinker from the border region, built on the ideas of nationhood in Rivera and Hinojosa as well as on the feminist writings of Enriqueta Vásquez and other foremothers. Anzaldúa elevated and extended the concept of borders, and their attendant hybridity, to other fields of study and, in the process, became one of the most influential Latino thinkers of recent years. Chapter 9 studies the development of Anzaldúa's innovative ideas, beginning with her concept of intersectionality of race, class, and gender, as well as the biculturalism of the border. In each of these categories, Anzaldúa sought to resolve binaries and oppositions in order to create a sense of what she called *mestizaje*, a hybridity. As a thinker, Anzaldúa always departed from her personal experience as a lesbian Mexican American, working-class border dweller. Whereas Tomás Rivera plumbed the depths of his community's and his own identity to connect with the rest of humanity, Anzaldúa elevated the state of in-betweenness, of hybridity, to bridge gaps and differences among people. As a creative writer, cultural and feminist/queer theorist, and healer, she sought to resolve conflicts and promote the ability to connect with wide swaths of humanity; because of the very essence of hybridity, it is possible to create a psychological wholeness in the individual and society. In practice, *neplanteras* (people who are border crossers) must be in the vanguard of social and international development. Thus, Anzaldúa has given Latino border crossers, bilingual/bicultural thinkers and actors, a vision to supplant nationalism and construct a more valid and humanistic relationship with cultures throughout the world.

Today, after some three decades of increased immigration, not just from Mexico and the Caribbean, but from Central and South America, the Latino community is much larger and much more diverse. And, in all truth, the intellectual thought and writing by Latinos in the United States has been much more diverse than can be comprehended from the above overview. Not all Latino intellectuals were or are considering questions of nationalism, gender, race, civil rights, and so on. The late twentieth and early twenty-first centuries also saw, for example, the development of scientists, engineers, economists, and others with different concerns who have had an impact on various fields, such as space exploration, medicine, physics, environmental science, and biology, fields in which Latinos have won Nobel Prizes. By the mid-twenty-first century, Latinos will make up as much as one-third of the U.S. population. Latino intellectuals will continue to envision and re-vision the nation within the context of this new demographic and cultural reality.

They will continue to contribute to knowledge in all fields of endeavor, especially as there is more access to education and more opportunity to develop intellectual pursuits. Whether they can succeed in incorporating their bilingual/bicultural identity into the nation, and whether that biculturation will lead them and the United States to more internationalist perspectives and policies, is yet to be seen.

CHAPTER 1

José Alvarez de Toledo y Dubois and Revolutionizing

One of the most perplexing and debated figures in the struggle for Mexican independence from Spain was José Alvarez de Toledo y Dubois (1779–1858), a Cuban-born Creole whose liberal ideas were tempered in the Cortes, Spain's parliament-in-exile, when Napoleon had conquered the country (all but the southern extremes of the peninsula). Alvarez de Toledo was one of the first Hispanic intellectuals in the United States to call for Cuban, Mexican, and Spanish American nationhood. Like the ideas of so many of his fellow exiles, his were influenced by secret societies in Cádiz, London, and Philadelphia and the writings of the Founding Fathers of the American republic. More than his actions and writings as a filibuster, a revolutionary, and, ultimately, a traitor, he may be considered an early representative of hybridity, of border culture and liminality, for he transcended nationhood when nations were just emerging. Perhaps this transcendence or ambivalence explains his being seen as a self-interested profiteer of conflict, distrusted by all parties, including representatives of powerful empires and the nascent republics of Texas and Mexico. He had profound transactions with and challenged the imperial authority of France, Britain, and Spain, while taking advantage of and later countering U.S. expansionist enterprises. He fought for and wrote on behalf of establishing independent republics in Spanish America, creating a pan-American confederation, and ejecting the French from the Iberian Peninsula and the French colonies in the Americas. His texts are also antecedents of the literature of Spanish American exile in the United States. He is a perplexing and misunderstood figure because, apparently, at one time or another he betrayed all of these nations and emerging nationalities.

Alvarez de Toledo was a prolific and eloquent orator, writer, and propagandist. In his dealings with government and military figures in the United States, he always presented himself as a freedom fighter planning for or engaging in revolutionizing Spanish America and the Caribbean. Despite his liberal persona, however, he was the target of suspicion and open attacks as a spy and/or self-serving mercenary in the employ of one or more of the major powers vying for control of Mexico, Texas, and the entire Gulf Coast; these included England, France, Spain, and the United States. While he appears to have spent most of his career in North America as a filibuster for the United States, under President James Madison's leadership, his final actions there seem to indicate that he was a double agent for Spain. To his credit, Alvarez de Toledo brought the first printing press to embattled Texas and published its first newspaper, *La Gaceta de Texas*, rebaptized *El Mexicano* in its second issue; his pamphleteering, issuing of manifestos, and filibustering were also the first call for Cuban independence and were indirectly responsible for the first independent republic of Texas.[1]

As tangled as was the web of intrigue being spun among the major colonial powers in North America and the Caribbean in the first decade of the nineteenth century, Alvarez de Toledo's actions were even more complex and labyrinthine. Born in Cuba to Spanish peninsular parents of noble lineage, Alvarez de Toledo was educated in Spain, rose to the rank of lieutenant in the Spanish Royal Navy, and battled against Napoleon's intervention in Spain. During this time, he developed relationships with the English, who were then allied with the Spaniards against the French; he actually commanded the *Tigre* as part of a British naval squadron (Warren 11). While joining other representatives from the Spanish American colonies in pressing for more rights and autonomy, Alvarez de Toledo became frustrated by the Cortes's rejection of liberal reforms on behalf of those colonies. A leader of the Spanish American protest, Alvarez de Toledo was accused of engaging in a plot with the English. The catalyst for his persecution by authorities and his subsequent flight, evidently, was his sending a report to his constituents in Santo Domingo on his disaffection with the Cortes and the alternative of independence from Spain; the report was intercepted and later published in the United States and circulated in the Caribbean.[2] On June 25, 1811, with the assistance of the American consul in Cádiz and the Masonic-inspired Caballeros Racionales, he fled from Spain in fear for his life. Before he left, however, the Spanish American delegation authorized him to revolutionize the northern provinces of New Spain, including Texas, and set up a government (Warren 12). Alvarez de Toledo arrived in London, where he participated in a chapter of the Caballeros Racionales, and then proceeded to Philadelphia, where in September the local chapter of Caballeros put him into contact with resident revolutionaries, such as the Mallorcan Juan Mariano Picornell (Warren 11; and see Riva Palacio López et al. 490–91; Rieu-Millán 55).

In Philadelphia, Alvarez de Toledo engaged in written polemics, publishing manifestos, letters, and his translated report in newspapers such as the *Aurora* (Dawn) (Alvarez de Toledo, "José Alvarez"). In his clear English-language prose (presumably translated by unnamed third parties), Alvarez de Toledo revealed himself to be a liberal propagandizing the two causes of liberation: Spain's shucking off Napoleon's yoke, and independence for the Spanish American colonies:

> I am moved by the fate of Spain; and . . . I suffer with her in her mortal agony, oppressed by her foreign enemies, and assassinated by that atrocious and barbarous Cádiz government, which ceases not to hasten her ruin. Above all, I desire the liberty and absolute independence of all the continent and islands of the hemisphere of Colon; I am an American, and with joy pour out my blood to contribute to this happy and glorious regeneration. These are the sentiments of my soul, and the great ideas which fill my imagination. (qtd. in Wells 75)

After meeting and conspiring with other colonial delegates to the Cortes, Alvarez de Toledo proclaimed his identity as "American," meaning a man of the Americas, and thus was an early promoter of Spanish American nationhood—a continental nation, the subsequent dream of Simón Bolívar and other revolutionists. As a Spanish American colonial activist for U.S.-inspired liberal republicanism, he won the attention of U.S. politicians and was soon on his way to Washington, D.C., to meet with Secretary of State James Monroe and President Madison. They discussed the possibility of freeing the Spanish Antilles and Mexico from Spain and forming a confederation with the United States (Warren 13). In Washington or Philadelphia, he met another freedom fighter, José Bernardo Gutiérrez de Lara, a blacksmith who had made his way to Washington from the Rio Grande Valley in pursuit of

American support for the revolutionary movement in Texas. The U.S. government and American businessmen encouraged and to some extent funded both men to conduct diverse filibustering activities.[3] However, Alvarez de Toledo's initial charge was to meet up with a U.S. representative in Havana, William Shaler, and revolutionize Cuba, Puerto Rico, and Santo Domingo. It seems, nevertheless, that Spanish ambassador Luis de Onís got wind of the mission and had authorities lying in wait for Alvarez de Toledo, which caused him to change his plans. Alvarez de Toledo would later meet up with Shaler in New Orleans and become his partner in revolutionizing Texas (on Alvarez de Toledo's motives and movements, see, esp., Dykstra; Riva Palacio López et al.; Trelles; Warren).

Manifiesto ó satisfacción pundonorosa

Through his proclamations, manifestos, letters to editors, and pamphlets, Alvarez de Toledo was one of the first Spanish Americans to establish a print culture of exile while actively providing a written ideology for the Spanish American colonies on which to base their independence movements. As would befit a guest in the birthplace of the American republic, in his first publications Alvarez de Toledo took as models the writings of the U.S. Founding Fathers, the Declaration of Independence, and the U.S. Constitution. On December 10, 1811, he published in Philadelphia the eighty-three-page *Manifiesto ó satisfacción pundonorosa, a todos los buenos españoles europeos y todos los pueblos de América, por un diputado de las cortes reunidas en Cádiz* (Manifesto, or Restoring My Honor, to All the Good Peninsular Spaniards and the Peoples of the Americas, by a Representative to the Cortes Meeting in Cádiz),[4] in which he anticipated many authors of Hispanic exile literature over the next two centuries in justifying his defection from the homeland and his taking refuge in the United States. Beyond being positioned from an "Americano" perspective, *Manifiesto*, as Kristin Dykstra illustrates (272), was a hybrid text, written in Spanish but based on the English-language print culture of the early American republic as practiced in Philadelphia. In addition to republican ideals, it is also inspired by the concept of the self-made man, especially represented by Benjamin Franklin. Alvarez de Toledo was anxious to create himself through his writings and through military action. But his typically fiery rhetoric in the oral style of a political harangue evinces his Hispanic culture,[5] as well as his class pride as an educated gentleman inciting his fellow Spanish Americans to rebellion: "Sixteen million inhabitants occupying this delicious Continent are never represented in the eyes of the Government and Rulers in Europe, except as a horde of miserable slaves who must blindly obey whatever they are ordered to, and in profound silence kiss those same chains that they have dragged since the time of Cortez and Pizarro" (49).[6]

In the pages of the *Manifiesto*, Alvarez de Toledo documents the abuses of the Cortes in rejecting the colonial representatives' list of desired reforms, including article 8, which stated that all citizens regardless of their Creole or Iberian birth, or Indian or mestizo ethnicity, should have equality of opportunity, to use today's concept (38). Thus, even from this early date, *mestizaje* is identified as a theme in Latino nation-building; the concept of *mestizaje* will continue to reappear throughout two centuries and ultimately be reimagined as transcending nationhood by Gloria Anzaldúa (chapter 9). The colonials' reasonable list of reforms was ignored and set aside by the Cortes, a fact that led Alvarez de Toledo to accuse the peninsular Spaniards of treating the colonials like *bestias* (beasts), condemning the citizens of Santo Domingo to "esclavitud y miseria eterna" (slavery and eternal misery), and subjecting these people to "leyes con estúpida insensibilidad" (stupidly insensitive laws) (53–54). Thus disillusioned, he explained, he wrote the ill-fated letter that would be intercepted and result in his persecution. In fear for his life, he also used the *Manifiesto* to take leave of his Spanish American colleagues in the Cortes and affirm his refuge in the United States: "The time had come for me to separate myself from you in order to evade the most atrocious of persecutions; and my last goodbye to that unfortunate land was interrupted by the emotional pathos of tenderness and pain. The memory of the good [peninsular Spaniards] will always be engraved in my soul with affection and respect; and that of the bad ones will serve me always as a lesson and a scandal" (74).[7]

In other parts of the *Manifiesto*, Alvarez de Toledo expressed the political strategy that would later lead him to play off one empire's interests against another's: the opportune moment was at hand for the Spanish American independence movement to take advantage of the rivalry between France and Britain, as they competed with each other for world domination (35). Also embedded in the *Manifiesto* was a separate document that on various occasions was printed as a broadside and distributed to northern New Spain and particularly to the resident population of Texas to incite revolt against

Spain. In general, this part of the document was an explicit call to all Spanish Americans to rise up in rebellion for their independence,[8] basing their mission on the rights of man and using language similar to the U.S. Declaration of Independence:

> Americans, you who inhabit the Isles and the immense continent conquered by the Ancient Spanish Empire: hear my words exhaled over the bountiful and peaceful shores of the Delaware River, exalted by the saintly love of humanity and the generous zeal for our Fatherland. Work to make happy the peoples of the New World, that it become the admiration and sweet envy of the prideful and tyrannized Europe. . . . It is incumbent upon us to sacrifice it all for the general good; and on the most purest and solid of bases construct an America that will be an immortal and admirable work for all future ages. . . . In the Constitution of the United States you can find beautiful things: select the good and avoid what may be deadly for America some day. (74–75)[9]

The heart of Alvarez de Toledo's embedded manifesto is a passionate and inspiring call to Spanish Americans to assume their responsibility for greatness:

> [Spanish] Americans: the world has placed its eyes on you; after three centuries of enslavement and ignominy, you will ascend to a sublime rank among the enlightened nations and join the place of Glory and the majestic power of ancient Europe. You have much to accomplish, but greatness is not achieved without great sacrifice, and without unalterable, generous, and superior constancy in the face of reversals and the twists of Fortune. Speed to the call of the omnipotent and august Right Hand of Providence, and remember that liberty is the most precious of all possessions; for you can never do too much to achieve it. (76)[10]

He ends his call as a Cuban who foresees the impending freedom of his homeland, like that of the entire hemisphere: "Oh sweet presentiment of liberty for my Homeland! If it becomes reality, I shall die full of joy, even if spilling all of my heart's blood to defend her rights and to terrify her enemies. This is my heart's desire; and hopefully this will also be desired by all of my brothers on the Isle of Cuba, and throughout the vast extension of the American hemisphere" (79).[11]

A second edition of the *Manifiesto* was issued in Charleston in 1812 by an attacker using the pseudonym Terso Machuca (loosely translated as "Clean Hit," "Clean Blow," or "On Target"). Machuca identifies Alvarez de Toledo as "el marte-filósofo de Delaware" (the warrior philosopher of Delaware). Machuca changed the title page from Alvarez de Toledo's original, where the long subtitle identifies the author's qualifications; instead, Machuca identified Alvarez de Toledo as "&a &a &a" (etcetera) to indicate the overblown, self-congratulatory nature of Alvarez de Toledo's presentation. The satirist then added contestatory footnotes in Spanish to the text, laughingly calling the author "the Spanish Achilles" (15) and the "Martyr of Liberty" (59), and remarking, tongue in cheek, "What a man! What extraordinary talents!" (24), "he'll be immortalized in the pages of History" (27) because of his "Quixotic adventures" (36). The satirist even went so far as to create a dramatic monologue spoken by Alvarez de Toledo's father, in which the senior bemoaned the ruin his son's treachery had visited on the family (28).

One main purpose of the anonymous deconstruction of Alvarez de Toledo's "infamatorio manifiesto" (infamous manifesto) was to demonstrate that the author was a bold-faced self-promoter and liar, as well as a coward for publishing his accusations so far away from Spain and in the safety of the United States (55). Machuca was referring not only to the *Manifiesto* here, but also to an article Alvarez de Toledo had published in Philadelphia's *Aurora* (84). On Alvarez de Toledo's exile, the commentator stated, "Spain is overjoyed by its separation from this spurious son of the Fatherland, considering him like an ulcerated and pestiferous limb" (67).[12] Machuca's last note to Alvarez de Toledo's text is a long apology for the Cortes, comparing its fair and just deliberations to those of the U.S. Congress and the British Parliament.

Alvarez de Toledo entered into another polemic on February 12, 1812, with the pamphlet *Contestación a la carta del Indio Patriota* (Answer to the Letter of the Patriot of the Indies), which he wrote in answer to a Platonic dialogue anonymously published as a gloss on the *Manifiesto.* In this anonymous work, titled *Diálogo sobre la independencia de la América Española entre un entusiasta liberal y un filósofo rancio* (Dialogue on the Independence of Spanish America between a Liberal Enthusiast and a Rancid Philosopher, 1812), a wise old "rancid philosopher" challenges the pie-in-the-sky idealism of a young liberal who has read Alvarez de Toledo's *Manifiesto.* The philosopher argues that an independent Spanish America will be easy prey for the

French, British, and nascent American empires, and accuses the rebels of being ambitious ingrates who have abandoned Spain in her hour of greatest need. He goes on to win over his young interlocutor, basically countering Alvarez de Toledo's arguments with the same language as Terso Machuca. However, he adds the charge that would stay with Alvarez de Toledo to this day: "Those who preach revolution have no other objective than to make a fortune in the middle of convulsions and the political developments in your constitution and government" (17).[13] In his *Contestación*, Alvarez de Toledo countered not only this anonymous writer but also Machuca, name-calling and imputing their sanity (22, 43), rebutting almost footnote by footnote Machuca's attack, and finally attacking Machuca's grammar and style, quoting some fourteen examples from Machuca's notes.

Mexicanos, llegado es el tiempo señalado por la Providencia

Before leaving for his adventures in Louisiana and Texas, Alvarez de Toledo had part of the embedded call in his *Manifiesto* reprinted in 1811 as a fiery broadside.[14] This broadside, titled *Mexicanos, llegado es el tiempo señalado por la Providencia para que sacudáis el yugo bárbaro [. . .]* (Mexicans, the Time Designated by Providence Has Arrived for You to Cast Off the Barbarous Yoke [. . .]), called for Mexican independence and denounced the tyranny of the Cortes. Here, the Cuban Creole Alvarez de Toledo appealed to emergent Mexican nationalism:

> Mexicans, the time designated by Providence has arrived for you to cast off the barbarous and insulting yoke that the most insolent of despotisms has ignominiously forced upon you for some three hundred years. Now that the Cádiz government has obliged you to continue dragging the same chains used by the kings of Spain to imprison you, those kings who had no authority over you except what you allowed them in governing you. . . . I advise you, oh illustrious children of the famous Montezuma, do not sheath your swords until you have established order and gained complete freedom for your country.[15]

Not only does Alvarez de Toledo acknowledge that there is such a thing as a Mexican nation, he also bases it on an Indigenous past or culture: that of the "illustrious children of the famous Montezuma." In doing so, he once again acknowledges Mexico's Indigenous past as a basis for its nationhood and also the existence of *mestizaje* as a founding principle of the nation.

It may seem unlikely that Alvarez de Toledo—or anyone else, for that matter—would be issuing manifestos to Mexicans from as far away as Philadelphia, especially given the difficulty of communications and the time lag of correspondence in the early nineteenth century. Nevertheless, this was precisely the time when Alvarez de Toledo was conspiring with a revolutionist from the Rio Grande Valley, José Bernardo Gutiérrez de Lara; documentation shows that Gutiérrez de Lara actually took copies of the manifesto with him to distribute during his invasion of Texas, with a force made up mainly of Anglo-American mercenaries and adventurers (Warren 25; see also Garret 290).[16] There is also evidence to suggest that Alvarez de Toledo penned another pamphlet, *El amigo de los hombres* (The Friend of Man), printed in Philadelphia by Blocquerst in 1812, that was distributed by Gutiérrez de Lara and his forces.[17] *El amigo de los hombres* seems to be a redraft of the call for independence, quoted above, as part of Alvarez de Toledo's *Manifiesto*.

When Alvarez de Toledo finally followed his coconspirator Gutiérrez de Lara to Texas, he recruited a Philadelphia printer, Aaron Mowry, and another pamphleteer, the Mallorcan freedom fighter Picornell from Venezuela, conscious of the need to create the propaganda that would win hearts and minds to the cause of independence. While Gutiérrez de Lara successfully expelled the Spanish forces from Texas, Alvarez de Toledo, Shaler, and other American filibusters despaired at Gutiérrez de Lara's poorly drafted constitution,[18] which announced independence not only from Spain but also from U.S. sponsorship and interests (Garrett 307). Alvarez de Toledo and Shaler, thus, plotted to wrest the newly founded Republic of Texas from his grasp and institute a government more favorable to the interests of their sponsor, the United States of America. Now thoroughly disenchanted with Alvarez de Toledo, Gutiérrez de Lara even accused the Cuban Creole of hiring assassins to kill him (Wells 59).[19] It was in part out of this effort that Alvarez de Toledo and Shaler published in 1813 Texas's first newspaper, *La Gaceta de Texas*, which would be renamed *El Mexicano* in its second number.[20] The *Gaceta* was typeset in Nacogdoches, Texas, at what is known today as the Old Spanish Fort or the Old Stone Fort, but Alvarez de Toledo and Shaler had to retreat to Natchitoches, Louisiana, before they could print it. Both issues of the newspaper proclaimed the benefits of independence but also directly attacked Gutiérrez de Lara and promised that U.S. support was forthcoming for the liberation and protection of an independent Texas. Alvarez de Toledo went to San Antonio and took over leadership of the movement, winning a battle but ultimately going down in defeat because of the infighting and factionalism of what was previously Gutiérrez de Lara's army.[21] This was the end of the briefly independent Texas, yearning for complete independence under Gutiérrez de Lara or for a relationship with the United States under the filibuster Alvarez de Toledo.

Alvarez de Toledo and Shaler, with a five-hundred-peso reward on their heads, dead or alive, subsequently took refuge in Louisiana. While in New Orleans, Alvarez de Toledo issued new proclamations in an effort once again to raise funds and recruit an army to invade Mexico, this time farther south, through Tampico (Riva Palacio López 485). This invasion never took place under his command. In 1814, he was arrested for violating the U.S. Neutrality Act, but there was insufficient evidence to prosecute him, and he was freed (Lockey 159). During this time, independence forces led by José María Morelos named Alvarez de Toledo *mariscal* (a low-ranking general) of the Northern Army, elevating him to full general in 1815. In New Orleans, Alvarez de Toledo purchased a ship, the *Petit Milan*, and delivered armaments to the rebels via Boquilla de Piedra, for operations in Oaxaca and elsewhere (Warren 128). In his role of Mexican representative to the American government and business interests, Alvarez de Toledo counseled the Mexican Congress to publish a declaration of independence and direct it to all the nations of the world, to explain and advertise the causes for the rebellion; in 1815, the Congress published such a document, the "Pururán Manifesto." He also advised the Congress to name an ambassador and other representatives to the United States and to send as much money as possible, given that in the United States, "nothing is difficult when there is money; but when there is none, nothing can be gotten" (Lemoine Villicaña 558).[22] The newly named ambassador, José Manuel de Herrera, brought with him a copy of the Mexican Constitution, drafted at Apatzingán, and had thousands of copies of that constitution printed and distributed in the United States.

Fernando VII returned to Spain and resumed his rule in 1814, taking some of the wind out of the sails of those struggling for independence, who, like Alvarez de Toledo, had used ridding the peninsula of Napoleon as partial rationale for their rebellion. After Morelos was captured and executed on

December 22, 1815, and the independence movement in New Spain found itself financially strapped, Alvarez de Toledo made a shocking decision. In 1816, he contacted Spanish ambassador Onís and prepared to make amends with the Spanish Crown and deliver intelligence about the revolution to the Spanish authorities. Harris Gaylord Warren concludes that "Toledo was first a traitor to Ferdinand VII and then to the Mexican insurgents. He served one master always, and that one was José Alvarez de Toledo" (138).

Unaware of Alvarez de Toledo's betrayal, two other revolutionary leaders, Francisco Xavier de Mina and José Servando Teresa de Mier, left London and sought to hook up with Alvarez de Toledo in either Philadelphia or New Orleans. In Philadelphia and Washington, D.C., Alvarez de Toledo did all in his power to stymie their progress, even interrupting their fundraising and recruitment of an army, but ultimately Mina prevailed and sailed off to the Gulf to revolutionize the Internal Provinces of New Spain through Soto la Marina.

By 1816, Alvarez de Toledo was engaged in a bizarre plot that Ambassador Onís had hatched to incite the British to attack the American republic. The United States had slowly but surely been eroding Spanish dominance along the Gulf Coast by supporting filibusters and rebellions and later by establishing relations with parts of the breakaway Spanish colony. From New Orleans and later Washington, Alvarez de Toledo promoted plans to invade Florida and plant the Mexican flag there, at which point Spain would sell Florida to the British—an offer that Alvarez de Toledo, representing Spain in London, would tender in person. In 1816, Alvarez de Toledo's talent as a propagandist once again swung into full force, when he published a letter in the *Louisiana Courier* and elsewhere warning of a plot hatched by Britain to take over not only Florida, but also Cuba, or at least the Port of Havana:

> The question brought forth by Spain relating to West Florida, did not originate in the cabinet of Ferdinand; its source springs from a higher and deeper authority; it may be traced to the councils and policy of Great Britain. That Spain had ceded *her rights* to the Floridas to Great Britain, no doubt exists in my mind, and that the great *maritime port of Havanna* may likewise be required and ceded to England, is highly probable.
>
> England in the possession of the Floridas and the port of Havanna, would hold in her hand the keys of the commerce of the Mississippi

> and the Mexican Gulph, and would be ready in case of necessity or policy to take the empire of Mexico into her *safekeeping*. All this and more may be attempted in this age of political miracles.
>
> If the girdle that was proposed at Ghent to encircle this country, could not be accomplished, that is no reason why Great Britain will hesitate now to plant her scepter in the vicinage of the United States.

Alvarez de Toledo closed his inflammatory letter with his patented appeal to nationalism, this time speaking to U.S. citizens:

> Americans be on your guard. Be assured that the *coalition of legitimates* of Europe are disposed for a crusade against whatever people or country that have hoisted the banner of liberty.
>
> Mexico free and independent, and allied to the United States by interest and gratitude as well as by the laws of nature, would be of more importance to the human race and the civilized world than any event that has occurred since the 4th of July, 1776. (27 Apr. 1816, original emphasis)

The complex plot, basically a hoax planned by Onís and Alvarez de Toledo, was a quixotic plan to prepare a path for the Spanish to reconquer Louisiana while enjoying British protection against U.S. filibustering in Texas and Mexico (Lockey 169–70). At least a few parties were drawn in. Joseph B. Lockey maintains that it was Alvarez de Toledo and Mina who inspired Sir Gregor MacGregor to seize Amelia Island off the Florida coast; it was all part of the plan to start a war in which "England and another European power, or powers, would be brought to the side of Spain" (163, 168).[23] Needless to say, the Alvarez de Toledo–Mina invasion never took place; Mina instead headed to revolutionize Mexico with ships purchased in the United States. Alvarez de Toledo was silent, seemingly not involved. Did this whole bogus affair place pressure on the U.S. government to possibly hasten its timetable for acquiring Florida? Lockey asserts that a number of subsequent U.S. invasions of Florida territories were the direct result of Alvarez de Toledo's machinations (176).

On July 1, 1816, Alvarez de Toledo wrote a letter to Father Antonio de Sedelia of New Orleans, requesting he serve as a messenger to Ambassador

Onís and the Spanish Crown. In the letter, he proposed his reintegration into the good graces of the king and his plan to defect from the Spanish American revolutionary effort; as part of the arrangement, Alvarez de Toledo offered not only to render service to the Crown but also to report important intelligence on the revolutionaries and their movements. By the end of 1816, news of Alvarez de Toledo's defection from the revolutionary cause was made public in a letter from the governor and captain general of Havana to Onís that was intercepted and published in Baltimore's *Country Courier* on December 9.[24] Another letter—this one written in 1818 by Onís, reviewing for Fernando VII the whole history of Alvarez de Toledo and the reasons for his re-allegiance to the throne—was intercepted by a rebel corsair, and the contents of the letter were published in the *Baltimore Patriot* (Riva Palacio López 326). His cover blown, Alvarez de Toledo went into hiding to escape from an order of execution issued by the Spanish American rebels; he hid for a fortnight in Onís's home and had no choice but to return to Spain. For all the inside information he reported about the independence movements and the parties involved in filibustering, Alvarez de Toledo was rewarded with an ambassadorship to Naples.[25] As mentioned above, Mina raised forces and financing in the United States and, following Alvarez de Toledo's example, brought Baltimore printer Samuel Bangs and his printing press along with his expeditionary forces to Northern Mexico.[26] Bangs later became a resident printer in various towns of a free Northern Mexico and eventually the first resident printer in Texas, where he issued in Galveston some of the first newspapers (see L. M. Spell).

Throughout all of Alvarez de Toledo's machinations, accusations were repeatedly made of his being a spy and collaborator, either in the employ of the Spanish, the French, the English, the Americans, or all of them at once, his seeking personal profit from the highest bidder. While meetings with Ambassador Onís, as well as with French agents and American politicians and businessmen, have been documented, Alvarez de Toledo's closest ties seem to have been to U.S. interests, and he even fought in Andrew Jackson's army against the British in the 1815 Battle of New Orleans. It was, in part, to combat some of these accusations that Alvarez de Toledo penned and published his *Manifiesto*, pamphlets, and letters to the editor. In retrospect, they should be considered as some of the first Latino texts in the United States to emerge from the borders or margins of nations intersecting, overlapping, and challenging one other. They were texts composed by an author who at various times and for diverse audiences positioned himself as one or more of the following nationalities: Spanish, Spanish American, Cuban, Mexican, and U.S. American (at least in spirit and rhetoric, and possibly employ). The implicit ambivalence and ambiguities of his biography may qualify him as one of the original border dwellers, a man on the cusp of biculturation before nations even were solidified.

CHAPTER 2

Félix Varela and the Origins of Latino Intellectual Thought in the United States

Félix Francisco Varela y Morales (1788–1853) may be considered a foundational Latino thinker, as he became the primary model for examining and discussing in print the founding principles of the American republic while actually working to establish them as the basis for Spanish American independence movements, specifically for the effort to liberate Cuba from the Spanish Empire.[1] Beyond his militancy, Varela left a foundational legacy through his long career as a priest and theologian in the Catholic Church of the United States. Varela was bilingual and published his work in either Spanish or English, depending on the audience.

Varela was born on November 20, 1788, in Havana, Cuba. At age three, Varela was sent to live with his paternal grandfather, a military commander at Saint Augustine in the Spanish colony of East Florida. At age fourteen, he entered the San Carlos Seminary in Havana to train for the priesthood. Upon becoming a priest and earning his baccalaureate in 1811, Varela began teaching philosophy at San Carlos. Over the course of time, he became known as Cuba's foremost philosopher, leading to his involvement in politics, even to his becoming elected in 1821 to the Spanish Cortes (a type of parliament in exile during the Napoleonic rule of Spain), where he met and worked with other leading thinkers from throughout the Spanish colonies in the western hemisphere; they soon would conspire for their colonies' liberation. That same year, he published a political tract that set him at odds with the monarchy, *Observaciones sobre la constitución política de la monarquía seguida de otros trabajos políticos* (Observations on the Political Constitution of the Monarchy, Followed by Other Political Writings), which sustained the idea that justice and political rights are inborn in man and derived from God. At the Cortes he proposed political autonomy for Cuba, the abolition of slavery, and support for the independence of Spanish America. Because of his political ideas, Varela had to take refuge in exile in the United States in 1823.

In Philadelphia, that same year, he founded and published one of the first exile newspapers, *El habanero: papel político, científico y literario* (Havanan: Political, Scientific, and Literary Paper); in Philadelphia and New York he also published in the historically important *El Mensajero Semanal* (Weekly Messenger), which was issued by exiled Spaniards and Spanish Americans supporting independence. In 1826, he anonymously published the first historical novel ever written in the Spanish language, *Jicoténcal,* a novel in which the narrator takes the side of the Native Americans (the Tlaxcalans) in Mexico during the Spanish conquest.[2] Varela set the precedent for Cubans and Puerto Ricans to print and publish in exile and have their works circulate in their home islands. In fact, Varela's books on philosophy and education (many of which were published abroad) were said to be the only "bestsellers" in Cuba, and Varela himself was said to be the most popular author in Cuba in the first third of the nineteenth century (Fornet 73–74)—despite there being in effect a conspiracy of silence, in which his name could not be brought up in public on the island.

Carmen A. Lamas (47–54) points out the importance of Varela's annotated translation of Thomas Jefferson's *Manual of Parliamentary Practice* (1801)—which was aimed at the double audience of Spanish Americans in the United States and those abroad—arguing that in his thirty-five notes he compared the parliamentary systems of the United States and Britain with the Spanish Cortes in order to choose the best practices and in doing so contest some of Jefferson's concepts. More salient, however, were the pains he took to articulate concepts about protecting the rights of minorities, which of course placed him squarely as a foundational figure for Latinos in the United States.

Throughout his career as a writer, theologian, and working priest who often tended to the immigrant populations in New York, Varela continued writing philosophical and theological tracts, such as his *Cartas a Elpidio* (Letters to Elpidio, 1835), on piety, fanaticism, and superstition. From 1834 to 1843, Varela co-edited the monthly *Catholic Expositor and Literary Storehouse.* He also edited the *Children's Catholic Magazine* (1838), *Young Catholic's Magazine* (1840), and *Catholic Expositor and Literary Magazine* (1841).

Varela was a leading voice in the debate over secular and religious education in the United States, and he succeeded in establishing a role for parochial schools in the country (Lamas 36–47). In 1850, Varela retired to the town of his childhood, Saint Augustine, where he died on February 18, 1853.

Luis Leal and Rodolfo Cortina, in their introduction to their scholarly edition of Varela's *Jicoténcal*, note that Varela's residence and revolutionary activity in Philadelphia were consonant with his activism for Cuban independence, given that the City of Brotherly Love had been a center for the Spanish American conspiracy for independence from Spain (xiii). Varela did not arrive in the city until late 1823 or early 1824; he was preceded there by scores of Spanish American intellectuals who had for nearly two decades prepared the ground that he would tread and expand. He followed their example of issuing from Philadelphia protests and publishing revolutionary ideas, translating and commenting on the documents that had successfully freed the thirteen colonies and allowed them to establish the United States as a sovereign republic.

The publication of books and periodicals supporting Spanish American independence by Hispanics living in exile in the early American republic began in three cities: New Orleans, Philadelphia, and New York.[3] However, the early American printers of Philadelphia were the most prolific in issuing the Spanish American tracts to support their pursuit of independence. An examination of more than one hundred books and pamphlets published between 1800 and 1820 in these cities reveals that the motive for writing and publishing many of these in the United States by Spaniards and *criollos* (Creoles) from throughout the Spanish colonies was political.[4] That is, many Spanish and Spanish American intellectuals and revolutionaries had taken up exile in the new American republic precisely to study its ideology and government institutions firsthand, in order to learn from, translate, and adapt them, and finally to export their version of republicanism and the creation of nationhood to incite or support independence movements in their homelands.

During the first two decades of the nineteenth century, numerous other revolutionists preceded Varela in utilizing American presses to issue tracts that they then smuggled into their homelands (see Kanellos, "Hispanic Intellectuals"). In the case of the Spanish exiles, their efforts at first were predominantly aimed at restoring a parliament and a liberal king in opposition to the puppet government set up by Napoleon. Colonials from as far south as the Río de la Plata, on the other hand, openly militated for liberation of their colonies from the Spanish Empire. Though their aims were opposed, colonial *criollos* and Spanish liberals associated with each other and met in secret societies to further their political plots. Also, both groups had access to the highest ranks of the American government and raised funds from American businessmen, who were usually interested in trade concessions when the new political order was established in the Hispanics' homelands (see Lazo, *Writing*).

At a time when the Spanish, French, and British Empires and the newly expansionist United States were jockeying for geopolitical and territorial advantage over one another in anticipation of revolutionary movements in the Americas, the printing press (with its use in propagandizing, filibustering, and spreading revolutionary ideology) was breaking new ground among Hispanic intellectuals, who turned to the printed word as an instrument of war and politics. Hispanic émigré writers in the United States not only studied republican ideology and governance of the early American republic, but also took up and continued the tradition, studied by Bernard Bailyn and others, of debating in print form democratic ideas in preparation for founding their nations when freed from European imperial administration.[5] Unlike the pamphleteers of the New England colonies, however, Spanish American intellectuals were in the main living in U.S. exile without a local public sphere in which to issue their books and pamphlets; rather, they engaged a community of readers and responders who were sparsely concentrated in Philadelphia, New York, and New Orleans, but mostly located in their homelands, where they could only be reached by writings smuggled to fellow colonials in Cuba, New Spain, New Granada, and points south. If Jürgen Habermas was correct in arguing that print discourse created a public sphere separate from that of the state and civil society, in which individuals could assert their autonomy and citizenship through reading and publishing and begin to imagine themselves as a nation, then the sphere of discourse that Hispanic intellectuals were creating at the beginning of the nineteenth century was immense, stretching from Cádiz and the Spanish Cortes to cells of revolutionaries operating in London, Philadelphia, and New Orleans, as well as throughout the Spanish colonies in the Americas.[6] It is hard to imagine how their published writing, spread so thin over so large a geographic and cultural area, with diverse Indigenous and mestizo communities, could duplicate the relationship of print discourse and revolution as, according to Michael Warner (3), it had developed in the geographically compact and more homogeneous population of New England.[7] Nevertheless, in battles articulated in Spanish, English, and French, books, periodicals, and pamphlets crisscrossed the Atlantic and the Caribbean; invading liberation forces were literally equipped with printing presses operated by professional printers; and revolutionary manifestos were issued on broadsides and in pamphlets to be smuggled and used for proselytizing the colonials. Expatriates from the Spanish Cortes and from as far away as Buenos Aires, Lima, Caracas, and Mexico City gravitated to Philadelphia, seen as the center of what for many intellectuals was the miracle of American democracy (see Lazo, *Letters*). They set up *tertulias* (discussion groups) and secret societies, and they raised funds from compatriots at home and abroad, as well as from like-minded American liberals and astute businessmen in the United States, for underwriting their publications and for enlisting invasion forces and the matériel of war. The Spanish and Spanish American exiles who took up residence in Philadelphia encountered a flourishing, uncensored print and publication culture. This culture had emerged with the democratic discourse in the public sphere that had helped produce the American Revolution and create the concept of the United States as an "American nation." For the most part the Spanish American exiles' early polemics in print were typeset and printed in the shops of early American printers, such as John Mowry, Thomas and William Bradford, Mathew Carey, J. F. Hurtel, and Thomas and George Palmer.

Among the books printed in Philadelphia meant for exporting American liberalism to Spanish America were an 1810 translation of the U.S. Constitution by José Manuel Villavicencio; an 1811 translation of selections from Thomas Paine's writings by Manuel García de Sena, entitled *La independencia de la Costa Firme justificada por Thomas Paine treinta años há: extracto de sus obras, traducido del inglés al español por D. Manuel García de Sena* (The Independence of the Continent Justified by Thomas Paine Some Thirty Years Ago: Selections from His Works Translated from English by . . .); an 1812 edition of John M'Culloch's *A Concise History of the United States*, also translated by García de Sena; and *Manual de un republicano, para el uso de un pueblo libre* (Manual by a Republican for Use by a Free People), issued anonymously in 1812. Other books and pamphlets sought to inspire patriotism and revolution in the Americas, such as the unsigned *El amigo de los hombres: A todos los que habitan las islas y el vasto continente de la America española; obrita curiosa, interesante, y agradable seguida de un discurso sobre la intolerancia religiosa [por] el amigo de los hombres* (The Friend of Man: For All Those Who Inhabit the Vast Continent of Spanish America; a Curious, Interesting, and Pleasurable Work Followed by a Discussion on Religious Intolerance by the Friend of Man, 1812);[8] *El triunfo de la virtud y del patriotismo* (The Triumph of Virtue and Patriotism, 1813), signed Patriota Sensible; *Diálogo sobre la independencia de la América española* (Dialogue on the Independence of Spanish America, 1812), by another anonymous author; and *El triunfo de la libertad sobre el despotismo* (The Triumph of Liberty over Despotism, 1817), by Juan Germán Roscio. Still others were printed in English and aimed at influencing U.S. policy and generating financial support for their movements: Manuel Torres's *An Exposition of the Commerce of Spanish America: With Some Observations upon Its Importance to the United States [. . .]* (1816); Manuel Palacio Fajardo's *Outline of the Revolution in Spanish America, or An Account of the Origin, Progress and Actual State of the War Carried on Between Spain and Spanish America: Containing the Principal Facts Which Have Marked the Struggle, by a South-American* (1817); *Appeal to the Government and People of the United States in Behalf of the Independent South American Provinces*, signed Anonymous (1818); and Vicente Pazos Kanki's *Letters on the United Provinces of South America, Addressed to the Hon. Henry Clay: Speaker of the House of Representatives of the U. States* (1819). In addition to promoting U.S. support, these tracts frequently promised future commercial or political advantages for the United States and its businesses.

It was Philadelphia, the seat of American independence and the first capital of the United States (until 1800), as well as the earliest seat of Masonic lodges in the Americas, that drew the greatest number of Hispanic intellectuals and revolutionaries. During the first two decades of the century, the secret Masonic society Caballeros Racionales (Rational Gentlemen), also known as Lautaro, which also had lodges in London and Cádiz, received the expatriates and furthered their communication with one another as well as with American government and business officials, who sponsored filibustering missions and probably their publications as well. The expatriates, whom Rodrigo Lazo prefers to call a "trans-American elite" (*Letters* 22),[9] ranged from José Alvarez de Toledo y Dubois, a Cuban-born former Spanish naval officer and representative for Santo Domingo in the Cortes; to José Bernardo Gutiérrez de Lara, a blacksmith from Revilla on the Rio Grande, who took it on himself to initiate the separation of Texas from New Spain; to Vicente

Pazos Kanki, a onetime advocate of a return to Inca dynastic rule (Kanki was the illegitimate son of an Aymara woman and a Spanish soldier). Among the many others who made their pilgrimage to conspire in the City of Brotherly Love were some of the most important figures in the struggle for Spanish American independence and establishment of nationhood, including Fray Servando de Teresa y Mier, Juan Germán Roscio, Vicente Rocafuerte Bejarano, and Valentín de Foronda.

Foronda (1751–1821) was an early Spanish pamphleteer in Philadelphia who, from 1801 to 1809, almost yearly issued statements on how to reshape Spanish government and politics along liberal lines (see Benavides and Rollán; Spell). While at first serving as a Spanish consul in Philadelphia, Foronda soon became a translator and promoter of the liberal ideas he encountered in the American republic. Born in the Basque region of Spain, Foronda studied in France and became a schoolteacher, known for disseminating the ideas of the French encyclopedists in Spain. He was persecuted by the Holy Inquisition between 1795 and 1798 for owning and reading prohibited books, and must have made his way to Philadelphia by 1801, when somehow he was named consul to the United States, which brought him directly into contact with some of the Founding Fathers and their liberal ideas.[10] During his years in the city, he became a member of the Philosophical Society as well as the Chemical Society of Philadelphia. As a follower of the Enlightenment and of American liberalism, Foronda had a broad base of knowledge, encompassing such fields as history, classical learning, politics, geography, science, and technology. Most of his written works reveal this broad knowledge, as well as his desire to introduce a constitutional monarchy to his homeland and build democratic institutions often based on American models. His works published in Philadelphia generally took the form of long, rhetorical letters, dialogues, and polemical essays, such as his *Carta sobre lo que debe hacer un príncipe que tenga colonias a gran distrancia* (Letter on What a Prince Who Has Colonies a Far Distance Away Should Do, 1803), in which he advised the king to free his colonies; *Cartas presentadas á la Sociedad Filosófica de Philadelphia* (Letters Presented to the Philosophical Society of Philadelphia, 1807); *Cartas escritas por Valentín de Foronda encargado de negocios y cónsul general de SMC. Fernando VII cerca de los Estados Unidos de la América septentrional relativas a lo acontecido en España* (Letters Written by Valentín de Foronda, the Business Charge and General Consul of His Majesty Fernando VII about the United States of America Related to What Happened in Spain, 1808); and *Apuntes ligeros sobre la nueva constitución proyectada por la Magestad de la Junta Suprema Española y reformas que intenta hacer en la leyes* (Quick Notes on the New Constitution Proposed by the Supreme Spanish Commission and the Legal Reforms It Intends, 1809).[11] Upon his return to the Iberian Peninsula in 1811, his liberal and constitutionalist activities intensified, until he was arrested in 1814 and exiled to Pamplona, where he died on December 23, 1821.

José Alvarez de Toledo y Dubois's ideas and publications anteceded Varela's but, for reasons explained in chapter 1, ultimately failed to provide a basis for the Spanish American and Latino thinkers to follow in the nineteenth and twentieth centuries. Nevertheless, Alvarez de Toledo should be remembered as having brought the first printing press to embattled Texas and publishing its first newspaper; his pamphleteering, issuing of manifestos, and filibustering were also the first call for Cuban, Mexican, and Spanish American independence and were indirectly responsible for the first constitution of an independent Texas. Like so many other Spanish American revolutionists, Alvarez de Toledo was a representative in the Spanish Cortes, became disaffected and steeped in Masonic thought, and escaped into exile. He made his way first to London and then to Philadelphia, where in September 1811 the local chapter of Caballeros Racionales put him into contact with such resident revolutionaries as the Aymara Vicente Pazos Kanki, the Venezuelan Juan Germán Roscio, and the Mallorcan Juan Mariano Picornell (Warren 11).[12]

Immediately preceding Varela in Philadelphia was Vicente Rocafuerte Bejarano (1783–1847). Rocafuerte had been educated in Spain and also in France, where in 1803 he met the future liberator, Simón Bolívar. He returned to Guayaquil in his home country of Ecuador long enough to be elected in 1812 to the Spanish Cortes in Cádiz, but he renounced his position in protest after King Fernando VII set up an autocratic monarchy upon his restoration to the throne in 1814. From then on Rocafuerte plotted for Spanish American independence, in league with Bolívar. He made his way to Philadelphia and, in 1821, published his treatise *Ideas necesarias a todo pueblo Americano independiente que quiere ser libre* (Necessary Ideas for All the Independent Spanish American People Who Wish to Be Free), which was written as a prologue to his translations of essays by Thomas Paine and John Quincy Adams, as well as the Articles of Confederation and the U.S. Constitution. After Mexico gained its independence and Agustín de Iturbide declared himself emperor of Mexico, Rocafuerte expressed his opposition to the tyrant in his second book, *Bosquejo ligerísimo de la revolución en Mégico, desde el grito de Iguala hasta la proclamación imperial de Iturbide* (A Brief Outline of the Mexican Revolution, from the Shout of Iguala to the Proclamation of Empire by Iturbide, 1821).[13] Upon Iturbide's fall, Rocafuerte was named secretary to the Mexican legation in London. While in London, he published *Cartas de un americano sobre las ventajas de los gobiernos republicanos federativos* (Letters by an American on the Advantages of Federated Republican Governments, 1826). His career from then on was made up of a series of political positions in Mexico and later in Ecuador, during which time he continued to write political tracts to be published in Mexico and New York. His last publications in the United States were his *Ensayo político, el sistema colombiano popular, electivo y representativo, es el que más conviene a la América independiente* (A Political Essay, the Colombian System of Popular, Elected, and Representative Government Is the Most Appropriate for the Americas, 1823) and the elementary textbook *Lecciones para las escuelas de primeras letras, sacadas de las Sagradas Escrituras* (Lessons for Grade Schools, Selected from the Holy Texts, 1823). Back in his homeland, he continued producing a body of work that served as the intellectual underpinnings of Spanish American liberalism and constitutional government, including treatises on religious tolerance (see Rodríguez O.). Rocafuerte's career had its low and high points, including a stint as a political prisoner and a term as president of Ecuador (1834–39).

A contemporary (and probably coconspirator) of Varela's in exile was Félix Megía. The future journalist, playwright, and historian was born in Ciudad Real, Spain, in 1776, into a working-class family. He nevertheless was able to obtain an education, probably at the University of Toledo, and some minor government positions. Megía was a liberal who opposed the French intervention in Spain and later was part of a conspiracy to declare in 1820 a liberal constitution in opposition to the monarchy of Fernando VII. Throughout the early century, Megía expressed his liberal ideas in his journalistic writing for such newspapers as *La Colmena* (Hive), *Periodicomanía* (Periodicalmania), and *El Constitucional* (Constitutional). He edited *Cajón de Sastre* (Tailor's Drawer), in which he published short stories and poems. In 1821, he and Benigno Morales founded an immensely popular, militantly political newspaper, *El Zurriaga* (Spanking), in favor of establishing a Spanish republic, for which Megía was jailed for almost a year, received challenges to duels and even an assassination attempt, and saw his house in Seville razed. Finally, he was sent to almost certain death at a prison in the Canary Islands, but he escaped on an English vessel and made his way to Philadelphia in 1824. In Philadelphia, he associated with the Caballeros Racionales and conspired with other Spanish American intellectuals in preparing the independence of their nations. In the City of Brotherly Love, Megía became even more productive, writing a history of the liberal revolution in Spain, a biography of his executed co-revolutionary Rafael del Riego, and biographies of William Tell and Francisco Pizarro. In order to celebrate and promote what he learned of democracy and republicanism in the United States, Megía wrote a play and published it in both Spanish and English: *Lafayette en Mount Vernon* (1825). In this play, as well as in his *No hay unión con los tiranos morirá quien lo pretenda o sea la muerte de Riego y España entre cadenas* (One Cannot Align with Tyrants, and Those Who Try Die, or the Death of Riego and Spain in Chains, 1826), Megía produced political allegory in romantic style, even personifying the liberal constitution as a woman. He also anonymously published two books attacking the Spanish monarch: *Vida de Fernando VII* (Life of Fernando VII, 1826) and *Retratos políticos de la revolución de España* (Political Portraits of the Spanish Revolution, 1826). Megía left Philadelphia in order to support the liberal war in Guatemala, where he promptly founded the newspaper *Diario de Guatemala* (Guatemala Daily) in 1827. In Guatemala, he had various offices in the liberal government until the dictator Rafael Carrera took power, and Megía escaped to Cuba and Puerto Rico in 1838. In 1841, he returned to Spain, where he died in 1853.

Except for associating with secret societies, which Varela foreswore,[14] the revolutionary priest went through the same steps as many of those liberal authors mentioned above: serving in the Cortes, escaping Cádiz, taking refuge in Philadelphia, and associating with other Spanish and Spanish American revolutionists and American government officials. In addition, he had his novel *Jicoténcal* printed in the shop of William Stavely, the same printer used by some of his predecessors and contemporaries, most notably Félix Megía. Varela even trafficked with some of the same government officials and filibusters in pursuit of American intervention and sponsorship of Cuban independence from Spain.[15] While Varela was certainly one of the most erudite, prolific, and accomplished intellectuals of his time, and was original in many of his writings, including *Jicoténcal*, the path he walked while in exile in Philadelphia and New York was well worn by the revolutionary writers and intellectuals who preceded him.

But even more salient as a forerunner of Latino dilemmas and sensibility was Varela's position between two nations and cultures, captured so well by Carmen A. Lamas:

> Varela's life and biography give voice to those who, like him, cannot return to their place of origin or refuse to do so, but who, at the same time, cannot find themselves fully at home in the world of the United States. Varela, who refused to return to Cuba and at the same time refused to take US citizenship, exemplifies the double bind of a Latina/o history that lies between political exile and social assimilation, between the possibility of natal return and immigrant belonging. Or perhaps his life exemplifies the expanded political possibilities of refusing the narrow parameters of both colonial and national delimitation. (54)

Indeed, many writers and thinkers profiled in the following chapters of this book found themselves in the same quandary and in the same interstitial space between nations. Over time, they proposed varied definitions of identity as possible solutions to their quandary, as we shall see.

CHAPTER 3

Francisco Ramírez

The Disillusionment of Embracing the Expanding American Nation

El Clamor Público (Public Outcry), a groundbreaking newspaper that voiced early Latino concerns after California had recently achieved statehood, was published in Los Angeles from 1855 to 1859 by just one man. This man read and researched diverse newspapers brought in by steamship and stagecoach, selected from their pages news items to be translated and reprinted, and gathered a small sampling of local news. He also set the type by hand himself, printed the paper, and most likely hand-delivered it. And, he forcefully, even aggressively, expressed personal opinions on the issues that he believed mattered most—or that he wanted to matter most—to his Spanish-speaking readers, made up of a diverse group of the descendants of the original Spanish/Mexican settlers of Southern California, as well as Mexican and other immigrants from the Hispanic world. Precisely because of Francisco Ramírez's Spanish-English-French trilingualism and his access to newspapers from throughout the hemisphere, he was able to develop a broad understanding of the intentions and effects of U.S. imperialism on Mexico, Central America, and the rest of the hemisphere to the south.

Like so many other frontier editors, Francisco Ramírez (1837–1908) never ceased to celebrate the U.S. Constitution and its benefits for American citizens. He looked forward to Californios reaping the benefits of American citizenship and inclusion in a nation that had instituted highly liberal ideas in its founding documents. He encouraged his readers to learn English and to learn all they could about the new government that had incorporated the formerly Mexican northern province of Alta California. But from the outset of his newspaper career, Ramírez perceived a glaring disjuncture between the rights promised to citizens and those that native Californios actually received. Among the rights that came with U.S. governance, most dear to him as a journalist, of course, were the rights to freedom of expression and freedom of the press. Those rights he tested with every issue of his newspaper.

Like many a frontier editor, he faced threats of violence and censure for the positions he took in his editorials, positions that frequently challenged the ideology of Manifest Destiny. He sought to link this ideology to American imperialism, with its attendant, rampant racism and genocidal tendencies. He censured the U.S. filibustering, territorial conquest, and expansionism that had resulted in California becoming a state—and Mexico, considered by Ramírez as "nuestra antigua patria" (our old homeland), losing half of its national territory. Ramírez did not side with the majority of frontier editors, many of whom had originated in the southern United States, on the continuation or expansion of slavery.[1] Although, like many Californios and Spanish Americans, he was usually negative toward Native Americans, he never called for their control or extermination, as did the Anglo press (see Benavides). And, of course, *El Clamor Público*'s greatest distinction of all was that it was Southern California's first Spanish-language newspaper, run solely by a native Hispanic Californian, serving his local Spanish-speaking community. While the few other newspapers publishing in the state at that time often had a Spanish-language page, no other Spanish-language periodical in Southern California existed independently of Anglo-American or French control and was solely beholden to the Spanish-speaking community.[2]

Despite its embrace of the U.S. Constitution and the system of partisan politics, *El Clamor Público* was to become an organ of resistance to the expanding American empire. As such, this very early periodical achieved a level of social and political analysis that was well beyond the years of its young editor and even beyond what Hispanic intellectuals in Texas, the Eastern Seaboard, and much of Spanish America were offering at this time. Many contemporary Hispanic intellectuals, both in the United States and in Spanish America, had just participated in liberating their countries from the Spanish imperial yoke. As documented in the previous chapters, these revolutionaries employed the ideas they had assimilated from the American Founding Fathers and the U.S. Constitution. The afterglow of the creation of the United States as the first, model republic, was still burning bright as the Spanish American republics confronted the disorder, wars, and invasions that followed the establishment of their own independence. Both Cuba and

Puerto Rico were still struggling for their liberation from Spain, relying on U.S. support, or even intervention, in one form or another.

Francisco Ramírez understood the discourse and dynamic of empire, even before the United States added an exclamation point to the era of Manifest Destiny with the 1898 economic, military, and political subjugation of peoples and territories in the Caribbean, Central America, and the far-off Pacific. What has not been fully understood about Ramírez, however, is how he struggled in his attempts to define his community, developing a national identity at the margin of the expanding American empire. He further struggled to defend it against the second wave of imperialist onslaught, which came in the form of rapid immigration from the east and the overwhelming ideology of Anglo superiority that was proclaiming all things Mexican and Hispanic as inferior, backward, mongrel, bastard, and worthy of obliteration from the face of the earth. As Ramírez himself once stated, what some Anglos wanted was for all Mexicans to have just one neck that could collectively be severed ("que los Mexicanos todos no tuvieran más que un solo pescuezo para cortárselo," *El Clamor Público*, 28 Aug. 1855).

In the early pages of *El Clamor Público*, Ramírez was not yet clear as to exactly who or what his community was. At first, he directed his efforts to the people he called "californios," "nativos californios," "la raza española," "de ascendencia española" (of Spanish descent), or "la comunidad española."[3] When he used the term *mexicanos*, he was probably referring to Mexican immigrants. *Hispano-americanos* for him referred to all Hispanic-origin peoples, both immigrants and natives. Gradually, he began to foment and promote a unity of both the natives and the immigrant *hispano-americanos*, even entitling an editorial "A Nuestros Conciudadanos Hispano-americanos" (To Our Fellow Hispanic American Citizens, 10 May 1856). By the time he closed shop on *El Clamor Público* on December 31, 1859, he included his own Californio community in what he called "Hispano-América" and "La América Española," despite its recent political incorporation within the Anglo-American empire. As José Martí would later phrase it, the Californios and "conciudadanos hispanoamericanos" were residing "in the belly of the beast." At closure of his newspaper, Ramírez stated that his mission had been "the defense of the moral and material interests of Southern California . . . at the service of my native California compatriots, generally, of all the hispano-americanos" (31 Dec. 1859).[4] Throughout the five years of his editorializing, Ramírez was wont to refer to these readers and communities in the first-person plural, using such adjectives and pronouns as "nosotros," "nuestros," "nuestro pueblo," and "nuestra raza" (14 June 1856), thus solidifying the community identity, claiming his membership in that community, and positioning his *El Clamor Público* as its voice. That Ramírez had intended *El Clamor Público* to become this site of identity formation and enunciation from the very beginning, as well as protector and defender of the Californios, is evident from his naming the paper "Public Outcry."[5] In addition, Ramírez, like his contemporaries Californio leader Pablo de la Guerra and Texan Juan Seguín, also referred to his disenfranchised group as "extranjeros en su propia tierra" (foreigners in their own land, 19 Jan. 1855).

Historian Rodolfo Acuña sees Ramírez as evolving from "an assimilationist to a nationalist" (150). However, from the beginning, Ramírez exerted resistance to Anglo-American encroachment and domination even while celebrating the U.S. Constitution and the other benefits of American liberties and rights. Throughout the years of *El Clamor Público*'s publication, he always struggled to define his community, to embrace a national identity, in the face of growing Anglo domination. Ultimately, he developed a transnational consciousness, even to the extent of promoting pan-Hispanism. During the life of *El Clamor Público* and afterward, Ramírez continuously crossed borders, territorially as well as culturally and politically, in his search for community and nation. It was an odyssey that led him to embrace the broadest Hispanic constituency possible, in opposition to the Colossus of the North.

The following discussion will trace Ramírez's intellectual journey from his opening editorial on June 19, 1855, when he addressed his readers as "¡Californios!" and "extranjeros en su propio país" (foreigners in their own country), up until his farewell of December 31, 1859, when he addressed them as "compatriotas nativos de California" (native California compatriots) *and* "todos los hispano-americanos" (all the Hispanic Americans). From the very first issue, Ramírez sought to identify and build a concept of community with Californios, people he defined as natives to California who traced their lineage back to the Spanish settlers: people "de ascendencia española" (of Spanish descent) or "raza española" (Spanish culture). Pointedly, he did not mean pure European racial stock when he employed the term *raza*, but was referring more to culture and historical antecedents. It is especially clear that he included such mixed-race Californios as Andrés Pico in this group and was aware of the extensive racial mixing (in Anglo-American terms) that made up Californio genetic history. He also defined this group by its issues, which gained frequent coverage and editorial comment, including through the reprinting of articles from the San Francisco newspapers *El Eco del Pacífico* (Pacific Echo) and *La Crónica* (Chronicle). Those issues included, first and foremost, Californios' right to life and property, which Ramírez argued not only by using the U.S. Constitution as an authority, but also by addressing the violence and lynching visited on Californios. In contesting the expropriation of lands, Ramírez challenged state and federal laws that were passed against Californio land tenure and in favor of squatters' rights and court intervention to confirm titles and land grants (intervention that favored white settlers).

As Californios were continuously dispossessed of their lands, Ramírez decried, "The people are struggling under the oppression of the judges, and so effective have been the injustices committed by them . . . what good does it do for a man to possess something, while being exposed to losing it all because of legal technicalities or the maliciousness of judges and their conspirers?" (2 Dec. 1855).[6] Referring to state laws passed to protect squatters and settlers, on April 5, 1856, he rebutted, "Here we have the licentiousness and immorality that, as of seven years ago [i.e., since the signing of the Treaty of Guadalupe Hidalgo], isolates and destroys the interests of honorable families, authorized now by a state law! Is there no limit to the arbitrariness of the strong over the weak, of the conqueror over the conquered!"[7] And on June 14 of that same year, he took on the legislature frontally: "a legislature as hungry as it is unjust has decreed that all the lands will be considered public property. . . . Can there be a more bald-faced affront to the solemn treaty of Hidalgo!"[8] He continued: "Many of the elder Californios who some six years ago saw themselves tranquilly enjoying the ownership of the lands left to them by their parents now see themselves in the most lamentable poverty and indigence because of the litigation they have been subjected to in order to prove their land titles."[9]

Ramírez also crusaded for division of California into two states to ensure the political and economic power that would accrue to the denser Californio population in Southern California. The issue was also related to taxation, with those in Southern California paying up to thirty-five times more taxes per person than those living in the northern counties, which also had more legislators in the state assembly; the inequity resulted from the high tax assessment placed on heads of cattle, the major economic base of Southern California (Romo 24).

Ramírez did not take on Protestantism, though he repeatedly covered Catholic Church news and festivities and penned scathing editorials against the Mormons, warning of their politics and cultural influence. As important as were language and Hispanic culture in defining his community, it was the ancestral territory and legal treaties, he believed, that could not be contravened as the basis for his people's existence and rights. Thus, Ramírez also based the definition of his people on the rights vouchsafed by the 1848 Treaty of Guadalupe Hidalgo, which ended the war between the United States and Mexico and ensured the rights of Californios, and all Mexican inhabitants of the ceded territories, to American citizenship and protection of their civil and property rights. In an 1856 editorial commemorating Mexican Independence Day (for which he once again reviewed Californio history), he not only made reference to this treaty but also made a rare early reference to his people as "Mexicans": "Mexicans! The time has now come for us to show the entire world that we merit the land on which we were born. More than any other people, we have certain indisputable rights in the nation where we now live. The Treaty of Guadalupe Hidalgo has conceded to us broad privileges to freely enjoy our rights and property" (27 Sept. 1856).[10]

Ramírez's Californio readership and community, thus, were initially defined by heritage, language, American citizenship, religion, treaty, territory, and land tenure. In his editorial "La Guerra de las Razas" (The Culture War, 5 Sept. 1855), Ramírez warned against reducing the Californio and Hispanic issues to a conflict of them and us, Anglo versus Hispanic. In many of his other columns, however, he blamed Anglo and European adventurers and criminals—in addition to state legislators, U.S. congressmen, and presidents of the United States—for the dispossession and ill-treatment of Californios.[11] This constant threat coming from outside the conceptual domain and rights inherited by Californios also helped Ramírez define what Benedict Anderson would call his "imagined nation," a community that he characterized as under siege on the newspaper's first anniversary: "we [i.e., the newspaper, or Ramírez himself] have mainly endeavored to serve as an organ serving the general sentiments in order to manifest the atrocious injuries suffered by the raza española in this country, where they were born and in which they see themselves in a status lower than even their most unfortunate persecutors" (14 June 1856).[12]

In the course of publishing *El Clamor Público*, Ramírez continuously broadened his view to recognize the conditions that Californios shared with

Hispanic immigrants—a population made up principally of Mexicans, Chileans, Peruvians, and Nicaraguans—and to evolve an understanding and an ideological posture that were more representative of colonial resistance to expanding imperial power. A defense of Spanish American immigrants would even drive Ramírez to crusade against the Know-Nothing Party and its virulent nativism: "Since the appearance of Know-Nothingism in U.S. politics, foreign immigration has decreased considerably" (2 Aug. 1856).[13] His calls for unity among the diverse groups in the Hispanic population became more frequent and desperate in order to try to assume some power, at least through voting and electing better representation (e.g., 16 Aug. 1855).

Ramírez was acutely aware that American filibustering had played a great role in Mexico's loss of its northern territory and that continued filibustering threatened to dislodge additional large segments from the Mexican nation. As early as March 10, 1855, *El Clamor Público* published a reprint from the *Buffalo Patriot* discussing the feasibility of annexing perhaps all of Mexico and policing the subjugated population. Ramírez was actively attempting to raise the level of consciousness of his readers as to the modus operandi of U.S. imperialism: filibustering missions in advance of revolutionary, separatist, and independence movements financed by U.S. business and government interests, and, finally, annexation to the United States. He stated, "Our readers ill understand why I make these observations about how these filibustering expeditions are organized in the United States of America. First of all, they were going to alienate a portion of Canada—then Texas and other parts of Mexico—and finally Cuba. Now, Nicaragua is in their sights and ambition" (19 Apr. 1856).[14] In fact, the United States had supported Cuba's revolutionary movements and had even tendered offers to buy Cuba from Spain to annex the island as a slave state—the subject of a later Ramírez blast against President James Buchanan (24 Oct. 1857; and see Lazo, *Writing*). But in his attacks on U.S. filibustering, Ramírez devoted the largest part of his attention to the Gadsden Purchase (1854) and to actions undertaken by the filibuster William Walker in Sonora, Mexico, in order to access the mineral wealth of that region.

The notorious Walker affair occupied scores of inches of *El Clamor Público*'s editorial vitriol. As early as August 28, 1855, Ramírez linked Walker to the tradition of Anglo-Saxon piracy—in fact, the term *filibusters* originally referred to buccaneers. For more than a year, he commented on Walker's filibustering missions in Sonora and Baja, California, and his bloody adventure on the way to becoming "president" of Nicaragua. The turning point in Ramírez's attitude toward U.S. citizenship and commitment to win a place for his people within the state of California may have been when President Franklin Pierce recognized Walker's government in Nicaragua (see *El Clamor Público*, 12 July 1856).

It is my contention that Ramírez's growing identification with Hispanic American immigrants and with *hispano-americanos* in general was related to his growing understanding that Californios were not exceptional in their relationship to the United States. They were just like *tejanos* and *nuevomexicanos*, who had become colonized and oppressed under American imperialist expansion; and the rest of Spanish America would fall victim to the same destiny. During 1857 and until the closure of *El Clamor Público*, Ramírez was more and more convinced of the hemispheric aspirations of the United States at the expense of Spanish Americans, from Alta California to Tierra del Fuego. He forecast invasion, conquest, and annexation, as well as the dispossession of all *hispano-americanos* owned, as they were converted to a landless, errant people. In the March 3, 1857, edition of *El Clamor Público*, Ramírez published a letter directed to the state of Sonora, picking up from his previous hypothesis: "in the end, Mexico would disappear from the catalog of nations, or would be like a batch of briar patches, sold at retail by the piece and by the yard, or like slices of cheese."[15] An article that appeared on the same day, entitled "La Actual Situación—Sonora—Baja California—Ambición de América del Norte, etc." (The Present Situation—Sonora—Baja California—North American Ambition, etc.), linked the situation in California, the Gadsden Purchase, and filibustering in Sonora to the destiny of all Latin America. He stated, "beginning with the cowardly Treaty of Guadalupe Hidalgo, and with the unnecessary sale of Mesilla, North America has become so vain and infatuated with itself as to believe it has been called upon to dominate the entire American Continent [i.e., the Americas]."[16] The article presented an overview of the population, riches, and vulnerabilities of Spanish America as much as of the United States. Ramírez calculated the population of Latin America as exceeding that of the United States by some fifteen million inhabitants, and the territory of Latin America as exceeding U.S. territory by some 1.5 million square leagues (4.5 million square miles). He further estimated that Latin America contained some of the richest resources in the entire hemisphere. Ramírez called for Latin American unity in the face of U.S. expansionism and advised Latin America to close its ports and commerce to the United States and forge commercial and political alliances with the Mediterranean states of Europe, with whom Latin America had so much in common. He further categorized U.S. expansionist adventures as quixotic and warned that California might be precisely the place where the United States was most vulnerable because of the alienation of the Latin American population in that state.

Through the remainder of 1857, until the closing of *El Clamor Público*, Ramírez devoted a great deal of attention to the efforts in Central and South America to forge a Hispanic American alliance, even to the extent of reprinting on May 16, 1857, the entire Continental Treaty of 1856. His coverage of the issue not only brought him to an outright comparison of the United States with the ancient Roman Empire, in an article entitled "El Imperio de los Estados Unidos" (The Empire of the United States), but also included reprint articles from newspapers in the major cities of Central and South America (26 Mar. 1859). Ramírez finally achieved an integrated vision of U.S. imperialism and Hispanic Americans in the United States and south of the border to the tip of Tierra del Fuego in his June 6, 1858, masterly essay, "Los Estados Unidos e Hispano-América" (The United States and Spanish America), which merits an extensive quotation to convey the eloquence and sophistication of Ramírez's analysis:

> In the land of Washington and Franklin, . . . at every juncture human rights as well as the natural way people live are violated, and the sovereignty of nations is invaded. The recent conquests effected in Mexico, dismembering half of the national territory, the scandalous events in Central America, the unjust initiatives against the natives of Panama in New Granada (Colombia), the protests from the Aves Island in Venezuela, the Galapagos in Ecuador, and Lobris in Peru, the initiatives against the Antilles, be they through force of arms or through separatist movements, which in the language of morality spoken by nations is the ultimate expression of ignominy, etc. etc. . . . Here is a compendium of maps outlined in the overabundant imagination of the Great Federal Republic, which will extend down to Buenos Aires if its course of conquest is not blocked. Is that fusion of peoples and languages, customs and religions, a practical base on which to establish one lone people made up of one hundred different nations, absorbing the Latin states and broadening continental democracy to the detriment of its

> neighbors' interests? No, a thousand times, no, is the people's cry, and, no, a thousand times no, is the echo repeated by all the descendants of Gonzalo de Córdoba and El Cid against this pernicious tendency protected by its laws and principles; each *hispano-americano,* like an eternal Hannibal everywhere, will fight to avenge the rapine and usurpation of their fatherland.[17]

Ramírez ends this essay by comparing American expansionism to that of France under Napoleon and foretells the ultimate failure of U.S. conquest and imperialism.

The evolution to this broader vision of *la raza latina* was both ideological and personal for Ramírez. As noted above, from the outset, Ramírez's publishing of *El Clamor Público* was motivated by a defense of Californios. The mistreatment of Californios and *hispano-americanos* that he documented in the newspaper's pages formed a leitmotif throughout the years. On May 10, 1855, Ramírez began making the case for emigrating from California to Sonora:

> California has fallen into the hands of the ambitious sons of North America, who will not abandon it until they have satiated their passions, outraged the first holders of this country's land, vilified their religion, and besmirched their customs. The injustices that are repeated each day represent one more reason for the unfortunate citizens of Mexico—who have always demonstrated their pure patriotism and who have sacrificed themselves in order to save the fatherland from inevitable ruin, consenting to be alienated with their property within the Republic of the United States—to go elsewhere to peacefully enjoy the fruits of their labors.[18]

Again on July 7, 1855, he repeated the call for emigration: "the Mexicans residing in California are resolved to emigrate to Sonora in order to flee this inhospitable country in which they have had to suffer so much. This emigration will be a stain on the history of the United States."[19] With the September 18, 1855, reprinting of an article from San Francisco's *La Crónica,* entitled "Hospitalidad Californiana" (California Hospitality), Ramírez endorsed broadening his focus to all Spanish Americans residing in California:

"los hijos de la América del Sur y en general toda la raza española" (the sons of South America and in general all of la raza española). In the course of the next few years, he carefully monitored and endorsed plans for not only Californios and Mexicans but also all Spanish Americans to emigrate from California to the Mexican state of Sonora, to live their lives free of the persecution they experienced in California: "all hispano-americanos have been subjected to a treatment that has no parallel in the history of any nation that has been conquered by either savages or civilized people. Everyone is convinced that *California is lost for all hispano-americanos*" (2 Aug. 1856, original emphasis).[20] Throughout 1858 and 1859, Ramírez reported on the meetings to organize the move of *hispano-americanos* to Sonora, and following the closure of *El Clamor Público*, Ramírez himself emigrated to that Mexican state (see, e.g., 16 Oct. 1859). Perhaps the straws that finally broke the proverbial camel's back were Ramírez's losing his election bid for state assemblyman in 1859, and the financial problems that led to the demise of *El Clamor Público*.[21]

Ramírez's evolution from a pioneering editor wishing to serve the needs of his Californios to an analyst of and defender against U.S. imperialism on a hemispheric scale, and ultimately to a refugee from U.S. imperialism, has much to do with his stance as an editor and publisher. While he, too, benefited from the periodicals that were brought from the East by stagecoach and steamship, Ramírez differed from Anglo-American newspapermen in that he was actually trilingual—he not only read French-language newspapers but often reprinted articles from them and at one point published a portion of his newspaper in French. Ramírez actually read the newspapers published in Spanish that were shipped from Valparaíso, Lima, Managua, and Mexico City, as well as from Texas and the East Coast (he stated at one point that he was reading as many as fifty newspapers a week). He thus was able to develop a bicultural perspective (perhaps even a tricultural one) and achieve a broad overview of the historical and contemporary political movements both in the United States and in Latin America. Ramírez's was an early understanding, forged on the anvil of personal experience as well as catholic reading tastes, of the dynamics of American imperialism and the threat it represented to Hispanic peoples throughout the hemisphere. His was precisely the kind of understanding that would later be enunciated in such foundational essays as Martí's "Nuestra América" (Our America). In addition, his ability to comprehend the differences of two national projects—those of Mexico and the United States—made him a true border dweller and interpreter, evidencing the type of biculturation that would reappear time and again over the twentieth century as Latinos pursued nationhood. Thus, the implications of the system of thought developed by the young editor of a modest frontier newspaper loom large to us today.

CHAPTER 4

Sotero Figueroa and Arturo Schomburg

Writing Afro-Caribbeans into the Nation

African American scholarship is replete with references and homages to Arturo Alfonso Schomburg (or Arthur A. Schomburg, 1874–1938), the Afro–Puerto Rican who became the archivist and bibliographer for the Harlem Renaissance and who assembled the most extensive collection of African diasporic writings of his time. Quite often, Schomburg is treated as unique in having transitioned from his Spanish-language, Afro-Hispanic background in Puerto Rico to American Negro culture, to use the term in vogue during his lifetime. But Schomburg was hardly unique in this regard, considering the number of Afro–Puerto Ricans and Afro-Cubans who settled in African American neighborhoods, intermarried within those communities, and adopted the language and ways they encountered there, while never truly giving up their Hispanic Caribbean identity (see Hoffnung-Garskof, "The World"). What is unique about Schomburg is that he as a lay historian and archivist-bibliographer contributed so much to establishing a history and awareness of the African diaspora. This chapter does not purport to review that well-traveled ground; instead, it studies a friend and antecedent of Schomburg's, Sotero Figueroa (1851–1923). Both men were Gramscian organic intellectuals who sought to document their people's story from the intersecting margins of the Spanish and U.S. empires.[1] Both had grown up in Puerto Rico as disadvantaged scions of mixed racial heritage, often called *mulato* or *pardo* because of skin color. Both were largely self-educated and learned crafts, especially typesetting, on the island; both migrated to the United States prior to the U.S. war with Spain; and both became associated with José Martí as they engaged in revolutionary activity to free Spain's

Caribbean colonies. And, finally, both men became subjects of the United States following this growing empire's victory over Spain.

Figueroa somewhat antedates Schomburg both chronologically and in his dedication to research and the writing of history, including the history of Puerto Rico's chapter of the African diaspora. Born to free parents of color in Ponce, Puerto Rico, Figueroa may have had some elementary education in San Juan from a famed Black teacher who instructed children of all backgrounds for free, Rafael Cordero (Hoffnung-Garskof, "To Abolish" 323). As I discuss below, Figueroa wrote passionately about Cordero in his book of biographies, *Ensayo biográfico de los que más han contribuído al progreso de Puerto Rico* (Biographical Essay on Those Who Have Contributed to the Progress of Puerto Rico, 1888). What is certain is that Figueroa, not having the financial resources for higher, private education, became an apprentice printer and learned the trade during the time when typographer-printers in Puerto Rico formed an intelligentsia among the working classes, akin to the leadership that *lectores* (readers) in Cuban tobacco factories maintained. The vast majority of printers at that time were men of color. With access to the liberal writings he printed, Figueroa became an autodidact who studied historical documents, edited and published newspapers, and wrote and published poetry and plays. In 1873, he was a member of a literary society, Club Artístico y Literario Borinqueño (Puerto Rican Artistic and Literary Club), for which he became the secretary (Toledo 23). Through his printing and literary interests, he became an important link to the working classes for white liberals seeking autonomy from Spain (Hoffnung-Garskof, "To Abolish" 323). In fact, Figueroa was arrested twice for his participation in the autonomist cause. In 1880, Figueroa founded his own print shop and began publishing newspapers, notably *El Eco de Ponce* (Ponce Echo) and *La Avispa* (Wasp); both enterprises eventually failed. He would continue to write for various periodicals and, in 1886, once again attempted to publish his own newspaper, *El Imparcial* (Impartial), which lasted a little less than two years (Toledo 30).

Before making the transition to the United States and becoming involved in the independence movement led by José Martí, as did Schomburg, Figueroa began researching Puerto Rican history and publishing the history of Africans and their condition on the island. He often was somewhat veiled and indirect in his writing, cloaking his aspirations for his people within general liberal causes. As Jesse Hoffnung-Garskof has shown, Figueroa (along with printer-poet and later revolutionary comrade Francisco "Pachín" Marín),

> sought to insert a radical politics of social equality into liberal projects, arguing that the abandonment of prejudice of rank and caste in favour of a system of reward based on merit should be at the centre of colonial reform. They sought to enshrine particular notions of social and racial equality as fundamental elements of a liberal Puerto Rican "regional" identity, and of modern, civilized, society. . . . [They] argued that prejudices of caste and rank, which they attributed to conservatives and Spanish officials, were a form of obscurantism. ("To Abolish" 314)

In much of his periodical writing and in his compilation of historical biographies, Figueroa argued for progress and civilization, often weaving in a leitmotif of eliminating the disadvantages of race and class and taking pains to include the names and biographies of Afro–Puerto Ricans he considered worthy of respect by the nation. In his fervor for researching and writing biographies, he antedates Schomburg's similar obsession. Figueroa continued to recognize African-heritage heroes in his later periodical writing as part of the independence movement in New York City. Figueroa's well-documented volume *Ensayo biográfico de los que más han contribuído al progreso de Puerto Rico,* which he dedicated to some of the most radical leaders of the autonomist movement, was written for a contest on biography, which the Afro–Puerto Rican autodidact won. It is obvious from the outset of his text that biography was for Figueroa a lens through which to explore Puerto Rican history and the construction of a Puerto Rican nation. Throughout the text, Figueroa makes use of the historian's tools, recovering and citing documents from the archive, citing newspaper stories and letters to the editor, and drawing on testimonies and accounts of contemporary witnesses to the biographical subjects. Along the way, he demonstrates his erudition, citing classical works, intellectual sources, and even the poetry of Luís de Camões (139). He refers to the words of educated historians and writers, such as Alejandro Tapia y Rivera and Salvador Brau, and offers alternative interpretations that conflict with their conclusions. He also corrects inaccuracies published in periodicals. In all, he assumes the role of historian with remarkable confidence and, at times, remarkable audacity, criticizing Spanish historical and contemporary authority and rule at a time when Puerto Rico was still a colony of Spain struggling for autonomy.

Figueroa begins his collection of biographies with sketches of missionaries and colonizers, but he dwells more extensively on the lives of personages of the nineteenth century. Despite his excellent documentation, Figueroa extends his biographies to include paragraphs on varied subjects as well as his own editorials on social life and conditions. In all, the *Ensayo biográfico* can be read in a number of ways because of Figueroa's criteria for selection and the leitmotifs that run through many of the thirty entries. Figueroa, ever aware of his unprivileged place in colonial society and his being deprived of a formal education, traces what education was available on the island and for whom, and records the lengths that many of his biographical subjects went to in making up for their lack of schooling. His interwoven history of education ties in neatly with his well-developed liberal ideas about the march toward civilization and progress on the island, despite the disregard of Spain for the welfare of its colonial subjects (61). Along the way, Figueroa also traces the history of slavery and its eventual abolition on the island; for him, slavery and its sociopolitical aftermath were the most serious barriers to enlightenment and civilization in Puerto Rican society—and the world. And, the greatest heroes in Figueroa's pantheon are those who pulled themselves up from poverty and disadvantage in that society and participated in bringing progress to Puerto Rican culture and making a Puerto Rican nationality; many of these were of African heritage. They were, Figueroa insists, self-made and unassisted by the white hierarchy; this, too, is a theme that Schomburg will repeat and expand.

Notably, the second biography in Figueroa's book is that of the *mulato* rococo painter José Campeche (1752–1809), who also served as a beacon for Schomburg in his gallery of race heroes. Besides the obvious renown of Campeche, Figueroa chose him because his life story offered the latter-day artisan the opportunity to editorialize on the lack of opportunity and privilege for people like him. He states that the painter would have been able to cross the Atlantic, see the works of antiquity, learn from the court painters of his time, and thus increase his fame—had he been born into a family privileged by the purity of Spanish blood and access to the financial resources to purchase an education (14). Figueroa states that Campeche's example teaches us, "what the creative power of genius can do, even without the help of education" (15).[2]

In the category of furthering education, Figueroa included Fray Benigno Carrión (1798–1871), Nicolás Aguayo y Aldea (1808–78), and Manuel Sicardó y Osuna (1803–64), whose entries gave the author the opportunity to comment on the lack of such opportunities on the island: "like so many sons of this country who do not have golden wings to fly to other regions to satisfy their hunger for learning, which is that much more stronger as greater are the obstacles that oppose it" (114).[3]

This theme of being deprived of access to education because of the lack of financial resources to travel to places with schools and universities runs throughout the *Ensayo biográfico* after being set up in the Campeche entry. However, the biographical entry dedicated to the self-taught teacher known in some circles as the "Father of Public Education in Puerto Rico," Rafael Cordero y Molina (1790–1868), is one of the longest entries. Here, Figueroa details at length this Afro–Puerto Rican tobacco worker's selfless contribution to teaching children of all backgrounds for free, perhaps even Figueroa himself at some point. He calls Cordero a "poor child of the people, branded with the stamp of degradation (that is what black skin was called in epochs of lamentable backwardness)" (141).[4] Cordero serves as a fundamental example in Figueroa's lobbying for public education, but also as an example of another self-taught intellectual like himself: "who rises up from the common folk, overcompensates in favor of his countrymen, and by his *own and exclusive effort* writes his name in the immortal temple of those who have benefited us" (141, added emphasis).[5] Figueroa speculates on the great tenacity it would have taken Cordero to overcome the barriers presented by the racist society of his day, when "Negros" were not allowed to attend the one school that existed in San Juan.[6]

In this chapter of his book Figueroa lambasts the institution of slavery and its deleterious effects on society, especially in terms of depriving that society of the genius and contributions that people of African heritage could have made to the nation had they just been offered the opportunity of an education. He affirms in many different ways that the color of one's skin has nothing to do with intelligence and talent, and argues that societies that discriminate in this way cannot be considered civilized. It is in this chapter as well that Figueroa brings up one of his greatest race heroes, the same one praised later by Schomburg: Toussaint L'Ouverture (1743–1803). Figueroa's choice is especially daring given the detestation felt for L'Ouverture by most white people, especially those in Figueroa's homeland of southern Puerto

Rico, where many refugees of the Haitian Revolution settled. But he sees in L'Ouverture the proof that people of African blood have rights and can be great men. He ends his diatribe with a call to philanthropists, even if they think their blood is superior, to educate Black people, including in Africa: "Perfect the Negro, philanthropists who believe yourselves to be of a privileged race!" (142).[7] He notes that even white Europe arose from a barbarian past, and goes on to cite legal documents dating as late as 1848 that allowed summary execution and maiming of enslaved people in Puerto Rico (143–45). In effect, Figueroa was turning the tables, asking who was the barbarian, the so-called *savage* African or the *civilized* white person?

Among the heroes who forwarded the abolitionist cause, Figueroa praises Ramón Power y Giralt, the above-mentioned Fray Benigno Carrión and Nicolás Aguayo y Aldea, Luis Padial y Vizcarrondo (1832–79), and various others, but he reserves his greatest praise and the longest entry in his book for Segundo Ruiz Belvis (1824–67). Belvis, explains Figueroa, tirelessly and through self-sacrifice worked to free the enslaved population in Puerto Rico, a deed that was finally accomplished in 1873, six years after he drafted the key document for abolition and died in exile. In the Belvis biography, Figueroa quotes extensively from Belvis's co-authored document known simply as the "Informe" (Report) and takes the opportunity to depict slavery in the longest editorial of his book. Slavery, he states, writing just fifteen years after its abolition, was "the iniquity of the centuries" (131).[8] He pictures the subjects of this iniquity as dehumanized "machines made of flesh that continually worked their way through plantations and agricultural fields, the lash of the whip accelerating the pace of their fatigued and exhausted bodies" (131).[9] In contrast with this horrible depiction, Figueroa follows with a poetic description of some thirty thousand enslaved workers receiving the news of their liberation: "Free! How great would they have expressed their emotion when they first heard that word! That is, finally supported by law, they were now *people* and not *things*. They now could maintain family ties, without the fear that their children would be torn from maternal breasts and sold to other regions. . . . Now, they could manifest their reasoning, have beliefs, start families without the fear that the brutal embraces of the foreman or of the owner, with their dignity intact, would violate the honor of their wives, the innocence of their daughters" (136–37, original emphasis).[10]

Lastly in the *Ensayo biográfico*, Figueroa memorializes artisans like himself, including Juan González y Chaves (1810–65) and Pascasio P. Sancerrit

(1833–76), among others. González y Chaves advanced Puerto Rican culture by being among the first to publish books and even a newspaper, *Fomento* (Development), on the island. Figueroa classifies him as a *laborioso obrero* (hard-working laborer, 122), thus emphasizing that the working classes can produce intellectuals, even if they are self-made. By recognizing González thusly, Figueroa implies that civilization can only be advanced in Puerto Rico by offering such people opportunities and supporting them. On the other hand, Figueroa makes clear that Sancerrit was of African heritage and became a distinguished typographer, poet, and newspaper publisher despite his lack of formal education, having accomplished so much all by himself (172): "what willpower aided by intelligence can accomplish" (173).[11] Figueroa also pays homage to Félix Padial y Vizcarrondo (1838–80) and José Pablo Morales (1828–82), who, although not of the artisan class, distinguished themselves as journalists. Padial took in Figueroa as an apprentice and initiated the young aspirant in not only literary pursuits, but also work on Padial's own newspaper, *El Progreso* (Progress); Padial also introduced Figueroa to political liberalism. Morales, insists Figueroa, was self-taught (*se formó solo*, 229), with his success due to his powerful intelligence and perseverance at a time when island culture was utterly backward and offered no training. Morales's biography gives Figueroa the opportunity to editorialize that withholding educational opportunities and keeping Puerto Ricans backward and ignorant were purposeful strategies of Spain to keep the population docile and governable (230), which, we might add, suppressed Puerto Rican nation formation.

Thus, it seems, unlike in traditional biographies and accounts of great men of the past—no women, of course, unfortunately—Figueroa's attention for the most part did not include politicians and many men of wealth and renown but favored those who worked to free the enslaved population and advance education on the island. His selection of biographical subjects was replete with artisans and men of African or Afro-European heritage, those who despite discrimination and lack of opportunity for them as free Black people or the children of manumission succeeded in intellectual or artistic endeavors *on their own*. That is, they were *self-made*.

In 1889, shortly after publishing his *Ensayo biográfico*, Figueroa left the island with his own printing press and equipment for New York, where he joined up with the leaders of the independence movement, as did Schomburg in 1891.[12] Both became active in the Partido Revolucionario Cubano

(Cuban Revolutionary Party) and associated with its leader, José Martí. Figueroa established a print shop, named América, where he published newspapers and books, among other types of documents. He was also the editor, from 1890 to 1892, of the renowned cultural magazine *Revista Ilustrada de Nueva York* (Illustrated Magazine of New York). On the presses of Imprenta América, Figueroa issued the revolutionary party's newspaper, *Patria* (Fatherland), which he edited when Martí was traveling. Among the qualities that drew Figueroa to associate with Martí and later to apotheosize him after Martí's death on the battlefield in Cuba was precisely the patriarch's well-known stance on doing away with all racial distinctions in the independent Cuba they were fighting to establish. Just as important was Martí's success in uniting the Afro-Cuban revolutionary forces with the traditionally white liberal ones and extending leadership to men of color, such as Figueroa and his printer-publisher colleague from Ponce, Francisco "Pachín" Marín, as well as Arturo Alfonso Schomburg, all three Afro–Puerto Rican autodidactic artisans.

In his periodical writing from within the revolutionary movement, Figueroa continued his leitmotifs of Afro-Caribbean contributions and the self-education of those from disadvantaged backgrounds, especially those of African lineage. For instance, he includes Toussaint L'Ouverture alongside Simón Bolívar, Miguel Hidalgo, and other famed liberators of the Americas in his article "Meeting de Proclamación" (Proclamation Meeting), in which he explains that "Toussaint, who arises from the darkness of slavery and demolishes the best of France's Napoleonic armies" is moved by "his love for the unhappy oppressed, his magnanimity for the vanquished" (*Patria*, 20 July 1895).[13] In this same article, he compares the fallen Martí to Jesus Christ and repeats his recurrent gloss on Martí's vision: "he does not recognize class distinctions nor skin color, only brothers in the fatherland and liberty."[14] But more strikingly, Figueroa repeats numerous times in editorials that the revolution will bring about equality of people, irrespective of their skin color: "the revolution in which they have fallen will be just if all Cubans pay no attention to [skin] color . . . (where) a man would only be distinct from another because of the warmth of his heart or the fire on his brow" (*Patria*, 14 Mar. 1892).[15] It is noteworthy that Figueroa actually interprets the actions of Martí as similar to those of Christ regarding class distinctions: "to sacrifice one's life for the redemption of his people, he emerges poor, dark, alone and defenseless across Judea to raise up in hearts the empire of justice, to abolish the law of castes, preaching the dogma enlightening the conscience and dignifying humanity, which can be summarized in three sublime words: Liberty, Fraternity, Equality." He continues the essay, warning that "those who [act] out of upper-class arrogance or social discrimination will not benefit from the revolution" ("Discursos" 2).[16] He proceeds in the same article to speak of the social justice and equality that must be enforced upon the success of the revolution, in which color and class discrimination must be abjured. In a front-page editorial, on October 2, 1894, he emphasizes that one reason for the independence movement was to abolish slavery, writing that "the colonial dominators . . . hardly ever paused to think that the slave could be free and that the creole could take care of his own business," thus proffering the analogy that abolition was to slavery as independence was to Creoles.[17]

Beyond referencing these recurrent themes, Figueroa assumes the confident stance of a true historian in many of the speeches and articles he penned and published in New York. For instance, in a series of seven articles entitled "La verdad de la historia" (The Truth of the History), which ran in *Patria* from March 19 to July 2, 1892, he traces the history of the independence movement in Puerto Rico, from its origins to the Grito de Lares (Shout at Lares) insurrection in 1868, correcting various published versions about the shout while foregrounding the role of Afro–Puerto Rican patriot Ramón Emeterio Betances (1827–98), who receives from Figueroa reverence similar to what he shows for José Martí. Another example is his published speech on the anniversary of Martí's death, "Primer Aniversario" (First Anniversary, *Patria* 29 Feb. 1896), in which he announces inscribing the names of the meritorious fallen in the pages of history. In the speech, he summarizes the independence movement and war, taking pains to enumerate the heroic fallen. And this, once again, gives him the opportunity to name Afro-Caribbean heroes in his pantheon: Victoriano Garzón (1847–95), Francisco Adolfo Crombet Tejera (1851–95), Alfonso Goulet (1865–95), and the famed carpenter turned general José Guillermo Moncada (1841–95). All these men died in battle the same year as Martí, and in Figueroa's shorthand they merit the same respect as their white comrades.

Notably, in the same speech, he returns to the need for education of the poor, now seen as an outcome of the revolution: revolutionary man will educate "the working class so that it can consciously march forward to conquer its rights." Maintaining the humility of the working classes, he emphasizes again, the "modest man who will give of himself without ostentation."[18]

Soon after Martí's death, Figueroa was marginalized by the white liberals in the movement in New York (Toledo 69–70), which led him to leave *Patria.* Jesse Hoffnung-Garskof attests that "after Martí left for Cuba in 1895 [four months before he died], the leadership of the party increasingly excluded men like [Rafael] Serra and Figueroa from decision-making and from editorial input in *Patria*" ("The World" 81). Figueroa then established his own newspaper, *La Doctrina de Martí* (Doctrine of Martí), which he published from 1896 to 1898 with the help of other Afro–Puerto Ricans, including Marín and Serra. *La Doctrina de Martí* sought to continue what Figueroa interpreted as Martí's "socially and racially progressive view of the revolutionary cause" (Hoffnung-Garskof, *Racial Migrations* 17), thus challenging the current conservatism of *Patria.* Among his diverse writings in his newspaper, Figueroa began a series of seven articles, from September 16, 1896, to March 2, 1897, defining what for him was the discipline of history and the role of historian, while he attacked and deconstructed Cuban newspaper publisher Enrique Trujillo's recently issued book *Apuntes históricos* (Historical Notes, 1896).

After the war with Spain was concluded and the United States obtained its Caribbean colonies, Figueroa in 1899 migrated to Cuba, intending once again to transport his printing press and set up shop to print and publish for the new nation; his plans were frustrated, however, when the same conservatives who had pushed him out of *Patria,* most notably Tomás Estrada Palma, intercepted the importation of his Imprenta América (Toledo 91). In Havana, he nevertheless continued to participate in political life and write Afro-Caribbeans into history through articles in such newspapers as *La Discusión* (Discussion). In 1900, he became a founding member of a political group, Asociación de Emigrados Revolucionarios Cubanos (Association of Cuban Revolutionary Emigrants), and by that same year he became a founding member of the revived Partido Revolucionario Cubano, which aspired to maintain the values of the independence movement from Spain; Figueroa became the editor of the party's newspaper, *Independencia* (Independence) (Toledo 98–99). In 1902, when Cuba became an independent republic—although under U.S. interventionist clauses in its constitution—he was named director of the republic's official organ, *La gaceta oficial* (Official Gazette). In 1904, Figueroa wrote a column for the newspaper *El Mundo* (World) entitled "Nuestros héroes" (Our Heroes), in which, along with well-known Creole revolutionary figures, he made a point of including biographies of Afro-Cuban heroes such as Antonio Maceo, José Maceo, Néstor Aranguren, and Vidal Ducasse. Figueroa's mission as journalist and historian, as well as protector of the Afro-Caribbean legacy, was continually frustrated to the point of his living his later years in penury. The conservative forces led by U.S.-supported President Estrada Palma prevailed in suppressing Afro-Cuban movements for equal rights, and a disillusioned Figueroa retired from public life while having to sue for his pension as a veteran of the war for independence (Toledo 110–11).

Alfonso Arturo Schomburg was born to an unwed laundress or midwife of free African heritage and a father of German or mestizo heritage who seems to have abandoned his wife and son (Sinnette 8). Although Schomburg himself made references to some education of one sort or another while growing up in Puerto Rico, there is really no evidence that he received any type of formal education, especially because there were practically no free public schools on the island during the nineteenth century and his impoverished mother certainly could not have afforded private tutelage.[19] Indeed, his lack of formalized study and degrees or certificates bothered Schomburg throughout his life and was an obstacle to his pursuing education and a law degree in the United States (Sinnette 9, 35). This lack was evident to his university-educated Black American brethren, such as W. E. B. Du Bois and Carter Woodson, as they willingly received his documentary research but slighted his insight and understanding, even his accented speech and poor writing style, which needed extensive editing (Sinnette 41, 52, 55). And, ironically, when Schomburg was a candidate to be hired to curate the collection he had sold to the New York Public Library, Du Bois and his followers opposed the hire because of his lack of formal preparation. Despite his references to some type of schooling, Schomburg proudly referred to himself as self-made.[20] With opportunities bleak in Puerto Rico, especially for an ambitious mixed-race individual, Schomburg relocated in 1891 to New York, where he promptly found employment among tobacco workers. For the most part, they were actively involved in the Cuban and Puerto Rican independence movements, and, like Figueroa, he soon became a member of revolutionary clubs, such as Club Borinquen and Las Dos Antillas. He, too, became associated with José Martí (Piñero de Rivera 178–79). It would strain credibility to think that a bibliophile such as Schomburg did not read Figueroa's *Ensayo biográfico* or that the two comrades did not exchange ideas, especially about the struggle for racial equality and Afro-Caribbean history. Both activists were essential in articulating the struggle for racial equality as part of the movement for independence from Spain.

During this early period in New York, Schomburg, like Figueroa, sent articles and letters in Spanish to periodicals in support of the revolution. He also had occasion to visit independence chapters in New Orleans and travel in the South, where he observed the conditions of African Americans (Sinnette 22). Unlike Figueroa, however, Schomburg stayed in the United States after the war, when Puerto Rico became a colony of the United States. He and his fellow Afro-Caribbeans also set up a bilingual Freemason lodge, El Sol de Cuba (Cuban Sun), which in 1911 changed its name to the Prince Hall Lodge and accommodated a growing African American membership. Hoffnung-Garskof calls attention to the lodge's reinforcement of Schomburg's constant preoccupation: "The brothers in the Prince Hall lodges glorified the image of the 'self-made man,' a message that appealed to Schomburg, the humble artisan, whose humiliation before the New York State Board of Regents was replayed multiple times at the hands of elite black intellectuals" ("The Migrations" 34). Despite racism among white Masons, Schomburg eventually became general secretary of the Grand Lodge of New York, becoming in this sense self-made; it was an intellectual distinction he was unable to duplicate in his work life as a humble mailroom clerk and messenger at a bank. After the United States took possession of Cuba and Puerto Rico, among the last colonies of Spain, Schomburg directed his intellectual energies toward studying the worldwide African diaspora and constituting its documentary history. In 1911, Schomburg and four others founded what eventually would be known as the Negro Society for Historical Research, and in 1914, he was elected to the American Negro Academy, whose membership was made up mostly of formally educated African Americans (Sinnette 38). Schomburg was now in full gear in his historical research and providing the documentary basis for Pan-Africanism, or what we might today call Black nationalism.

In his latter decolonizing archival work and writings, Schomburg strove to revise white man's history, create a space for African heritage, and even at times document African and Afro-Hispanic antecedence in developing "civilization." As he wrote in "The Negro Digs Up His Past," "History must restore what slavery took away, for it is the social damage of slavery that the present generation must repair and offset" (372). Where Martí may have tipped his hat to creating a multiracial society in Latin America, Schomburg on the other hand placed the African presence in the center of Latin American history (Meehan 78).[21] In this he departed also from Figueroa, who unflaggingly praised Martí's ideas on racial integration. And like Figueroa in preserving the heroic role of Toussaint L'Ouverture, Schomburg went a step further and proposed that one of the greatest gifts to the Americas was Black Haiti's blazing the path to independence from Europe ("The Economic Contribution"). Throughout his collecting and his essays and speeches, Schomburg took pains to recover African "firsts" in order to correct the historical record. And like Figueroa before him, biography became a mainstay in his research and writing methodology. Many of Schomburg's articles rescue the contributions of African-heritage figures to the development of the Americas. He filled the pages he wrote with biographies of philosophers, poets, politicians, artists, educators, and all types of accomplished individuals of African heritage who blazed paths in Europe and the Americas. Writing in "The Economic Contribution by the Negro to America" about the Africans who had been forcefully brought to the New World, Schomburg stated, "They were not the untutored savages we are expected to believe from modern histories." Thus, like Figueroa as well, Schomburg here and in most of his works was motivated to challenge and correct official history, as he makes clear in the closing remarks of this essay: "Suffice it to say that the position which the Negro and his mixed progeny of European or Indian blood had won in South America, they have also earned, if even they have not as yet received, due recognition therefore in North America." Among the numerous historical figures he rescues are the colonial Mexican poet Juan Cortez; "the first Negro librarian," Manuel del Socorro Rodríguez; and the Cuban poet Plácido.[22] Schomburg coincided with Figueroa in drafting essays on such heroes of the independence movement as Antonio Maceo and José Martí, but a notable recovery was his biographical exaltation of the same Puerto Rican painter that Figueroa had researched before him: José Campeche. Thabiti Asukile asserts that in his lifetime and even today, Schomburg's contributions as a writer and scholar were not and are not valued, largely because he did not have the sanctioned training and use the accepted scholarly methodology (79). Thus, Schomburg relied on biography as a means to rewrite Western history by bringing to light historical figures of African heritage, challenging ideas of African inferiority, and combating stereotypes that were widely held even among the educated classes.

Aside from the biographical methodology employed by the autodidact Schomburg, his writings reveal a similar leitmotif to Figueroa's: the value of self-education for Afro-Caribbeans and others, who despite tremendous barriers have made impressive contributions to civilization.[23] He declared the need for "Negro" history, a call that speaks to the value of knowledge produced by nonacademic as well as academic sources: "We need in the coming dawn the man who will give us the background of our future; it matters not whether he comes from the cloister of the university or the rank and file of the fields" ("Racial Integrity" 69). Schomburg, more than Figueroa, most certainly faced this quandary of producing scholarship without the academic credentials that his rivals, such as Du Bois and Alain Locke, had and held over him. Schomburg defensively asserted the value of being self-taught and experienced rather than just formally educated, as affirmed in his 1913 Masonic speech: "The university graduate is wont to overestimate his ability, fresh from the machinery that endows him with a parchment and crowns him with knowledge, he steps out into the world to meet the practical men with years of experience and mother wit" (qtd. in Hoffnung-Garskof, "The Migrations" 34). Sossianna Arroyo has also noted the role that Masonic thought played in reaffirming Schomburg's confidence in being self-made: "During his life, Schomburg would intertwine his definition of the Masonic workshop with his own story as a self-made man, which included his interaction with other Masons who were also free-born slaves who became leaders and mentors of other African Americans (such as John Bruce), and his work as a bibliographer and historian of the African diaspora" (12). But while Hoffnung-Garskof acknowledges that the Prince Hall Masons offered Schomburg continuity with the African-heritage societies he and other self-taught Afro-Hispanic intellectuals joined, neither he nor Arroyo highlights how this self-making was a common theme among the accomplished but unschooled African-heritage organic intellectuals in the Caribbean. And, no one has previously identified Figueroa as his antecedent and probable discussant on this and other issues, such as history, biography, and nation-building.

In summary, the renowned collector-historian Arturo Alfonso Schomburg carried out a decolonizing project that had its roots in the Puerto Rican and Cuban independence movements, using approaches and concepts that were anteceded by his elder and associate Sotero Figueroa. Earlier than Schomburg, Figueroa had inserted Afro-Caribbeans into history as part of his decolonizing mission and had used biography not only to expand and correct official history, but also to define a nation. And, furthermore, the archive Figueroa created in *Ensayo biográfico* and his articles and speeches was just as much a counterarchive as Schomburg's. Cognizant of the educational deprivation of enslaved people and their descendants, Figueroa also anticipated Schomburg in emphasizing the meritorious role that self-education, drive, and native intelligence played and should play in making the independent, freed man who would construct his people's identity, with pride in a racial past that needed to be brought forth from the shadows. One must conclude that Sotero Figueroa contributed to the construction of African American and Latino identities directly and through the writing and activity of the renowned Arturo Alfonso Schomburg. They both expanded the concepts of "American" and "Latino" to include Afro-Caribbeans.

CHAPTER 5

Developing an International Working-Class Consciousness Instead of a National Identity

With the beginning of large-scale Hispanic immigration in the mid-nineteenth century and the proletarization of the native Mexican and Mexican American population of the Southwest, as well as the advances in travel and communications within the North American continent, Hispanic or Latino workers began to develop a sense of solidarity as "wage slaves" oppressed by factories, railroads, shipyards, agribusiness, and mining corporations, among many other employers of manual labor. The move to organize labor during the late nineteenth century was often marked by competing ideologies about how to unify, whether along ethnic lines, by industry, or as a working class defined by various socialistic movements. Latinos participated in most of these movements, except when they were excluded because of ethnicity or race.

As early as 1883, cowboys were organizing in the Texas Panhandle under the leadership of Juan Gómez, and by 1888, the first Hispanic labor union, the Caballeros de Labor, was founded in New Mexico as an affiliate of the Knights of Labor, which had been founded in Philadelphia in 1869. Tobacco workers had organized in Cuba and Puerto Rico from the mid-nineteenth century, and they brought their worker consciousness to cigar factories in Key West, Tampa, Long Island, and elsewhere. In Puerto Rico, a workers' political party, Partido Obrero Social (Workers' Socialist Party), was established in 1899 and later became affiliated with the American Federation of Labor (Kanellos, *Hispanic Firsts* 133–35). In 1903, Mexicans and Japanese field hands in California formed the first farmworker union as the Japanese-Mexican Labor Association. When Latinos were not organized in unions, their mutual aid societies often filled the breach (Rosales, *Chicano!* 115–17). The strike was the workers' greatest weapon, and they used it frequently throughout the late nineteenth and early twentieth centuries, with tobacco workers in Tampa, for instance, striking in 1899, 1901, 1910, 1920, and 1931. Miners repeatedly went on strike in Arizona, beginning with the historic Clifton-Morenci walkouts in 1903. The Japanese-Mexican farmworkers went on strike in 1903, the street railroad workers in Los Angeles in 1910, the grape pickers in Fresno in 1922, the berry pickers in El Monte in 1933, the pecan shellers in San Antonio in 1938, and so on (Almaguer 183–203; Jamieson 76–77, 100–105; Kushner 20–21, 68–76; McWilliams 190–95; Rosales, *Chicano!* 119–22).

Many of these worker movements and unionizing efforts were inspired by and often supported by what government representatives and industrialists would consider radical groups and their socialistic ideologies. One of the most pervasive and influential of these systems of thought, which was taught to workers on factory floors as well as off-site in mutual aid societies, union halls, and worker education centers, was anarchism. Among the most misunderstood movements in U.S. labor history, anarchism was popular among working-class leaders from the late nineteenth century up through the Depression years. It is still felt in working-class culture in the liberal leanings of today's Latino workers and intellectuals in the United States, only to be counterbalanced by the conservatism of Latino nationalism and religiosity, as will be seen in chapter 6.

Anarchism in its heyday is best understood as an anti-authoritarian political philosophy that promoted absolute equality of people, including across gender, and opposed the state as unnecessary and harmful, preferring nonhierarchical associations such as labor unions for making decisions (see Goldman). In general, anarchists may have supported labor unions as a necessary and temporary step to creating their utopia, but they were unified in opposing all organized institutions, including government and religious institutions. They also opposed private ownership, especially of the means of production, and considered workers to be slaves in capitalist society. In a real sense, anarchists were enemies of the state, classist society, and institutional religion; thus, they posed a discomfiting threat to the established order, and the most extreme anarchists resorted to organizing violent revolutions and taking over or abolishing those institutions they opposed. On the positive side, anarchists led or joined efforts to shorten the workday and work week, to eliminate child labor, and to treat women as equals in the workplace and the home; many anarchists opposed marriage as an institution of women's oppression and instead supported free love as the natural human state. However, to the negative, the most extreme anarchists were responsible for assassinations of government leaders and bombings of institutions, such as the financial capital of the United States: Wall Street.

When American scholars venture to address the subject, their focus is reduced to known American anarchists of varying ethnicities, especially those involved in key labor movements, and their causes célèbres, such as the Haymarket Square riots and the trials of Joe Hill, Sacco and Vanzetti, and the Scottsboro Boys. Outside of anarchist publications written in English, and some Italian, Yiddish, and German ones, little is known of other ethnic-based movements expressed in the vernacular of various immigrant groups in the United States. While authorities at one time considered Italian anarchists the greatest internal enemies of the country, they mostly overlooked much of the extensive organizing and publishing by Spanish-speaking anarchists, even while many Hispanic leaders and their entire organizations maintained intimate ties with their Italian brothers and sisters, as well as with mainstream anarchist movements. As an example, Paul Avrich in his bibliography of anarchist newspapers lists only five Spanish-language ones, when in my estimate more than one hundred appeared in the United States between 1890 and 1940.[1]

While following many of the same political theorists as mainstream American anarchists, such as Peter Kropotkin, Pierre-Joseph Proudhon, Mikhail Bakunin, and others in Spanish translation, Hispanic anarchists were anarcho-syndicalists. According to Murray Bookchin, they worked for the complete "elimination of capitalism, not merely the amelioration of . . . labor conditions"; in reality, the movement was based on "an economic organization of workers—a revolutionary union as distinguished from a political party—[that could] take over society by means of a general strike" (132–33).

Many anarcho-syndicalist organizations, along with their study groups, political activities, and periodicals, were clustered around the industries that most employed Spanish-speaking immigrants and natives. Nevertheless, a number of these groups subscribed to more militant and violent anarchist actions designed to bring down the state; these groups were often influenced by Luigi Galleani (1861–1931), whose followers in the United States conducted a series of assassinations and bombings that included Wall Street in

1920. Galleani's essays were published in his newspaper *La Questione Sociale* (Social Question) in Paterson, New Jersey, and from there were translated and reprinted in the Spanish-language anarchist press as far away as Los Angeles and Tampa. He maintained close ties with the Catalonian Pedro Esteve, who became the editor of *La Questione Sociale* in 1899. Galleani was deported by various governments and settled in 1902 in Barre, Vermont, where he wrote and mailed out his influential newsletter *Cronaca Sovversiva* (Subversive Chronicle), until it was terminated by U.S. government authorities under the Sedition Act of 1918. Then, they deported him to Italy in 1919, not for publishing his chronicle, but for publishing a bomb-making manual (Pernicoe; "Luigi Galleani").

The hundred or so Latino anarchist periodicals that were published and distributed in the United States before World War II ran the gamut from newspapers published by anarcho-syndicalist organizations to periodicals put out by working-class intellectuals in exile from Spain or Spanish America. The anarchist content in the periodicals evolved over time, from a more pure and militant anarchism in the late nineteenth and early twentieth centuries to a more practical outreach to forge solidarity with other Latino community groups during the Depression, especially those organizing against fascism during the Spanish Civil War. While many anarchists tempered their radical stance in this outreach, others made the transition to communism during the Depression. The anarchist-oriented periodicals spanned the continent from New York, the most frequent place of publication, to California, Florida, Illinois, and Texas. They were published by and for mine workers in Arizona, agricultural workers in California, tobacco workers in Florida, steelworkers in Chicago and Lorain, Ohio, and factory workers in New York and New Jersey. Most of them only survived a few years, but others, such as *Cultura Obrera* (Worker Culture), edited by Esteve, lasted almost two decades. While Hispanic anarchists were active in most states of the union in the early twentieth century, according to places of publication and newspaper donor and subscriber lists published in these periodicals, the three principal areas of Hispanic anarchist activities were New York/New Jersey, Tampa/Ybor City, and the American Southwest. The groups operating in all three areas always maintained communications with one another, participated in one another's activities, and reprinted essays and news from one another's periodicals. Nevertheless, they differed in character and mission, especially in their relationship with labor unions, militancy, and subversion of government authority and the bourgeoisie. Almost all of them organized among Spanish-speaking immigrants hailing from distinct regions of the Hispanic world. While individual groups may have included Mexican, Spanish, Cuban, Puerto Rican, or other nationalities, they did not necessarily make ethnic, national, or racial distinctions.[2] This was in keeping with their anarchist ideology. The workers and the leaders of various backgrounds often crossed ethnic and geographic lines. Moreover, they maintained ties with the leaders of other labor and anarchist movements in the United States, joined in their rallies, invited their leaders to their own Hispanic functions, and translated and published their speeches and essays in their Spanish-language periodicals. For instance, Hispanic leaders such as Esteve accompanied Emma Goldman on speaking tours as translators.

New York/New Jersey

The New York/New Jersey shipping and manufacturing industries were heavy employers of Hispanic labor originating in the Caribbean and in Spain. The workers did not just follow the numerous Italian leaders active from Boston to Philadelphia. Immigrants from Spain, especially from Catalonia, long a center of revolutionary and trade union activity in the peninsula, also led Hispanic anarcho-syndicalists. Immigrants from Catalonia were especially experienced in labor politics. They had established the large, successful Confederación Nacional de Trabajo (National Confederation of Labor) in 1910 and met with wide-scale government repression, including the placing of Barcelona under martial law. The confederation went underground but nevertheless grew to have an estimated six hundred thousand to one million members (Bookchin 153). The perennially suffering economy in the late nineteenth and early twentieth centuries and the brutal official repression of worker organizing were major causes of the emigration of workers, many of whom were anarchist activists. Many of them came to the United States and found work in communities with sizable Spanish-speaking populations. Waves of Spanish political refugees also arrived when the Spanish Civil War broke out in 1936.

Categorized by the periodical *Propaganda*, on October 26, 1901, as "the most pronounced anarchist" in the United States, Catalonian immigrant Pedro Esteve (c. 1865–1925) was one of the major figures spreading anarcho-syndicalist ideology among Spanish-speaking workers on the East

Coast beginning in the 1890s.[3] The son of a working-class family (*Cultura Obrera*, 19 Sept. 1926), Esteve became a typesetter and in 1887 an editor with Barcelona's major anarchist newspaper, *El Productor* (Producer). After the authorities shut the paper down, Esteve fled, in 1893, to Cuba to proselytize (see Esenwein 139).[4] During his three months' stay, he published the weekly *Archivo Social* (Social Archive) and promptly became a persona non grata. He subsequently organized tobacco workers in Ybor City/Tampa, miners in Colorado, seamen in New York, and silk factory workers in Paterson, New Jersey.[5] In Ybor City, he edited *El Esclavo* (Slave) from 1894 to 1898 while working as a *lector* in a cigar factory (Avrich 391). According to Susana Sueiro Seoane ("El asesinato" 176), he also founded and operated an anarchist school called Escuela Francisco Ferrer, and a cultural center titled Antorcha (Torch).[6] Even while producing his newspapers in New York and New Jersey, he maintained an active travel schedule to further the anarchist cause in such places as Ybor City. From 1899 to 1906, he assumed the editorship of *La Questione Sociale* from Galleani in Paterson, where he also became the editor of the already existing Spanish-language *El Despertar* (Awakening) during the 1890s.[7] In 1911, while he was back in Ybor City again, vigilantes broke up his print shop, and he fled to New York (Avrich 393).[8] He immediately opened up a print shop on West Street and started publishing his most important and longest lasting newspaper, *Cultura Obrera*, which lasted from 1911 to 1927 (see Sueiro Seoane, "Spanish-Speaking"). At one point, he was arrested and threatened with deportation, but released with orders to cease publishing. He ignored the orders. Esteve also operated a small anarchist publishing house, appropriately named La Políglota (Polyglot) (Avrich 391–93).

Paterson was a major silk weaving center that attracted immigrant workers; in the early twentieth century, it experienced major strikes promoting reforms of child labor practices and an eight-hour workday. Esteve edited *El Despertar* in Paterson until 1908. As with many other anarchist publications serving ethnic communities, its pages included translations of the major European anarchism theorists. The paper also advertised and sold the books of these theorists. Throughout the life of *El Despertar*, Esteve published his own editorials and essays, and at least two of his own pamphlets: *A los anarquistas de España y Cuba: Memoria de la Conferencia Anarquista Internacional celebrada en Chicago en septiembre de 1893* (To the Anarchists of Spain and Cuba: Commemoration of the International Anarchist

Conference Celebrated in Chicago in September 1893, published 1900) and *Socialismo anarquista* (Anarchist Socialism, published 1902).[9]

Esteve, who became one of the leading and most celebrated anarchism theorists among Latinos, was reported to prefer publishing his thought in newspapers over books because of their relative accessibility to the working class: "Yes, books are beautiful, grand, but is their distribution possible? Can they reach those minds that after a rough day's work seek rest?" (*Cultura Obrera*, 19 Sept. 1926).[10] Concurrent with his work on *El Despertar*, beginning in 1905, Esteve published another periodical in Paterson, *Doctrina Anarquista-Socialista* (Socialist-Anarchist Doctrine). His lead essay in every issue explored a different theme of anarchist theory. Although most subscribers and donors were from New Jersey and New York, others lived as far away as California. It built a following by addressing current issues, but gave special attention to the cigar rollers in Tampa, where Esteve had maintained relationships (see Mormino and Pozzetta).

One of the few in-depth stories on Esteve in the English-language press came not from the New York–area press but from the *Dallas Morning News*, on June 7, 1903, after reporter Stephen Bonsal interviewed him. Bonsal reproduced in English one of Esteve's long speeches and made other observations in his four-column report. He stated that the "dago" printer was an expert polyglot of "wide education and culture" who seemingly devoted twenty-hour workdays to writing and single-handedly publishing his periodicals and pamphlets, and weekends to delivering fiery anarchist speeches.

Esteve's major contribution to anarchism appeared in New York's *Cultura Obrera*. Following the anarcho-syndicalist practice of serving specific workers, *Cultura Obrera* had a direct relationship with dockworkers and seamen, and became an official publication of the Marine Firemen, Oilers and Watertenders Union of the Atlantic and the Gulf, a union founded by Esteve's activist colleague and anarchist journalist Jaime Vidal (Sueiro Seoane, "El asesinato" 176). Not only was the newspaper for sale on ships, but its pages listed the donations and subscriptions collected, arranged by ship name. A Spanish-English bilingual paper in the beginning, *Cultura Obrera* printed translations of major anarchists, extensively covered union and strike activity by Latinos throughout the United States, covered the Mexican Revolution, and even collected donations for the defense fund of the Partido Liberal Mexicano (PLM, Mexican Liberal Party) and its exiled leader, Ricardo Flores Magón.[11] In its heyday, *Cultura Obrera* had the distinction of reprinting more articles from Flores Magón's newspaper *Regeneración* (Regeneration) than it did from any other source. Esteve's essays and correspondence, likewise, were among the most reprinted in *Regeneración. Cultura Obrera* also maintained a bookstore, which sold Esteve's pamphlets, including *Reformismo, dictadura, federalismo* (Reformism, Dictatorship, Federalism, c. 1922).[12] On Esteve's death in Weehawken, New Jersey, in 1925, *Cultura Obrera* commemorated his leadership and contributions with testimonials from the leading anarchists of the time. The paper went under in 1927 and was succeeded in New York by *Cultura Proletaria* (Proletarian Culture), under the editorship of one of Esteve's mentees, Marcelino García (1893–1977).[13]

The Spanish-born García had immigrated to the United States as a child and at fifteen worked in zinc mines in West Virginia; in New York, he did everything from working as a stevedore and a carpenter to operating an elevator. He also became a member of the *Cultura Obrera* group (Avrich 391). During the Spanish Civil War, he went to Spain and sent in two articles a week to the New York paper, but he was arrested by the fascists in Barcelona. Only with the intervention of Emma Goldman was he freed and able to return to New York to edit the paper (Avrich 174). In an interview García estimated that twenty-five hundred active Spanish anarchists and some two thousand sympathizers (not to be confused with an unknown total of anarchists from Mexican, Cuban, and other Spanish-speaking groups) lived in the United States during the 1920s and 1930s, and affirmed that *Cultura Proletaria* had four thousand subscribers at its peak, during the 1930s (Avrich 392).[14] García, nevertheless, regretted the intellectual focus of the paper, with the staff never really active in the trenches, at strikes and rallies, and blamed this for the paper's decline. This sentiment aside, *Cultura Proletaria* maintained an esprit de corps with its followers and a core group of about twenty-five volunteers who helped in its composition, printing, and mailing, as well as in the organizing of public lectures and events. José Hernández, one such volunteer, recalled, "When we had to mail out the paper each week, we all got together at the Center [Centro Internacional on Twenty-Third Street]. There was a long table and we all wrapped and addressed the paper and we mailed it the same day. To raise money for the hall and the paper we also had a monthly supper at the Center" (Avrich 394). The reach in numbers of both *Cultura Obrera* and *Cultura Proletaria* went beyond their staff's accounting as both papers were read aloud in workers' clubs and factories to many who never became subscribers or donors. Joachín Edo recounted that among Midwest steel and automobile workers, from Gary to Detroit to Youngstown, thousands of Spanish-speaking followers/readers often came together in conferences and picnics (Avrich 400).

Adrián del Valle (1872–1945), who wrote under the pseudonym Palmiro de Lidia, became an associate of Esteve's. Valle was a Catalonian anarchist who preceded Esteve on his route to New York and later became his collaborator. He, too, seems to have cut across all ethnic and geographic boundaries, and his writings, both political and literary, were featured in anarchist periodicals across the United States. Valle initially sought to establish a Spanish republic but was converted to anarchism when he regularly attended meetings of the freethinkers' club La Luz (Light) in Barcelona in the 1880s (Esenwein 131). After writing alongside Esteve for Barcelona's anarchist newspaper *El Productor*, he moved to New York City at the behest of anarchist leader Errico Malatesta in 1892, where he administered the newspaper *El Despertar* until Esteve took it over (Martin et al. 31; and see Shaffer). By 1898, he was writing for Brooklyn's *El Rebelde* (Rebel) in support of the Cuban war for independence—from which Esteve maintained his distance, not believing in nationalist movements. As co-editor of the paper, Valle published a weekly column titled Crónicas Subversivas (Subversive Chronicles, possibly titled in honor of Galleani's *Cronaca Sovversiva*), under his usual pseudonym. At the same time, he made a living by teaching classes in arithmetic, bookkeeping, Spanish grammar, and basic English (*El Rebelde*, 15 Sept. 1898). He also published literary works, such as the short play "Revista Tabaqueril" (Tobacco-Worker Revue, 15 Oct. 1898), for which he employed the pseudonym Lidón.[15] After the United States defeated Spain and occupied Cuba, Valle returned to the island in 1899 to support the anarchist cause by founding the newspaper *El Nuevo Ideal* (New Ideal) and a magazine, *El Audaz* (Audacious One). He made the island his base until his death in 1945, sending out political and literary works to be published in the Hispanic world, including in anarchist periodicals of the United States, such as New York's *Cultura Obrera* (from 1911 on) and *Inquietudes* (Disquietude, 1927), Tampa's *Nueva Vida* (New Life, 1924) and *Internacional* (1940), and, in Ohio, Steubenville's *Revista Unica* (Unique Magazine, 1928). Spanish-language commercial and community newspapers that did not promote an anarchist agenda, such as San

Antonio's *La Prensa* (Press), also published his work. Over the years, Valle's anarchist rhetoric was toned down, and he became more mainstream and popular in Cuba while still publishing in the United States.

Valle's and Esteve's anarchist successors in New York during the Spanish Civil War took on the task of bringing together the many Hispanic mutual aid societies and community organizations in a unified effort to restore the Spanish republic and expel fascism from Spain. The anarchists softened their radical rhetoric when they established the Sociedades Hispanas Confederadas (Federation of Hispanic Societies) and began publishing the federation's long-lasting newspaper, *España Libre* (Free Spain), which would appear in print from 1930 until 1977.[16] Departing somewhat from anarchist orthodoxy, the paper's working-class editors and many of its writers sought to forge a broader identity for the Spanish nation in exile and recruited a vast array of cultural workers from all the Spanish-speaking ethnic groups in and around New York City. The individual community groups hosted fundraising events, rallies, lectures, theatrical performances, picnics, and more. The newspaper, published as a weekly for most of its existence, was distributed through newsstands in the New York area and mailed to Spanish-speaking communities throughout the United States, Latin America, and Europe; underground correspondents in Spain distributed the paper on the peninsula and sent in reports of their work. According to Montse Feu-López, circulation peaked at five thousand copies (*España Libre* 114). Unlike many of the previously noted anarchist papers, *España Libre* limited reprints of anarchist theorists and devoted its eight broadsheet pages to news, Civil War coverage, political essays, personal narratives, opinion columns, community events, book reviews, cartoons, and so forth. The principal founder of the federation, the Andalusian José Castilla Morales (1893–1961), served as *España Libre*'s director from 1939 to 1961. Castilla Morales had written for labor newspapers in Cuba before fleeing to New York from dictator Gerardo Machado's repression. In Manhattan, he worked as a staff writer for the newspaper *Solidaridad* (Solidarity) and later became the assistant editor of *La Voz* (Voice). He also wrote for *España Libre* under various pseudonyms and emceed the federation's daily radio broadcast on WBBC (Brooklyn Broadcasting Corporation). Despite the number of anarchists working on *España Libre*, under Castilla Morales *España Libre* continuously campaigned against the spread of communism and fascism, which presumably led to its clean bill of health after being investigated by the FBI (Feu-López, *España Libre* 43, 122, 143).

Jesús González Malo (1913–65), who had served as a staff writer on *España Libre* since the 1950s, succeeded Castilla Morales in 1961; he had been an anarcho-syndicalist leader and militiaman in Santander, Spain, before going into exile in New York, where he first worked as a welder on the docks. González Malo's main concerns were to support the Spanish resistance—that is, to keep the issue in the forefront even after so many years of fascist rule—and to maintain the openness, egalitarianism, and diversity of *España Libre,* where all liberal ideologies were still welcome (Feu-López, *España Libre* 117, 123). Under González Malo's directorship, numerous women assumed greater leadership in the confederation and the newspaper. Carmen Aldecoa is a case in point; she had run an orphanage for Spanish refugee children in Lyon, France. In the 1940s, Aldecoa worked with various women's groups in the confederation and wrote articles for *España Libre* from women's perspectives. Then, in the 1950s and 1960s, she advocated an alliance of the working and middle classes; she also became a member of leadership committees, such as the confederation's International Advisory Committee, and was a leading organizer of protests in New York that sought to bring U.S. pressure on Spain (Feu-López, *España Libre* 102–4). After González Malo's term ended in 1965, *España Libre* gradually waned. It shut down in 1977, when the Spanish republic was finally restored.

Tampa/Ybor City

Tampa, Florida, and its historic neighborhood Ybor City became yet another concentrated center for anarchist action and publications. More than one hundred cigar factories relocated there from Cuba from the 1880s to the turn of the century, in part as a means to avoid the labor unrest that had been endemic to the industry in the Caribbean.[17] The factories were nevertheless plagued with anarchist and labor organizing and numerous strikes from their inception. Ultimately, the cigar workers formed the strongest unions of any Latino workers in the United States. One explanation for their success was that they were among the most literate and informed, especially because of the long-standing institution of the *lector*. *Lectores* were hired by the workers to read newspapers to them in the mornings and novels and labor/anarchist literature in the afternoons during their repetitive, often boring, artisan tasks. *La Aurora* (Dawn), the first worker's newspaper founded in Cuba, in 1865, had benefited from *lectores* among tobacco workers. Cuban,

Spanish, Italian, and Puerto Rican tobacco workers continued this tradition in Florida and founded a series of newspapers affiliated with their unions. Included among these were *La Federación* (Federation, est. 1890), *Boletín Obrero* (Worker Bulletin, est. 1903), *El Federal* (Federal, est. 1902), *El Internacional* (International, est. 1904), *El Obrero Industrial* (Industrial Worker, an Industrial Workers of the World [IWW] paper issued during the 1910s), *El Tabacalero* (Tobacco Worker, published by the Tobacco Workers Association in the 1930s), and *Vocero de la Unión de Tabaqueros* (Public Voice of the Tobacco Workers' Union, est. 1941).[18] All of these were highly influenced by anarchist teachings. However, the doctrinaire anarchist papers began even earlier, with Pedro Esteve's *El Esclavo*, in 1894.[19] *El Esclavo* was similar to Esteve's later papers in that it featured translations of the major anarchist ideologues; however, as the war for Cuban independence was still raging, *El Esclavo* supported the effort with essays and poems by major revolutionary writers, such as Francisco Sellén. It also featured several series of satirical columns by *cronistas* (columnists) under various pseudonyms; most notable of these was the column Crónicas Subversivas (Subversive Chronicles), written by anarchist writer and poet Palmiro de Lidia (Adrián del Valle) and published in *El Esclavo* in 1897 and 1898. The paper revealed its support of unions with its regular accounts of the strike committee's fund (Comisión de Huelga). As was the practice of many of these periodicals, their offices became centers for distribution of anarchist literature. The lists of publications that they distributed provide a sense of their reach. In one instance, *El Esclavo* listed some nine pamphlets published by El Ideal in Brooklyn that were available for free in its offices.[20]

Esteve's newspaper was followed by *La Voz del Esclavo* (Voice of the Slave), published in Spanish and Italian in 1900; *Liberación* (Liberation), published in 1912; and *Nueva Vida* (New Life), edited by Herminio González and R. Miqueli and published in 1924.[21] This last was one of the few anarchist newspapers to feature a weekly woman's column, Conciencia Femenina (Feminine Conscience), which was written by the co-editor's Cuban American wife, Violeta Miqueli de González. Overlapping the run of *Nueva Vida* was *El Boletín del Torcedor* (Cigar Rollers' Bulletin), published in 1924 by the Cigar Rollers Association and printed at Mascuñana Printers in Tampa. It too featured numerous weekly series of satirical *crónicas*, most notably those of "Don Mateo" (Antonio Calado). The newspaper often featured reprints from Esteve's *Cultura Obrera* and from Flores Magón's *Regeneración*, thus embracing the Northeast, Southwest, and West in its network of sister publications and affinities. In its militancy, *El Boletín* often engaged in polemics with *El Internacional.* It also listed anarchist publications for sale at its offices, including pamphlets imported from the Editorial La Protesta in Peru.

Some of these publications were issued at the Centro Obrero (Worker Center) in Ybor City, which had a press and served as the center of anarchist reading and discussion groups, union strategy meetings, and theatrical performances. Here, the most notable Latina anarchist, Luisa Capetillo (1879–1922), lectured and produced her plays; she also produced numerous essays that were published in the labor and anarchist press, not only in Tampa but also in New York, Boston, Los Angeles, and other cities on the continent and in the Caribbean (see Kanellos, *Greenwood* 1: 188–89). Her work as a labor organizer took her from her native Puerto Rico to Cuba, the Dominican Republic, Tampa, and New York; and in each locale she left her mark on local publications. As an early feminist, Capetillo promoted absolute equality of the sexes and advocated free love; she collected her essays and published them herself in four books during the first two decades of the twentieth century.[22] These included: *Ensayos libertarios* (Libertarian Essays, 1909), detailing her anarchist ideology; *La humanidad en el futuro* (Humanity in the Future, 1910), published to raise funds for her magazine; *Mi opinión sobre las libertades, derechos y deberes de la mujer* (My Opinion on the Liberties, Rights, and Duties of Women, 1911), developing her feminist ideology; and *Influencia de las ideas modernas* (The Influence of Modern Ideas, 1916), featuring many of her literary works and theatrical pieces.

Violeta Miqueli de González (c. 1893–1972), another anarchist to come out of the cigar factories of Ybor City/Tampa, was born to cigar-rolling parents in Ybor City but went on to attend the University of Havana and later obtained a master's degree in education from the Florida State College for Women. She was married to Herminio González, the co-editor of *Nueva Vida,* in which her weekly feminist column Conciencia Femenina ran in the 1920s. She also published articles in New York's *El Debate* (Debate) and *Nueva Era* (New Era). In subsequent decades, Miqueli continued writing in favor of women assuming more public roles in society while editing *Alpha* magazine in Tampa and publishing articles in Spanish in periodicals as far away as New York's *Cultura Proletaria* and *España Libre* (e.g., 15 Mar. 1940) and Buenos Aires's *La Prensa* (Press). A practitioner as well as a theorist, Miqueli ran a girls' school in Tampa for many years. Miqueli surfaced in

New York during the 1940s, where she performed in plays staged by the federation and published antifascist articles in *España Libre* (Feu-López, "Transnational" 139). Her most lasting and still referenced work, however, is her *Women in Myth and History* (1962).[23]

As the Depression hit, cigar-rolling machines displaced workers, and American smoking habits changed, many cigar workers in Ybor City/Tampa lost their jobs, and union and anarchist activity waned. They even assimilated into the cause of seeking to rid Europe of fascists during the war.

The Southwest

The third area of widespread anarchist publishing and organizing was the Southwest, where the most influential newspapers were founded or inspired by Ricardo Flores Magón (1873–1922) and his Partido Liberal Mexicano, which took on the task of deposing Mexican dictator Porfirio Díaz, eventually bringing on the 1910 Mexican Revolution.[24] By 1900, anarcho-syndicalist Flores Magón had launched his renowned newspaper *Regeneración* in Mexico City, where it was promptly repressed by the Díaz regime; before going into U.S. exile, Flores Magón was jailed four times for his radical journalism (see Kanellos and Martell 20–27). In 1904, he began publishing *Regeneración* in San Antonio, Texas; it transferred in 1905 to Saint Louis, Missouri, where the paper printed editions of twenty thousand copies (Hart 89); then the next year it was published in Toronto, Canada; and in 1908, he revived *Regeneración* in Los Angeles. No matter the location of its offices, *Regeneración* registered wide distribution throughout the United States and Mexico through various ingenious methods of smuggling the periodical. Flores Magón saw his group's commitment to the revolution in Mexico as the vanguard of liberation for all workers, and many anarchist newspapers around the country echoed those sentiments, even to the extent of making donations to *Regeneración*, the PLM, and defense funds to free Flores Magón and his followers when they were jailed. As had occurred with *Cultura Obrera* in New York during World War I, the U.S. government targeted *Regeneración* for breaking the Trading with the Enemy Act and the Espionage Act (both of 1917) and denied it mailing privileges (see Park 412–27). At least twice, authorities ransacked the offices of *Regeneración* and smashed its press. They also jailed and indicted Flores Magón on a number of occasions, including, on March 16, 1918, for publishing a manifesto to anarchists and laborers of the world. They arrested him again in 1918 for breaking U.S. neutrality laws; he was found guilty at trial and sentenced to twenty years at the federal penitentiary in Leavenworth, Kansas, where he died mysteriously in 1922.

Lázaro Gutiérrez de Lara (1870–1918) was one of the most active PLM members. He was jailed with Flores Magón and other members of the PLM in Los Angeles in 1909 for supposedly attempting to assassinate President William Howard Taft (*New York Times*, 26 Apr. 1940).[25] Under threat of deportation, Gutiérrez de Lara swore to authorities that he was not an anarchist, just a socialist and pacifist.[26] He was a lawyer, journalist, and writer who served as a member of the *Regeneración* editorial board. Contrary to his testimony in Los Angeles, which resulted in his freedom, he fought as a soldier in the heat of battle and was active in the famed miners' strike in Cananea, Mexico, an experience that he recorded in his 1907 anarchist novel *Los bribones* (The Scoundrels). He lost his life in Cananea, when he was captured and shot dead, his body burned and thrown into a river. Gutiérrez de Lara had defected from the PLM and joined the Francisco Madero camp, for which Flores Magón labeled him a traitor. From that point on, he presented himself as a socialist. Gutiérrez de Lara was one of the first writers to document the Mexican Revolution, with his *El pueblo mexicano y sus luchas por la libertad* (Los Angeles, 1914), which was published in New York that same year as *The Mexican People: Their Struggle for Freedom*.[27]

Another associate of both Flores Magón and Gutiérrez de Lara was Antonio P. de Araujo (1883–unk.), who had arrived in Cananea in 1905. With Gutiérrez de Lara and other associates of Flores Magón, he attempted to organize the miners as part of the effort to initiate the revolution against the Díaz regime; they founded the Club Liberal de Cananea as an affiliate of the PLM. The Cananea miners' strike broke out in 1906, and under pursuit by agents hired by the mining companies, Araujo, Gutiérrez de Lara, and others left and joined up with Flores Magón in Los Angeles. While Flores Magón was in jail or otherwise absent, Araujo edited *Regeneración*, but in 1908 he founded his own newspaper, taking as its title the motto of the PLM, *Reforma-Libertad-Justicia* (Reform, Liberty, and Justice). He would publish the paper at various sites, including El Paso, Austin, and Waco, Texas, and McAlester, Oklahoma, because of continued persecution. All the while, Araujo was organizing armed invasions of Mexico on behalf of the PLM. He was detained by federal authorities in Waco in 1908 and, like so many of his brethren, was sentenced to three years in Leavenworth (Flores Magón 132).

After his release in 1911, Araujo once again joined the battle, and in 1912 he was arrested in Calexico, California, for breaking U.S. neutrality laws. Once freed, he again picked up the duties of editor of *Regeneración* while Flores Magón was serving a sentence at McNeil Island in Washington State. It was during this time as editor of *Regeneración* that he initiated an international smear campaign against Juan Francisco Moncaleano and Rómulo S. Carmona for breaking with the Flores Magón group, as noted in detail below.

Like many anarchist newspapers, *Regeneración* advertised books and pamphlets and sold so-called *bibliotecas sociológicas* (sociological libraries); also, its affiliated anarchist bookstore, Librería Mexicana "La Aurora," owned and operated by Carmona, sold some eighty-seven titles published by *Regeneración* in the early 1900s. In addition to the *Regeneración* titles, Carmona bought books in Spain for the equivalent of five cents and sold them for fifty cents. His sources included the Francisco Sempere publishing house in Valencia and La Escuela Moderna in Barcelona. Among the four hundred titles he advertised in *Regeneración,* the newspaper also noted works from Spanish-language publishers in San Antonio, Saint Louis, and elsewhere in the United States. Carmona's relationship with Flores Magón went back to 1906–7 in El Paso: Carmona founded the Santiago de la Hoz liberal club there and was father to Flores Magón's lover and first wife, Paula Carmona. The senior Carmona also organized the Grupo Regeneración in Riverside, California (Barrera Bassols 11, 14–15).

With *Regeneración* as the Bible, so to speak, the PLM established chapters like the Riverside Grupo Regeneración and affiliated newspapers throughout the Southwest. Its affiliates included El Paso's *La Bandera Roja* (Red Flag), *Humanidad* (Humanity), *Punto Rojo* (Red Point), *Reforma-Libertad-Justicia,* and *Cerebro y Fuerza* (Brains and Power); Albuquerque's *El Demócrata* (Democrat); Los Angeles's *Libertad y Trabajo* (Freedom and Labor), *El Mosquito* (Mosquito), and *La Reforma Social* (Social Reform); and, from Del Rio, Texas, *El Liberal* (Liberal). As part of the anarchist movement, and PLM papers in particular, the role for women as editors and writers had expanded alongside their role as revolutionaries. In fact, a leader of the PLM, Práxedis Guerrero, in a long, front-page editorial in the October 18, 1913, issue of *Cerebro y Fuerza,* extolled the contributions of women revolutionaries.[28] Women's equality to men was to be part of the renovation of society that would take place with the triumph of the revolution.

Notable among the women who assumed leading roles in PLM-affiliated newspapers was Laredo's Sara Estela Ramírez (1881–1910). Born in Mexico, she was a schoolteacher in Laredo who gave fiery speeches at workers' meetings and published poetry and essays in the local Spanish-language press.[29] In 1901, she began publishing her own newspaper, *La Corregidora* (named for the heroine of independence, Josefa Ortiz de Domínguez, known as the Chief Magistrate); and in 1910 she started publishing the magazine *Aurora*, appropriating the popular anarchist metaphor for its title. Before her sudden death in 1910, she had written for Juana Gutiérrez de Mendoza's *Vésper: Justicia y Libertad* (Dawn: Justice and Liberty) and joined with her and other revolutionary women in founding Regeneración y Concordia (Regeneration and Concord), an organization to forward the interests of women, Native Americans, and the proletariat (Tovar 13).

Other PLM-affiliated periodicals under the direction of women were Teresa Villarreal's *El Obrero* (Worker) in San Antonio, Teresa and Andrea Villarreal's *La Mujer Moderna* (Modern Woman) in San Antonio, Isidra T. de Cárdenas's *La Voz de la Mujer* (Woman's Voice) in El Paso, and Blanca de Moncaleano's *Pluma Roja* (Red Pen) in Los Angeles. Many of these newspapers repeated anarchist rhetoric and spoke for and to women in order to enlist them in the revolutionary cause. The editors of *La Voz de la Mujer* demonstrated their militancy in exhorting revolutionary action in an editorial on July 28, 1907: "We face another challenge today, to take what we need, Liberty! We must become rebels. It is better to die than to allow our children to be made slaves. We, the mothers and wives, sisters or daughters, are responsible for meeting this challenge" (qtd. in translation in C. Lomas 302).[30]

According to the literary critic Clara Lomas, *Pluma Roja* placed women's emancipation at the forefront (300). The newspaper's motto on its masthead was "Instruid a la mujer y el triunfo de la Anarquía será breve" (Educate women, and the triumph of Anarchy will be at hand). Printed on the same press as *Regeneración*, *Pluma Roja* was founded and edited by Colombian anarchist Blanca de Moncaleano (dates unk.), who, with her husband, Juan Francisco Moncaleano (1883–1916), had been expelled for radical activities from Colombia, Cuba, and Mexico.[31] In the same building where both papers were printed, the Moncaleanos and Rómulo Carmona set up the Casa del Obrero Internacional (International Workers' Home), modeled after centers they had run in Bogotá and Mexico City.[32] Despite raids on the press by authorities, condemnation from fire marshals, competition and sabotage from the IWW, and attacks by the *Los Angeles Times*, Mexican workers were attracted to and benefited from the Casa del Obrero (Barrera Bassols 20). In *Pluma Roja*—as well as in *Regeneración* and other anarchist papers in which Blanca de Moncaleano published articles—she challenged patriarchal society, the state, and the church, and was severely critical of revolutionaries who were men not conscious of their own suppression and enslavement of women (C. Lomas 306).[33]

Blanca de Moncaleano's "Manifiesto a la Mujer" (Manifesto to Women), published in one of the few extant issues of Boston's monthly *Fraternidad* (Fraternity, Sept. 1915), is a revision of history from women's perspective and a militant call for women to break the chains that have suppressed their progress over the millennia, and consequently the progress of the entire human race. Moncaleano begins her polemic with a passionate, poetic invocation, redolent with oratory rhetoric that appeals to motherhood and situates women's exploitation across time and space:

> I direct these words to you, the sublime human shape that some ten thousand years ago the Vedas called the mother of Humanity; to you, who the Church fathers denied had a soul; to you, the unending source of life, the key to all that exists; to you, the slave of priests, governors, and the rich go my words; to you, who makes innumerable sacrifices to raise your children, and when they are all grown and robust and you are at the door to happiness, tyrants tear them away in the name of the fatherland and throw them into battle, where they are ripped to pieces by deadly lead, and they will become food for worms and crows: a sad end for that immense treasure of your love![34]

She then goes on, maintaining a poetic and declamatory tone and rhythm, to elaborate how enslaved women have responded by continuing to create life and continuing to love in response to the war and hate created by the church, the state, and the rich. And, while these forces have enslaved and maintained the poor in poverty and ignorance, their words of war and hate have drowned out "la voz redentora de Anarquia, que es vida y amor, como natura nos lo enseña" (the redemptive call of Anarchy, which is life and love, as nature has prescribed).

After expounding on the laws of nature that humans should obey and assigning all ills to the triumvirate of the church, capital, and the state, Moncaleano calls for women to break their chains:

> break that heavy religious chain and enter the sanctuary of rational science, where liberty will crown your brow, like a reward for your powerful effort. Listen to me. I approach you not like Veronica used her dusty robes to wipe up the tears of the cowering God; nor do I wish you to come crying to me like the mother of the crucified Jew; desolation has no place in my life; nor do I smile as I come to speak with you, like Safos and Mesalinas in convents, because my bitter lips only curse instead of bless. I am not here to whisper into your ear, as do those snakes in cassocks; I'm here to speak like a thunderstorm, I am a rebel and as such I speak to you; I'm not here to speak of the peace that debases the slaves, nor to murmur sorrowful words; I'm here to speak to you of rebellion and vengeance, I'm here to explain the cause of the evil that sickens you, and to designate the way to avenge yourself with dignity. So, listen!

Next, Moncaleano offers paragraphs of diatribe against the nests of vipers that religious institutions have been over time, debasing women and infecting popes, kings, and all forms of government with evil around the world and across time, "educando al mundo para la esclavitud" (educating the world for enslavement). She then traces the origins of the class system, the creation of militarist societies, and the causes of the wars afflicting the world. She invites women to ascend to a vantage point overlooking the carnage on battlefields across time and nations, battlefields created by the clergy, government, and capital, following the teachings of the Talmud, the Koran, the Bible, and other sacred texts.

Moncaleano invigorates this proposal with an image typical of socialist thought: "While the world becomes populated with widows and orphans, smoldering ruins and people disabled for industrial production, while the arts and industries are turned into skeletal ruins, the high and mighty, the impresarios of war, dance in the sumptuous ballrooms of their palaces and, clinking their glasses in insolent libation, they take account of the millions of workers who are left to be sacrificed in the slaughterhouse of war." At each step of the way, Moncaleano concretizes her vision for *tú*, her ideal female reader:

> and your children will be part of an army of beggars who, weak from hunger, will approach the marble steps of the lordly mansion pleading to the powerful man for charity, and he will answer with a strident demeaning guffaw that stifles the anguished cries in your throat. And your daughters will enter whorehouses after having lost their innocence in the arms of those same gentlemen who harangued the ignorant masses, depicting a beautiful future full of honor and glory that awaited them if they fought on behalf of the fatherland.

And, appealing to the maternal instinct, she declares: "Criar hijos para que se los coman los 'cuervos' es cosa horrible!" (It is horrible to raise children only for the crows to eat them!).

After all this accumulation of tragedy and exploitation caused by the hateful triumvirate, Moncaleano finally arrives at the call to action for women, the point of her manifesto:

> What can be done to avoid so much crime and to safeguard the lives of your children? Destroy the tyrant, attack that palace where the jailor of liberty lives, unite ourselves in order to conquer by force the rights we are born with. By destroying the religious yoke that makes women submissive slaves and workers vile pariahs. Yes, demolish that den from which the rich, the governor, and the priest officiate while they feast on proletarian blood; sweep away the barriers that obstruct our triumphant march, cutting off the heads of the executioners to the rhythm of our libertarian songs.
>
> To die breaking the chains is more dignified than kissing them. To die giving a world of liberty to children is to live eternally. Giving them a beautiful world where humanity, redeemed by education, will labor for its own welfare, without soldiers, priests, the wealthy, and governments. An anarchic world in which your children will be safe!
>
> Yes, woman, give vent to the ire in your breast, dry the tears in your eyes and light in them the torch of vengeance, make a fist and help me with mighty force to hammer down that enormous fortress gate

of unconsciousness imprisoning the ignorant masses groaning under heavy chains.

Help me, and be not afraid to tear down that millennial wall that divides man into races and states. Help me show the children that road that leads to the port of Anarchy. Be no longer hesitant. Join your effort to anger, help me destroy palaces and tyrants, jails, military quarters, churches, and convents. Help me build the eternal city of harmony and goodness, the city of Anarchy.

So strong was her writing that El Paso's *Cerebro y Fuerza* (18 Oct. 1913) called her "virile," a gendered term reserved for brave and bold exponents of revolutionary thought. Her writings, including a statement that appeared in the June 27, 1915, issue of *Pluma Roja*, lend credence to this view: "Lost in the supposition of their superiority, stupefied by their ignorance, men have believed that, without the assistance of women, they can reach the goal of human emancipation."[35] As would be expected, Moncaleano sought to break down the nationalist ideological linkage of woman to home, family, and procreation for the nation. Other women in the PLM offered equally caustic critiques of patriarchal men. Unlike the male leaders of the PLM, such as Ricardo and his brother Enrique Flores Magón, who believed that it was women's "'feminine duty'—to coddle men, nurture them, and dare them into becoming revolutionaries," Moncaleano "by contrast, ordered women from their prescribed functions entirely" (Pérez, *Decolonial* 69). Eventually, the Moncaleanos, accompanied by Rómulo Carmona and León Cárdenas Martínez, split with the Flores Magón faction, principally because they were more engaged in an educational and cultural project, in contrast with the Magonistas and their interest in armed revolution.[36] Jacinto Barrera Bassols, the leading historian on the PLM, opines that the best period of *Regeneración* came about when the Moncaleanos and Carmona were involved. After splitting with Flores Magón, Juan Francisco Moncaleano joined Martínez in editing *Cerebro y Fuerza*, which they used as a forum to attack the Magonistas (20).[37] Juan Francisco Moncaleano died on January 1, 1916, at the age of thirty-three. Remaining in Los Angeles, Blanca and their children, after seeing the fate of anarchists like Ricardo Flores Magón and suffering repression themselves, changed their name to Lawson and went underground. The Moncaleanos' grandchildren live in Southern California to this day.[38]

Of course, the Magonistas were not the only anarcho-syndicalists active in the West and Southwest in the early twentieth century. *Fuerza Consciente, Revista Ilustrada (Dedicada a la Propaganda Anarquista y Revolucionaria)* (Conscious Strength Illustrated Magazine [Dedicated to Anarchist and Revolutionary Propaganda]) began publishing on March 15, 1913, in New York City, but by October it had relocated to Los Angeles under the editorship of José Vilariño. As of March 7, 1914, Jaime Vidal had taken the helm of the magazine and changed its format to a broadsheet. Very little is known about Vilariño, except that in 1911 he was chairman of the Marine Firemen, Oilers and Watertenders Union, affiliated with *Cultura Obrera*. By 1915 he was working on the anarchist paper *Voluntad* (Volition) in New York. But Vidal was a well-known colleague of Pedro Esteve, had worked on *Cultura Obrera* and served as secretary of the aforementioned union, and even did a stint at *Regeneración*. As a personal friend of Francisco Ferrer i Guàrdia, the martyred founder of the Modern School, Vidal established organizations to continue Ferrer's socialist legacy but also, according to Sueiro Seoane ("El asesinato" 176–77), hatched plots to assassinate King Alfonso of Spain in revenge for Ferrer's assassination.[39] Vidal also founded the Comité Pro-Revolución Española (Pro–Spanish Revolution Committee), which was affiliated with the Revolutionary Party headquartered in Paris, France (see Goldman). While working with the union and publishing his own periodical, *Cultura Proletaria* (1910–11), Vidal also published articles in Spanish and English in *Cultura Obrera*, proposing among other things an international organization of workers to incorporate more than just anarchists, "to open a path and create the opportunity for the social ideas to develop among the slaves" (30 Dec. 1911).[40] In the March 24, 1912, issue, he published an extensive, but practical, essay on "How to Strike." *Cultura Obrera* featured numerous other writings by Vidal. In May 1912, Vidal and Esteve founded the magazine *Brazo y Cerebro* (Brawn and Brains), in New York. By 1913, the U.S. Post Office had refused mailing privileges to the magazine, at which point Vidal published a plea in *Regeneración* (11 Jan. 1913) and presumably other periodicals for volunteers throughout the United States, Mexico, Puerto Rico, Cuba, Canada, and Spain to distribute *Brazo y Cerebro* in their regions. *Brazo y Cerebro*'s format would be emulated and its contents simulated and reproduced by Vidal's next venture: *Fuerza Consciente*, which he began directing in March 1914 and promptly moved from Los Angeles to San Francisco. The government canceled its mailing privileges, and Vidal announced its pending closure in *Regeneración* on March 6, 1915. He issued the paper's last number in May. (On September 15, Vidal's essay "Trinchera Anarquista" [Anarchist Trench] appeared in Boston's *Fraternidad*, but this was not necessarily an indication that he had moved to Boston.) While *Fuerza Consciente* lasted, it reprinted essays by the leading European and Latino anarchists, such as Ricardo Flores Magón and Práxedis Guerrero. Its January 15, 1915, issue was notable in its focus on free love, which featured an essay by Luisa Capetillo on the subject. She contributed a number of essays to both *Brazo y Cerebro* and *Fuerza Consciente* by mail from Tampa, under the header of "Femeninas" (Feminine Themes). *Fuerza Consciente*'s lists of subscribers included readers from all over the United States, from New York to Corpus Christi, Texas, and even Havana and Panama City. The newspaper ran its own bookstore, where it sold many anarchist titles, including pamphlets by Jaime Vidal.

The Latino affiliates of the IWW in Tampa, the West, the Southwest, and the Midwest produced numerous labor newspapers that promoted anarchism.[41] While anarchists like Pedro Esteve had at times associated with the IWW, many became disillusioned and separated themselves from the organization and its publishing enterprises. Latinos in the West had a different experience from Esteve's with the Wobblies. Actually, early in its history the IWW was active in Northern Mexico and just north of the border, and by 1908 the IWW had built a hall in Holtville, on the California border, begun publishing a Spanish-language newspaper, *Libertad y Trabajo* (Freedom and Labor), and given strong support to Flores Magón and the PLM (Zimmer 238). IWW activity among Latinos extended from New York to the Midwest and Northern California, but in Los Angeles the Wobblies were more successful in working with Mexican laborers and in producing periodicals in Spanish.

One of these newspapers was *El Rebelde* (Rebel), published from 1915 to 1917 by the IWW Latin Propaganda League, under the supposed editorship of Doroteo Arango (Pancho Villa's real name). Elsewhere, Spanish poet and essayist A. V. Azuara appeared as its editor as well as the author of pamphlets for sale through the newspaper. These included *Una gran unión de trabajadores* (A Great Workers' Union) and *Viaje a Alaska* (Trip to Alaska), relating to his work in canneries in Alaska. Azuara had also worked in fisheries in California and mines in Arizona, where he was arrested for his activism in the Clifton and Morenci strikes (Harrison 146; *Regeneración*, 16 Sept.

1916). Unlike the Spanish anarchists of the East Coast, Azuara immigrated to Mexico and then made his way to California, where his union organizing activities for the IWW resulted in his imprisonment for twenty years at Leavenworth (see *I.W.W. Prisoners*).

Among the IWW periodicals published in Los Angeles were *Huelga General* (General Strike, est. 1913), edited by José Corona, and *El Obrero Industrial* (Industrial Worker, est. 1914). In Chicago, the Wobblies published *Solidaridad: El Periódico de los Trabajadores* (Solidarity: The Workers' Newspaper, est. 1923); and in Brooklyn they published a periodical also named *Solidaridad*, which ran for more than ten years, beginning in 1919. Communist newspapers, such as the mimeographed *Claridad Proletaria* (Proletariat Clarity), published by the Revolutionary League of the United States in the 1930s, also appeared in Chicago, Detroit, and New York. The most important of the Communist-led Latino papers was *Pueblos Hispanos* (Hispanic Peoples), edited by Puerto Rican poet Juan Antonio Corretjer, who had recently gained his release from federal prison in Atlanta but was prohibited from returning to Puerto Rico to resume his radical activities. He moved to New York and immediately founded *Pueblos Hispanos*, a newspaper that covered liberation movements throughout the Americas and the world and included some of the most renowned Puerto Rican writers and intellectuals in New York between 1943 and 1944.

Aside from ideological differences, what set this anarchist group of periodicals apart from the hundreds of commercial and community-based newspapers was their lack of, or indifference to, the national or ethnic makeup of readers, and their unwillingness to change their identity or ideological stance. As they were opposed to national identities, which separate the workers of the world, they also did not believe in borders. They were unified in opposing capitalism and the exploitation of working people, which they considered synonymous with Americanism. What also united these workers' intellectual efforts was their publishing in Spanish and building an audience or community among Spanish speakers regardless of their ethnicity or nationality. In that, they were in the vanguard of implicitly building a Latino consciousness in the United States, a consciousness that is only today really being celebrated, especially for channeling the economic and political power of today's much larger Latino population. A clear example of unifying the diverse Latino populations in a political cause, other than anarchism, was *Es-*

paña Libre's willing suspension of radical rhetoric in order to bring together a broad range of community organizations to raise funds and subvert the fascist government in Spain. Always implicit in that compromise, however, was a return to educating the laboring masses to bring about a social revolution in Spain, once democracy was restored, and presumably to produce social revolution in the United States and the world.

CHAPTER 6

Conservative Culture and Religiosity

The role of religion, in all its diversity and historical evolution, in building Latino culture in this country has, until recently, not been adequately studied or understood. In the past few decades, however, a number of studies have been published regarding religious thought and practice in the diverse Latino communities of the United States. They begin to document the role of Latinos in building the Catholic, Presbyterian, Methodist, and Mormon Churches and Latino Judaism, among others. They also investigate popular and alternative religious practices, such as Santeria and spiritism among Caribbean-origin Latinos, the Penitentes in New Mexican life and culture, faith healing, Hispanic festivals, and religious pageantry (see Stevens-Arroyo and Díaz-Stevens). Such studies as J. P. Dolan and Allan Figueroa Deck's *Hispanic Catholic Culture in the U. S.* (1994), Moisés Sandoval's edited collection *Fronteras* (1983), and Tim M. Matovina and Gerald E. Poyo's edited collection *Presente!* (2000) go a long way to providing previously unknown knowledge to even the church itself about Latino Catholicism. Likewise, Paul Barton's *Hispanic Methodists, Presbyterians, and Baptists in Texas* (2006), R. Douglas Brackenridge and Francisco García-Treto's *Iglesia Presbiteriana* (1987), Joshua Grijalva's *A History of Mexican Baptists in Texas, 1881–1891* (1982), and Aviva Ben-Ur's *Sephardic Jews in America* (2012) are among the publications that have elucidated a history of diversity in Latino religiosity.

Notwithstanding these books, the history of Latinos and their religious thought and practices needs much further and deeper study, as does the development of Latino culture in the United States as a whole. During the nineteenth century, the United States incorporated lands and peoples by conquest and purchase; by the end of that century, great waves of Hispanic immigration ensued; it persisted throughout the twentieth and persists in the twenty-first century. The most important historical events that resulted in the growth of the Latino population were U.S. expansion south and then west to occupy lands either expropriated or purchased from the Spanish Empire and later Mexico during the course of the entire nineteenth century; the massive immigration of economic, political, and religious refugees from the Mexican Revolution, beginning in 1910; the Spanish-American War of 1898 and the subsequent incorporation of Puerto Ricans as American citizens in 1917; and, throughout the twentieth century, the building of large enclaves of Hispanic immigrants and refugees (the immigration often as a result of U.S. foreign policy and interventionism), enclaves that became centers of Latino minority culture in the urban centers of Boston, Chicago, El Paso, Los Angeles, Miami, New York, Philadelphia, San Antonio, and Tampa. Today, we are still receiving the economic and political refugees of Central American civil wars that were supported by the United States.

The religious affiliations and diverse religious practices of Latinos have been critical to their evolving as ethnic and minority groups in the United States. Part of the Americanization process of Puerto Ricans on the island and on the mainland was their being targeted by Protestant missionaries. An integral part of the practice of Mormonism is the conversion of Latin Americans and Native Americans, thus the need for missionary experience in Latin America for the Church of Latter-day Saints. During the Mexican Revolution, the Catholic Church set up its hierarchy in exile, in Texas and Southern California, and this helped solidify the Catholic identity of Mexicans and Mexican Americans in the United States. In Mexico, an entire war was fought (and funded in part by religious exiles and immigrant communities in the United States) over the role of religion in Mexican life: the Cristero War of 1926–29. From the 1920s through the 1950s, churches and church societies were the most stable and unifying institutions in the immigrant communities of Cubans, Mexicans, Puerto Ricans, and Spaniards. Quite often, the first institution that immigrants constructed in their new home was a church named for their patron saint; affiliated with the churches were the numerous lay organizations they founded. One such society was the Círculo de Obreros Católicos San José (Saint Joseph Catholic Workers' Society) in East Chicago, Indiana, in the 1920s and 1930s, which preserved language, faith, and culture by performing plays, sponsoring fundraising dances and bazaars, publishing newspapers, and even organizing civil rights protests.

As much as the historical role of religion in building Latino communities is unrecognized, even the religious background of civil rights, land rights, and workers' rights movements in the 1960s and 1970s is often ignored or minimized by political scientists and historians. The beginning of the Chicano Movement, with the farmworker strikes and boycotts, as well as the school walkouts, was largely successful not only because churches and religious personnel, both Catholic and Protestant, offered meeting facilities, guidance, and funding, but also because the leaders and participants were themselves spiritual, often openly praying and invoking religious symbolism to inspire and motivate participants. Even the militant struggle of the late 1960s to recover ancestral lands in New Mexico was led by a Pentecostal minister, Reies López Tijerina. And the contemporary literary movement that has helped define Latino identity in the United States has done so by exploring spirituality and religious practices, so clear in such foundational works as Piri Thomas's *Down These Mean Streets* (1967) and *Savior, Savior, Hold My Hand* (1972), Tomás Rivera's *. . . y no se lo tragó la tierra / And the Earth Did Not Devour Him* (1971), Pat Mora's *Chants* (1984), and Rudolfo Anaya's *Bless Me, Ultima* (1972). Numerous other religious beliefs and practices have helped define a Latino identity; for example, the development of salsa music is inconceivable without Santeria, which also informs the Nuyorican poetry movement, especially as practiced by Sandra María Esteves and Tato Laviera. Similarly, Santeria is evident in such Cuban American visual arts as the canvases of Paul Sierra. Devotion to the Virgin of Guadalupe has informed much of Chicano easel and mural art, as practiced by Yolanda López and Patssi Valdez, and Chicano theater, especially as pioneered by the movement's founder, Luis Valdez, in such works as *La Carpa de los Rasquachis* (The Tent of the Underdogs, 1974) and *La Pastorela* (The Shepherd's Play, 1975).

Since 1992, the University of Houston's Recovering the US Hispanic Literary Heritage program has been locating, preserving, and studying a large body of religious thought written by Latinos during the nineteenth and early twentieth centuries. In that treasure trove of manuscripts and printed material are hundreds of religious periodicals, previously unknown to scholars, that circulated in Spanish-speaking communities during this time span: Baptist, Presbyterian, and Methodist newspapers for wide circulation; weekly newspapers by church-related groups that served as a major source of information for the ethnic enclaves; Catholic magazines for a general readership; and Sephardic newspapers from New York and California, written in Ladino, an archaic form of Spanish, but printed in Hebrew characters. The varieties of language expression—monolingual, bilingual, at times trilingual—reveal further diversity of the reading habits and abilities of the congregations over time.

Equally unknown, and now unearthed for the first time, are the hundreds of Spanish-language books published by and for Latino faithful from such cities as El Paso, San Antonio, Kansas City, and Chicago, where religious refugees settled and immigrant communities developed. They run the gamut from Bibles, catechisms, and books of sermons in Spanish to autobiographies of converts and ministers, memoirs of religious-political exiles, and books detailing the role of religion in social and political life. In addition, the Recovering the US Hispanic Literary Heritage program has brought into its archives thousands of manuscript sermons, pieces of correspondence, book manuscripts, photographs, reports, and studies that are becoming the raw material for scholarly examination and commentary.

In the Southwest, publishers, editorialists, columnists, novelists, poets, and playwrights were almost unanimous in developing and promoting the concept of a *México de afuera* (a Mexican nation abroad). Essentially an ideology of exile, it promoted the idea of a Mexican colony existing outside of Mexico, in which it was the duty of the individual to maintain the Spanish language, keep the Catholic faith, and insulate the children from what community leaders perceived as the low moral standards practiced by Anglo-Americans. Basic to this belief system was an imminent return to Mexico, when the hostilities of the revolution were over. Mexican national culture was to be preserved in the midst of what intellectuals considered an iniquitous Anglo-Protestant culture that aggressively degraded and discriminated against Latinos. On the other hand, the expatriates believed that Mexico was so transformed by the socialist hordes that had conducted and won the revolution that the only true Mexican culture survived in exile, precisely in their exile and immigrant *colonias* (colonies) (see Bruce-Novoa, "*La Prensa*"). The ideology was most expressed and disseminated by cultural elites, many of whom were political and religious refugees from the Mexican Revolution. They represented the most conservative segment of Mexican society in the homeland; in the United States, their cultural and business entrepreneurship exerted leadership in all phases of life in the *colonia* and solidified a conservative substratum for Mexican American culture for decades to come. While these political and religious refugees truly believed this ideology, they exerted themselves to promote it through publications to the economic refugees, that is, the immigrants whose descendants make up the largest portion of the Mexican American community today.

With the Cristero War, initiated as a reaction to the governmental persecution of the Catholic Church stemming from the anticlerical tenets of the 1917 Mexican Constitution, a fresh batch of political refugees founded newspapers and publishing houses to attack the Mexican government and to serve the needs of the religious community in exile. During the buildup of conflict between church and state in Mexico, such periodicals as *La Guadalupana: Revista Mensual Católica* (Guadalupan: Catholic Monthly Magazine, est. 1922) and *El Renacimiento: Semanario Católico* (Renascence: Catholic Weekly, est. 1923) were founded in El Paso (along with others elsewhere, such as *La Esperanza* [Hope, est. 1924] in Los Angeles). In fact, El Paso became the destination of choice for many Spanish-language religious presses, not just for Catholics, as Mexican Baptists, Methodists, and others also took refuge in Texas. The influence of the Cristero refugees was felt in many immigrant newspapers, not just the religious ones; the already conservative counterrevolutionary papers naturally focused on the religious persecution in Mexico and the atrocities committed by the government of *bolcheviques* (Bolsheviks). A spate of books appeared defending the church and decrying the atrocities committed against the clergy in Mexico. But, more important, a Spanish-language religious publishing industry that issued books and periodicals became cemented in El Paso, where it still functions today.

Aside from religious leaders in exile during the revolution, one of the most powerful political, business, and intellectual figures in the Mexican immigrant community was Ignacio E. Lozano (1886–1953), founder and operator of the Casa Editorial Lozano publishing house and of the two longest lasting and best distributed Spanish-language dailies: San Antonio's *La Prensa* (Press, est. 1914) and Los Angeles's *La Opinión* (Opinion, est. 1926), the latter still publishing today.[1] With the business training and experience that he received in Mexico, Lozano contributed professionalism and business acumen to Latino journalism in the United States, reflected in his hiring of well-trained journalists, including Teodoro Torres, the "Father of Mexican Journalism," as editor of *La Prensa*. The ideas of men like Torres and Lozano, such as the ideology of *México de afuera,* reached thousands not only in San Antonio but throughout the Southwest, Midwest, and Northern Mexico through a vast system of newsstand sales, home delivery, and mail. In its day, *La Prensa* was indeed influential, not only as a medium of communication, but also as a vehicle of the intellectual leadership of Lozano and many of his prominent writers and editorialists in Mexican and Mexican American communities.

Within the print and intellectual culture of the Mexican Southwest, however, no one was more influential in laying a basis for Latino conservatism than the exiled politician and publisher Nemesio García Naranjo (1883–1962). Not only did he represent both facets of Mexican exile—political and religious—but he was what today we understand to be a transnational figure, one who moves between two or more national cultures, serving as an intermediary or actually creating new cultural forms out of hybridity. If such is true of García Naranjo, then he was a figure ahead of his times, for Mexican American culture by definition would develop during the 1930s to the present through a process of hybridization. As such, the writer, orator, and magazine publisher García Naranjo may be better understood in terms of what today is seen as border culture, which in itself is a hybrid phenomenon. Ironically, despite his bilingualism, hybridity, and ability to function as an insider-outsider, García Naranjo espoused the conservation of a Mexican national culture and a religiosity that flourished in the late nineteenth century during the dictatorship of Porfirio Díaz.[2] García Naranjo had served in the national congress during the Díaz administration, and for the rest of his life, both in U.S. exile and in Mexico, he remained a staunch defender of the tyrant. The Díaz regime, for him, "had been a time of civic virtue, personal honor, cultural, economic, and intellectual progress" (R. García 238). As probably the most influential Mexican exile in the United States, García Naranjo had command of various print media and such an eloquent, expository style that he became the most popular speaker in Mexican communities throughout the Southwest.

García Naranjo was born on March 8, 1883, close to the northern border of Mexico, in Lampazos, once known as the Athens of the North for its flourishing high culture (and also the birthplace of a number of anarchist instigators of the Mexican Revolution in the Villarreal family: Andrea, Antonio, and Teresa). García Naranjo's first exile took place during childhood, when his politically active parents were expelled to Encinal, Texas; there, he attended elementary school and learned English. The family later returned to Mexico, where García Naranjo attended Monterrey's Colegio Civil. He graduated in 1902 and went on to study law in Mexico City, where, upon graduating in 1909, he worked as a professor at the National University and the National Military College (Camp 93). From 1910 through 1913, he served as a *diputado* (member of the national congress) representing various states; he rose to become the general secretary of the congress. Next, he served in President Victoriano Huerta's cabinet—Huerta had come to power after a coup supported by European powers and the United States—as the minister of public instruction and fine arts. He is remembered for having emphasized the humanities and arts, as well as morality in education, which were themes that reoccurred in his speeches and writings throughout his life. When Huerta was forced out of power and fled into exile, García Naranjo also went into exile in the United States. His English-language ability landed him a job at *Cosmopolitan* magazine to cover Mexico, but he never worked this job; instead, in 1915, after spending some time in Central America, he landed in San Antonio, where he founded the magazine *Revista Mexicana* (Mexican Review) and worked intermittently for *La Prensa* as a journalist and editorialist (López Portillo Tostado 76–77). In 1923, he and his family returned to Mexico under a general amnesty. In the prologue to a collection of García Naranjo's speeches, his fellow exiled compatriot and lifelong associate Querido Moheno stated that García Naranjo founded the magazine in San Antonio because the "populace is still ours, because it still prays to the Virgin of Guadalupe and praises Father Hidalgo."[3] Moheno further elaborated that the motive for establishing the periodical was *hacer patria* (to create homeland) (*Discursos* 20–21). Thus, religious and national identities were inseparable as motives for García Naranjo in establishing his magazine, as they were for most of his lifelong work as a public intellectual.

Revista Mexicana became the most respected forum for expatriate opposition to the revolution, particularly for exiles throughout the Southwest and as far north as New York to attack the revolutionary regime of Venustiano Carranza. García Naranjo often expressed proudly that it was the best designed, most intelligent, and highest quality magazine produced by Hispanics anywhere. Indeed, the quality of the essays and editorials, poetry and creative prose, and political cartoons reveals the high level of confidence the publication earned in the expatriate Mexican community. Together with *La Prensa*, it served as base to popularize García Naranjo's beliefs as well as his personal leadership in exile and immigrant organizations. And, as Maura L. Fuchs has asserted, *Revista Mexicana* was as much a transnational product as García Naranjo himself, and should be considered in both U.S. and Mexican scholarship, incorporating English- and Spanish-language sources and references (41). But as a hybrid product, *Revista Mexicana* was subject to U.S. government censorship. In fact, García Naranjo was indicted for violation of U.S. neutrality laws, was tried and found guilty, and had to pay a $500 fine as well as translate and file with the government the magazine's editorials that mentioned President Woodrow Wilson, General John Pershing, and Secretary of State William Jennings Bryan (García Naranjo, *Memorias* 8: 356–67).

García Naranjo's editorials in *Revista Mexicana* served as a forum for exile thought, railing against the turmoil and disruption of life in Mexico during the revolution and its leaders, especially General Carranza. However, his editorials also revealed and popularized his stance about the resident Mexican American population of the Southwest, a population that at the time represented a quandary for many immigrants and refugees: these locals were a diverse people who often looked like them but who spoke an antiquated, English-influenced version of Spanish and were an oppressed national minority. Whereas most journalists and creative writers visited opprobrium on these *pochos* (non-Mexicans) and satirized their embrace of Anglo-American culture as *agringados* (gringoized) and *renegados* (renegade by denying their Mexican heritage), García Naranjo, perhaps because of his own hybridity and his many years among Mexican Americans, embraced them as cultural heroes. Perhaps, as a participant observer, he intuited the future, when many children of the immigrants and exiles raised in the United States would find themselves in similar hybrid circumstances, despite all the pressure on families exerted by the widespread ideology of *México de afuera.*

In fact, in the front-page editorial of the inaugural issue of *Revista Mexicana,* published on August 1, 1915, and featuring a full-cover portrait of Porfirio Díaz, García Naranjo appealed to Mexican Americans by assuring prospective readers that the magazine would elevate the image of *la raza* (culture) and fight stereotypes: "We propose to elevate the credit accorded our people; eradicate the calumnies promoted against our culture . . . contribute to the betterment of those compatriates who have for fifty years lived in this country."[4] Notable here is not only that one mission of the magazine is the defense of the resident Mexican American population, but also that its stance includes viewing them as *compatriotas*, that is, admitting them into the Mexican nation. Fuchs sees this stance as a reaction to the segregation, even lynchings of Mexican and Black people in Texas during this period (299). In an effort to document this oppression, García Naranjo included in the September 29, 1915, issue a letter by a former Brownsville sheriff, Emilio C. Forto, originally published in the *Pan American Laborer*, that called attention to the attacks and even murders of Mexican Americans by the Texas Rangers and other authorities, who tried to force the residents off their lands: they "make so many laws and codes that it is imposible for the poorly educated Mexicans to understand them" (Fuchs 299).

In editorials published on October 22 and November 26, 1916, García Naranjo took on the issue of segregation in public education, under the headlines "Debe admitirse a los niños mexicanos" (Mexican Children Should Be Admitted) and "La educación de la servidumbre" (The Education of the Servant Class). In both, he censures the exclusion and/or separation of Mexican-origin children in poor, substandard schools. However, in the latter, he goes on to connect this racial discrimination to the United States' imperialistic practices in Latin America. He states, "one of the points of U.S. foreign policy precisely is to humiliate Latin people, dissolve their institutions, pulverize their traditions, convert them into something inferior, despicable, and devalued."[5] García Naranjo in his broad understanding of the implications of Yankee imperialism, like Francisco Ramírez before him (see chapter 3), broadens his perspective beyond Mexico, choosing to focus on the U.S. domination of one of its colonies: Puerto Rico. In the editorial, he judges the island colony to be "de abyección y esclavitud" (abject and enslaved); where once existed a well-evolved and respectable Hispanic culture, now exclusive instruction in English has been imposed on public schools, a new unjust judicial system has been instituted, and Puerto Ricans have been dislodged from their ancestral land. This is a new phase of imperialistic conquest, one in which no blood is spilled, but, "instead of fighting they attempt to defile; instead of wounding with Mausers [rifles], they slowly but surely break down dignity and pride; and over two generations, they meet their objective: conquering the desired lands and creating a servant class for exploitation."[6] Where Ramírez had been prescient in his 1850s editorials, warning countries south of the border of the imperialistic designs of the United States, some sixty years later García Naranjo not only proved him right, but went further by elucidating the relationship of U.S. colonialism to the country's internal colonies, in this case that of Mexicans in the Southwest after the United States had incorporated them as a result of the 1846–48 war, which converted them into a proletariat. But also obvious to García Naranjo was that the same conversion or degradation was being effected on the children of Mexican immigrants. Another lesson for his times in this editorial was, of course, the linkage that García Naranjo was establishing among the diverse Hispanic peoples: Puerto Ricans on the island or on the continent, Mexicans in Mexico or in the United States, and Central and South Americans targeted by U.S. imperialist or neocolonial design.

García Naranjo was a border Mexican, a hybrid, a transnational, an insider-outsider. In fact, he broke into journalism in 1900, writing for a border newspaper: Nuevo Laredo's *El Demócrata Fronterizo* (Border Democrat). He achieved his perspective and formed his conclusions on the United States and Mexico, conclusions that are so current today among cultural theorists and political scientists, because of his transnationalism. Thus, I do not agree with Fuchs, who ascribes García Naranjo's view of U.S. imperialism to his status as an exile (303). The fact is that hundreds of other Mexican writers in exile (not to mention writers of other nationalities in U.S. exile) limited their commentary to the interior politics of their homelands rather than addressing the external-internal colonialism of the United States. In fact, many other exiled writers denigrated Mexican Americans as *pochos*, *agringados*, and *renegados*, as I mentioned above, and used them as reverse examples of the *México de afuera* prescriptions.

García Naranjo concluded his incisive essay with a call to Mexican Americans to follow the example of Puerto Ricans and resist sending their children to inferior schools. He further used the issue of segregation to reinforce the tenets of the *México de afuera* ideology: it is the responsibility of the family to educate the children in the Spanish language and Mexican culture and religiosity.

Beyond the realm of print, García Naranjo used oratory to express his opinions to the illiterate masses. He was considered in his time to be one of the most eloquent speakers, whose high-toned rhetoric propelled the *México de afuera* ideology and general Mexican nationalism to crowds of hundreds. His speeches gained further currency when they were printed word for word in newspapers throughout the Southwest. Because of all this exposure, García Naranjo became one of the best known leaders of the Mexican expatriate community during the revolution. In his speeches, which were often contracted to commemorate special days on the Mexican patriotic calendar, he elaborated many of the same themes as in his editorials: counterrevolutionary attacks and warnings about the degradation of the Mexican state and culture in general; nostalgia for the homeland; the Catholic identity of Mexicans; the preservation of Mexican identity in the United States; and, of course, eulogies in honor of the national heroes being celebrated, such as Ignacio Zaragoza, Miguel Hidalgo, José María Morelos, Agustín de Iturbide, and Benito Juárez. On numerous occasions he promoted the deposed dictator Porfirio Díaz as the symbol of the Mexico that once was. In a speech in honor of Díaz at the Strand Theater in Laredo on July 2, 1919, not only did he eulogize the dictator but he also took the occasion to vilify the revolution for the destruction wrought on the homeland: "all that was a fortunate place of work and bonanza a decade ago became sterile, all destroyed" (*Discursos* 43–44).[7]

García Naranjo, this man who throughout his life trumpeted the glories of Mexican, Venezuelan, and Cuban dictators, and even had a relationship with Francisco Franco's government in Spain, spoke repeatedly throughout the Southwest in homage to the national heroes of independence, Hidalgo and Morelos, but also sang the glories of such dubious figures as Iturbide, who, shortly after the country had won its independence from Spain, crowned himself emperor of Mexico. Without missing a step, García Naranjo used an Iturbide homage at Liberty Hall in El Paso on September 27, 1921, to attack liberals and even the Partido Liberal Mexicano (PLM, Mexican Liberal Party), which was a spark igniting the revolution: "Pase Iturbide al altar de los heroes" (May Iturbide be admitted to the altar of heroes). Iturbide, like Porfirio Díaz, was for the orator, "un símbolo de orden" (a symbol of order) (*Discursos* 66–67).

It was in these speeches that García Naranjo also came to articulate a frame of thought that develops in many exile communities, regardless of their national origin: the idea that the expatriate community's culture is the only authentic national culture, given that the internal politics of the homeland have degraded and destroyed the original culture within its borders. His November 2, 1920, speech in honor of newspaper publisher (and his brother-in-law) Ignacio E. Lozano presented an eloquent argument for a deterritorialized nationality, the true basis of a *México de afuera*, purer and more authentic than the *México de adentro* (Mexico within the geographic borders). He began by stating that being Mexican is spiritual more than physical: "the spiritual Homeland that is more beautiful than the geographic Homeland"

(*Discursos* 128).[8] From there he went on to claim that the spiritual homeland is eternal, whereas the geographic one can be invaded and even disappear from the map, which led him to compare Mexican history to that of Athens and Poland, the latter of course having been wiped off the map in 1795. Nevertheless, these nationalities survived in their art and culture—in contrast with such peoples as the Phoenicians and the Carthaginians, who did not have culture and thus perished for all time. Mexico does have culture and will survive for all time as a nation, he sustained. This all led up to the inclusion of the Southwest and Mexican Americans as part of Mexican national culture:

> And we have not died in these lands separated from the Homeland some three quarters of a century ago. The Mexican spirit continues to empower us, the Mexican expatriates, north of the Rio Grande, as if the incomparable skies of Anahuac were protecting us. And not just those who have come from Mexico think of the absent Homeland: also those who were born and raised here continue to be pure undiminished Mexicans. They all carry the name of Mexico set in their hearts like a diamond. (*Discursos* 129)[9]

As stated earlier in this chapter, the ideology of *México de afuera* also prescribed preserving the Catholic faith, especially because the purveyors of this thought system believed that Catholicism was under assault by the predominant Protestantism of the United States. As a principal exponent of *México de afuera*, García Naranjo often articulated that Mexican culture was exclusively Catholic and had been so since the very founding of the Mexican state. In his eulogy of Iturbide, he stated, "Iturbide identified himself with the Catholic religion, which continues to dominate the Republic from one border to the other."[10] And although the Catholic Church, which is not the same as the religion, chose political sides in historical conflicts, that fact did not change "the spiritual unity of the country. . . . Mexico lives under the Christian Cross and was purified in the fires of the New Testament" (*Discursos* 80–81).[11]

The anticlericalism of the revolution—and the associated limits imposed on the church—further inflamed the counterrevolutionary spirit of García Naranjo, as can be appreciated in his February 2, 1920, speech in Laredo: "And it is sadder to observe how the physical landscape of a country is destroyed . . . it is much more impactful to see the faith of a people shattered to pieces, heroic traditions shamefully and openly incinerated, the national character buried under the lava of hate, and one hundred years of noble and fruitful work undone because of criminal rancor and impotent revenge" (*Discursos* 137).[12]

True to his insider-outsider personality—in reality, he was an outsider in both Mexico and the United States as an exile and immigrant—García Naranjo did not limit his critical commentary to internal Mexican politics but also censured his host country. Being bilingual, he remained fully informed on life, culture, and politics in the United States, especially as these related to Mexico and Mexicans. His particular target for criticism was President Wilson and U.S. foreign policy, especially the invasion of Veracruz, the U.S. Army's pursuit of Pancho Villa within Mexican national territory, and U.S. support of Venustiano Carranza during the revolution and his subsequent presidency. García Naranjo also expanded his vision to the study of U.S. foreign policy toward Cuba and Central America, which he lumped in with U.S. policy toward postwar Germany in an analysis of the mechanisms of the American empire. In the same *La Prensa* article (1 May 1921), he indicted U.S. hypocrisy and compared its imperial designs on Mexico to the nineteenth-century French intervention in Mexico under Napoleon III: "Wonderful! The worst was that Mr. Wilson wanted to 'save' the Mexicans. Napoleon III some sixty years ago also wanted to save our country."[13] Even during his third exile in the United States, beginning in 1926, when he moved to New York, García Naranjo continued to comment on American policy toward Mexico and Spanish America. In 1930, while he was working for American oil companies, he penned a series of four essays in English, presumably for publication in the American press, entitled "John Pierpont Morgan in Mexico," decrying the collusion of the U.S. government, American banks, and the American plutocracy in ruining Mexico's credit.[14]

In late 1919, President Carranza called an amnesty for political refugees, including the return of some of their previously expropriated lands to them, and many began to return home. With a good portion of its readership lost, *Revista Mexicana* had to close shop in 1920. Nevertheless, García Naranjo declared, in a January 4, 1920, speech at Liberty Hall in El Paso, that he would sacrifice himself by remaining in exile rather than give up his political ideals.[15] He further stated that those who stayed behind, like the group in El Paso, were the true conservators of the Mexican nation: "During the last year, oh, exiled patriots in El Paso, you have been the main sustainers of the flag" (*Discursos* 261).[16] With *Revista Mexicana* shut down, García Naranjo needed to sustain himself and his family otherwise, and his brother-in-law Ignacio E. Lozano hired him to work as a regular journalist and columnist for *La Prensa*. García Naranjo began publishing scores of opinion pieces criticizing Mexico's internal politics, particularly the *rojo* (red) national government (see, e.g., 24 Apr. 1921). The work at *La Prensa*, however, was not enough, and in 1923 the García Naranjo family returned to Mexico. Los Angeles's *El Heraldo de México* (Herald of Mexico) announced on May 4 of that year that he would be heading for Monterrey, where he was contracted to give a series of speeches. On January 13, 1924, *La Prensa* announced that García Naranjo had opened up a legal practice in Mexico City. He subsequently ran ads in San Antonio's *La Prensa* for a couple of years promoting his legal services in the capital and occasionally sent articles for publication to *El Heraldo de México* and *La Prensa*. The presumed reason for advertising in San Antonio his Mexico City legal office was to offer legal services to expatriates in the United States who had issues in the homeland; thus, once again, García Naranjo was functioning as a bridge between two cultures, two nations.

Despite his having paid dearly with his years of exile for his political stances and affiliations, once back in Mexico, García Naranjo maintained his critical stance toward the reforms instituted by the revolution. And, as conflict increased between the state and the church in Mexico, García Naranjo began publishing more religious articles, even in Baptist periodicals such as El Paso's *El Atalaya Bautista* (Baptist Watchtower) (see, e.g., 24 Sept. 1924). He proceeded to voice and print direct attacks on the regime of President Plutarco Elías Calles (see, e.g., *El Heraldo de México*, 25 July 1924), who subsequently accused him of inspiring subversive acts during the Cristero War and gave him seventy-two hours to leave the country or face the consequences (López Portillo Tostado 80). In 1926, García Naranjo and his family went back into U.S. exile, interrupted at times with stints in Europe and Venezuela. On his way to exile in New York, García Naranjo participated in the Pan American Congress of Journalists in Washington, D.C. (April 8–9, 1926), where in an interview he lobbed a grenade at the anticlerical regime in Mexico, stating that the more repressive the government was, the more the faithful would fight back, even to the extent of fanaticism (*La Prensa*, 7 Apr. 1926).

Thanks to his bilingualism and legal training, García Naranjo secured work as a lawyer for American oil companies while also continuing to write for newspapers in San Antonio and Los Angeles as well as for others in South

America and Cuba. And, thanks in part to the Pan American Congress of Journalists he attended in Washington, D.C., García Naranjo became even more widely known throughout the hemisphere. During his presentation, he stated that journalism needed to take into account the national culture of each country, arguing for instance that Catholic culture did not condone divorce, unlike what was a common practice in the United States. Thus, he lobbied for employment of Hispanic reporters in the American news services. García Naranjo obviously found sympathizers who then invited him to send opinion and journalistic pieces to their newspapers abroad (López Portillo Tostado 81).

His work in the oil industry during the Cristero War accounted for an additional nine years in exile (1926–34), and García Naranjo found the time to continue his oratory in Latino communities in New York and in the Southwest, even going on lecture tours to cities along the Rio Grande Valley and up the California coast. It was a particularly fertile writing period, in which he argued his ideas on religious freedom, published at least one article per week in *La Prensa,* and produced a number of books.[17] These books were basically long, glowing biographies of his heroes, including *Venezuela and Its Rulers / Venezuela y sus gobernantes* (1927 English, 1930 Spanish), *Porfirio Díaz* (1930), and *Simón Bolívar* (1931).

During the heat of the Cristero War and the arrival of thousands of religious refugees, García Naranjo published *El quinto evangelio* (The Fifth Gospel, 1928), a novelized version of the New Testament, presumably extending its reach in more readable form to Catholics.[18] True to his conservatism, the representation of Christ, Mary, and the apostles is for the most part traditional. Noteworthy, however, is his casting blame for the betrayal of Christ and the Crucifixion entirely on the Jews. One important departure from the New Testament reinforces Catholic anti-Semitism, where he includes a spurious tale of the Jews having taken down Jesus's cadaver from the cross so that the apostles would not recover it and claim miracles.[19] He goes into great detail about their inability to carry the body, which weighs as much as if it were made of lead, presumably because of their shame; ultimately the Jews have to turn the body over to Mary and the apostles, who carry it away, light as a feather (152). In all cases throughout the book, the apostles are treated as if they were not Jews.

García Naranjo returned to Mexico in 1934. He found the country much changed but managed to accommodate himself to the new culture. He continued to write, speak out, and find work in cultural industries, including writing for the national newspaper *Excélsior*. Despite his conservatism and occasional exclusion from cultural events because of his reactionary stances, García Naranjo was elected to the Academia Mexicana de la Lengua (Mexican Academy of the Spanish Language) in 1938 and the Real Academia Española (Royal Academy of the Spanish Language) in Spain in 1956. He was a frequent writer for national magazines *Todo* (All), *Hoy* (Today), and *Siempre!* (Always!), as well as for regional newspapers. He died in Mexico City on December 21, 1962.

During his lifetime, Nemesio García Naranjo was one of the most influential cultural figures in the Mexican-origin communities in the Southwest. Across some four decades, through the power of his considerable verbal talents and broad learning, he articulated and reinforced in oral presentations, journalism, and opinion writing, as well as in entire books, a latent and traditional conservatism in Mexican exiles and immigrants as well as in Mexican Americans. He successfully combined both the community's Catholic faith and the political reaction of exiles and immigrants dislodged from their homeland into a coherent doctrine we call *México de afuera*. Many ideas and attitudes rooted in those times are still bearing fruit today and continue to exert a tension against the progressive ideas promoted by the labor movements that were studied in the previous chapter of this book.

CHAPTER 7

Tomás Rivera and the Creation of Nationhood

It is generally acknowledged that the Chicano civil rights movement was sparked in 1965 by the organizing of farmworkers in Delano, California, by César Chávez and Dolores Huerta. Hundreds of community-based organizations across the Southwest followed suit in the pursuit of employment, housing, and educational and political rights. Latino artists and writers of every stripe, as well as community and college-based journalists, joined in support of the effort, not only with their arts but also with their activism. It is not really known who or what organization started the movement or exactly when it became known as the "Chicano Movement," but the literary and dramatic writers and performers, abetted by the nascent movement newspapers and magazines in local communities, were essential in propagandizing and popularizing the movement at the grass roots and at universities. From the outset, in consonance with the farmworkers, the movement had a working-class ideology, even among this first large generation of Latino college students, who saw themselves as children of the working class. Two young professors at Berkeley, subsequently, founded in 1967—in the city of Berkeley itself, independent of the university—the most respected and best distributed magazine of the movement, *El Grito: A Journal of Contemporary Mexican-American Thought.* Three years later, these two individuals, Octavio I. Romano and Herminio Ríos, founded the even more successful publishing house Editorial Quinto Sol.[1] The pair quite deliberately set about defining Chicanismo by what they accepted and rejected for publication (see Bruce-Noboa, *RetroSpace* 132–45), especially in the first two anthologies Quinto Sol issued—*El Espejo—The Mirror* (1969) and *Voices: Readings from*

El Grito (1971)—both of which began to be used as textbooks in nascent ethnic studies courses at universities throughout the United States. These universities, through their curricula and their bookstores, would become the primary market for Quinto Sol's publications and what became its most influential effort: the establishment of a national award for Chicano literature, the Premio Quinto Sol, in 1970 (López). In fact, the first three books awarded the prize and subsequent publication have been treated since the early 1970s as the foundation of a Chicano literary canon: Tomás Rivera's . . . *y no se lo tragó la tierra / And the Earth Did Not Devour Him* (1971), Rudolfo Anaya's *Bless Me, Ultima* (1972), and Rolando Hinojosa-Smith's *Estampas del Valle y otros relatos* (Sketches of the Valley and Other Works, 1973). To award the first-ever prize for Chicano literature to Rivera's novel highlighted the publishers' "commitment to address issues of social class and economic exploitation" while maintaining a link to the farmworker struggle, for Rivera himself was a former migrant farmworker (López 185). And Rivera (1935–84) was already associated with *El Grito* and apparently agreed with the cultural nationalism espoused by the editors in their own essays and in the selection of works they published. However, it should be emphasized that authors like Rivera and Hinojosa had been writing since before *El Grito* ever existed and before the Chicano Movement started.

I met the first three winners of the award in 1972, and we forged a relationship that has lasted; I eventually became the editor and publisher of the complete works of Rivera and Hinojosa, and also of a poetry book by Anaya. The occasion of our first meeting was a historic event in itself: the first symposium on Chicano literature, at which I was invited to read a paper.[2] That year, the three of them agreed to be on the editorial board of our nascent magazine *Revista Chicano-Riqueña* (Chicano-Rican Review)—Luis Dávila and I were the editors, and we published Rivera's wonderful short story "Looking for Borges" as a sort of *ars poetica*. Rivera's prizewinning novel . . . *y no se lo tragó la tierra* (or simply *Tierra*) still remains his most significant work in a truncated career—limited by academic administrative duties and by an untimely death—that also produced a number of short stories and essays.

Tierra was the first novel promoted by Quinto Sol as a model of Chicano literature, despite the fact that nowhere in the narrative does Rivera use the term "Chicano" or refer to his characters as "Chicanos."[3] In fact, in his essay "Chicano Literature: Fiesta of the Living," Rivera explicitly states, "To claim that my own writing is representative of the Chicano experience is not my intention" (*Tomás Rivera* 274). Nevertheless, from its initial publication to the present, professors have framed the novel as representative of the literature of Chicano ethnic identity, a type of bildungsroman and a way for Chicanos to discover themselves (see Calderón, "At the Crossroads"). Arnulfo D. Trejo encapsulated this idea about Rivera narrating Chicano identity: "The author's message is that if the Chicano builds on his strengths and accepts his weaknesses he will find his identity and determine his own destiny" (202). Many scholars and teachers have repeated these sentiments to the present. Many Mexican American works have followed that use *Tierra* as a model or, at least, a major inspiration, including Sandra Cisneros's *The House on Mango Street* (1984; see Gonzáles-Berry and Rebolledo), Denise Chávez's *The Last of the Menu Girls* (1986), Evangelina Vigil's *Thirty an' Seen a Lot* (1981), and Helena María Viramontes's "The Moths" (1985). I believe, however, that Rivera's experimental novel *Tierra* has often been misunderstood, from its interpretation as a novel of exclusion in an early academic review by William H. González, to Joseph Sommers's three approaches to interpreting *Tierra*, to the way that professors often situate the novel in the curriculum as promoting a "Chicano" identity.[4]

Contrary to these approaches, which to some extent have become conventions in the classroom and the published criticism, I want to talk about *Tierra* as iconoclastic, even revolutionary, rather than reformist. I also want to talk about Rivera's vision and his approach to reconstructing the institutions that he attacked in his novel and other works. In his stories, poems, and essays, Rivera indicted three institutions in American society: a capitalist economic and political system, the education system, and the church.

Rivera, just a few years after having left the migrant worker circuit himself, was writing his community into literature and art. In doing so, he was not writing autobiography—many have approached *Tierra* as such—but focusing on the collective experience and consciousness of his migrant community.[5] As he stated in his essay "Recuerdo, Descubrimiento y Voluntad en el Proceso Imaginativo Literario" (rewritten by Rivera in English as "Remembering, Discovery and Volition in the Literary Imaginative Process"), "My mission was to allow a collective voice to be expressed" (*Tomás Rivera* 359).[6] In doing so he not only celebrated the collective voice of migrant workers but also denounced the victimization of these workers, all the while providing a vision for their future. Just as important, he wrote in the oral narrative style that his ideal readers were accustomed to and could readily understand, basing his style on the rhythm and colloquial language of his community of migrant workers (and beyond). As Manuel Martín-Rodríguez has stated, "Rivera's endeavor to 'imitate' popular narrative forms should not be interpreted as just a stylistic resource. Rather, . . . it needs to be seen as a communicative strategy that seeks to engage the reader in an active process of literary (re) creation." That Rivera was able to reproduce these linguistic registers and at the same time produce a poetic text only speaks to his mastery of as well as respect for the inherent artistry in working-class culture, what Martín-Rodríguez identifies as "his readers' storytelling practices" ("Reading" 27).

An important antecedent to, but not an influence on, this express mission was Daniel Venegas's *Las aventuras de Don Chipote, o cuando los pericos mamen* (The Adventures of Don Chipote, or When Parakeets Suckle Their Young, 1928), the first novel that we know of to have a "Chicano" character as protagonist and to be written specifically for a "Chicano" audience—in the early twentieth century, "Chicano" meant poor Mexican immigrant, that is, an economic refugee. Like Rivera, Venegas drew the characters and experiences he narrated from his own life as an immigrant laborer. In Venegas's case, he had crossed the border at El Paso and found employment in the slavery-like conditions of laying track across the southwestern desert. Arriving in California, he found other menial jobs in restaurants and in road construction, paving the Golden State highways. Most likely a self-taught or minimally educated writer, Venegas went on to found a modest theatrical troupe that performed his plays and to publish a weekly newspaper, *El Malcriado* (Brat), for which he wrote all the articles (using different voices and registers of speech), drew all the illustrations, and set the type by hand himself. In his newspaper and later in his novel, he experimented with writing in the voice of Mexican immigrant workers. It is clear in *Las aventuras de Don Chipote* that the author strove to write the Chicano culture of the times into art and literature; he was creating an identity in print for the poor Mexican immigrant. To do so he not only used Mexican working-class dialect (mostly related to northwest Mexico) in his narration and dialogue, but also made wonderful use of the folkloric sayings, songs, and worldview of *los de abajo* (the underdogs). Venegas's text also reflected the social environment of slave-driving bosses and foremen, abusive police, and lumpen that preyed on the ingenuous, greenhorn immigrants. Like many immigrant writers of the time, as mentioned in previous chapters, Venegas censured the *agringados* and *renegados* (gringoized and cultural renegades). Venegas called for Mexicans to return to the homeland because staying in the United States would never make them prosperous but instead strip them of their identity; in this his message was distinct from García Naranjo's insistence that Mexican identity could prevail outside of the *patria* (fatherland). Venegas departed from the strategies that Tomás Rivera would use later in his writing by directly inserting himself into the narrative as a historical witness and protester to the exploitation and discrimination experienced by migrants; Rivera's protest, in contrast, was subtle, expressed through plot development, characterization, and dialogue, without interrupting the narration. But overall, Venegas's project was very similar to Rivera's: to create literature and art based on the life and culture of a specific community, Mexican (American) migrants in the U.S. Southwest. Both authors were on a mission to democratize literature and create a sense of identity—nation, if you will—for their respective communities, which were previously unrepresented in literature.[7]

Tierra's narrative structure presents a collection of disparate tales, monologues, dialogues, thoughts, and observations whose relationship only becomes apparent in the last episode of the book as representing the recollections and experiences of a young man attempting to make sense out of the continued hardship and tragedy that befall his family and community. In fact, it is precisely through *memory* that he is able to *discover* the reasons for that hard life and decide (*volition*) to continue to recall and relate the fragments of experience to understand not only who he is but also who his community is. The character's volition to remember his life experiences and his observations of others' thus becomes a metaphor for the creative act, for writing literature—these are Rivera's three principles either extrapolated from or applied in his masterful text. However, this highly literary endeavor may also be read as a protest novel. In Rivera's advocacy mission, he specifically targets the three institutions of capitalism, education, and the church to raise the level of consciousness about the pernicious power these institutions hold over people. The denunciation of the capitalist political economy is foremost in *Tierra*, present in its depictions of the practical enslavement of the workers, who are treated as just another resource, like the earth and the seeds themselves, while producing consumer goods like boxing gloves that are more resilient than the workers themselves, as elucidated in one chapter. Rivera also indicts the education system numerous times in the novel, depicting its intolerance of Spanish speaking, its racism in expelling Mexican American children, and its intolerance toward working-class knowledge and wisdom, even the art of a folk poet such as the character Bartolo. Of course, the church—represented by nuns, Catholic priests, and Protestant ministers and missionaries—receives a number of blows in *Tierra* as corrupt, mystifying, and obsessed with sex. After denouncing these institutions and their imposing on Mexican Americans an identity bereft of language, history, and culture, Rivera posits implicitly in the novel that the common man, working-class man, indeed has a community strong and dignified enough to create and sustain its own identity, language, and culture, as well as a culture strong enough to foster art and literature and to take over and reform the institutions that oppress it.[8] Out of this microcosm, if readers and teachers can apply the example to all Mexican American/Chicano, Latino, or other colonized communities, all the better—but they will have to expand the message from the particular example of migrant workers. As Rivera stated in his essay "Recuerdo . . . ," by going deep into one's own community, a person can reach and connect to other communities, whether national or international, or what teachers like to call "universal": "I think that everything is imbued with the specific. The more man is placed within his environment, the better he will be understood by all. The more national he is, the more international he will become. . . . That is to say, the more the specific man is shown in his natural and dialectic element, the more his human universality is revealed" (published translation, *Tomás Rivera* 303).[9]

Out of respect for the worker, the folk base of society, his own family, and his community, Rivera constructed a literary language (a Spanish dialect of migrant workers, with their Anglicisms, folkspeak, and code-switching) that his community had never seen represented in books or education. In short, Rivera created a language that not only migrant workers, but also Mexican Americans in general, could recognize as their own dialect. He used that language, in the most poetic but also the most direct and understandable terms, to depict how institutions had mystified and fragmented his people's understanding of their lives and their place in society. In *Tierra*, he demonstrates how Mexican Americans are marginalized not only because of their minority-language usage in relation to English, but also because of their bilingualism, and thus biculturalism, which consigns them to the no-man's-land between the United States and Mexico. Tomás Rivera, emerging from this liminal space himself, shows implicitly in his writing, well before

Homi K. Bhabha enunciated it, that that liminal space is eminently innovative, eminently creative in its challenge to imposed national identities and canons, but that real people live and suffer and dream and create life, culture, and art there.

Through the written word, Rivera led the way to his people's recognizing themselves in literature and in society; he led them into building community and led that community into claiming its rightful place in societal institutions and into making decisions in those institutions. This he did in his writing as well as in his work with academia and other cultural institutions of the United States.

In his writing, Rivera showed people—including the hundreds of thousands of students who have now read *Tierra* in its Spanish original or in its various translations—the need to recognize and embrace their collective and individual histories and to build their sense of community from there.[10] Despite all the forces (the economic and political system, the schools, the church) that deny the people's worth and their individual and communal identities, and despite the fragmenting effect of these institutions, people can construct, can create, themselves from within. Rivera's respect for them recognized their inherited and collective knowledge, their own intuition, their inherent skepticism, the strength of their connection to the land and to nature, and their ability to draw from their internal resources to empower and create themselves (Rivera's *voluntad,* volition), just as Rivera and the cadre of writers and professors that he led carried on to create what they called "Chicano literature." They did this out of intuition, out of force of will, out of collective memory, out of respect for human dignity . . . and with full knowledge that where there is a people, there is a culture and a language and a literature (as colonized people they were thought not to possess culture, language, or literature). They could accomplish this as an act of volition, as is indicated in the all-important conclusion to *Tierra,* "Debajo de la casa" (Under the House) (*Tomás Rivera* 120–24), which implies that the main character will create himself and his community through memory, the act of writing out of sheer will. Rivera himself indicated as much in his essay "Recuerdo . . .": "He invents himself . . . a purely volitional act" (published translation, *Tomás Rivera* 306).[11]

Tomás Rivera was an iconoclast and a critic of institutions, but he was also a builder of institutions. He was a pioneering dean, vice president, and then chancellor of institutions of higher education and leader in democratizing higher education in the United States—a career track that pretty much ended his literary productivity and also resulted possibly in the loss along the way of a completed novel manuscript, *La casa grande* (The Big House). Ultimately, Rivera's spirit lives on in the academic institutions and programs he led and helped shape. It also lives on in the students and scholars he helped shape, people who continue to follow his example of bringing the community into academia, respecting the culture of working people, and furthering his brand of humanism—that's what he called it in his essay on writer Richard Rodriguez—in the way we teach and write and dream the future (see *Tomás Rivera* 341–49).

As a longtime resident in the halls of academia, I want to briefly state that in many ways the ivy-covered walls are the thickest and most stubbornly resistant to change, and that the toll exacted on anyone who seeks to scale, penetrate, or otherwise topple them is very high . . . and I believe that Rivera paid the ultimate price, exacted with his untimely death.

Now, I want to memorialize in particular the role Rivera played in pioneering and institutionalizing Chicano and Latino literature. He did this of course as a foundational writer, one who showed the way, blazed the path for others to follow. Rivera was also foundational as an organizer and sponsor of writers, magazines, and publishing houses, and a presence at conferences and conventions that wanted nothing to do with Chicanos and Latinos back in the 1970s. Having won the first national award for Chicano literature and provided a text eminently useful for high school and university classes, Rivera was in high demand as a speaker at universities and conventions around the country, where mostly Latinos invited him. Much to the chagrin of event organizers, however, in his prepared statements he often not only spoke about the accomplishments of Chicano literature but also used his allotted time to read from the works of other writers. Those presentations eventually took the form of his published essays—"The Chicano in Literature," "Chicano Literature: Fiesta of the Living," "Recuerdo, Descubrimiento y Voluntad en el Proceso Imaginativo Literario," "On Chicano Literature," and "The Establishment of Community"—which include an extensive collection of poems and prose excerpts from the works of writers today considered among the first Chicano literary generation. Among the writers he highlighted were Alurista, Sergio Elizondo, Rolando Hinojosa-Smith, José Montoya, Ricardo Sánchez, Raúl Salinas, Jesús "El Flaco" Maldonado, and Luis Valdez—all men.[12]

Rivera and the first generation of Chicano literary critics targeted academic societies for inclusion of sessions and panels on Chicano and Latino literatures. Among those, of course, were the Modern Language Association (MLA), the Popular Culture Association, the Western Literature Association, the American Association of Teachers of Spanish and Portuguese, and the International Society of Hispanists. Quite often, Rivera, all of us, had to suffer snide attacks from senior professors, the ones who did not hire or who denied tenure to scores of Chicano assistant professors. They had no qualms about uttering such prejudice-laced statements as, "How interesting, there are Chicano literary critics, when there is no real Chicano literature!" The MLA was notorious for either turning down panel proposals and papers or, when they were accepted, scheduling them for nine in the morning or nine in the evening on Saturday, when no one would attend. In those early years, Rivera, Hinojosa, Luis Dávila, Frank Pino, Judy Salinas, Chuck Tatum, Tomás Ybarra-Frausto, myself, and others would read our papers to one another, when no one, or perhaps two or three others, attended. The three or four panelists and two audience members would form a circle of chairs, read the papers, and discuss other issues regarding institutionalizing our literature in both English and Spanish departments. They turned out to be great strategy and bonding sessions, with Rivera and Hinojosa often cheerleading.

Actually, my life as an editor and publisher began in part because of Rivera's confidence in me. Back in 1972, when Dávila and I were planning to publish the Latino literary magazine *Revista Chicano-Riqueña*, not only did Rivera agree to join our editorial board, but he also recruited other major figures for the board and encouraged writers to submit works to us. In 1973, Rivera was highly sought after, as I said, having won the Premio Quinto Sol. He nevertheless gave us his story "Looking for Borges" to publish. The short story is a powerful statement against literature being disconnected from community and from life. Rivera gave it to us, I would guess, as a gamble on two young men who were neophytes in academia as well as publishing. I was fresh out of graduate coursework and had not even written my dissertation yet. He entrusted the story to us, not requesting or even expecting a fee or royalties, only getting in return a handshake and our obvious respect. There would be no payback for him, no raise at the end of the year as a faculty member, no royalties, probably not even the respect of his faculty colleagues. It meant absolutely nothing to his department that he published a story in an unknown ethnic magazine. He would not get a promotion, tenure, or even a raise for writing and publishing Chicano literature. He mostly got insult and heartache, some of which I witnessed: his being turned down for a position at the University of Texas at Austin, likewise for a position at the University of Houston, where I eventually ended up as a professor and institutionalized *Revista Chicano-Riqueña* and Arte Público Press. Rivera gave us the masterpiece "Looking for Borges" to help our nascent magazine, to further the literature, to empower us all. Today, Arte Público Press, which grew out of the magazine, keeps all of Tomás Rivera's literary writing in print and e-book editions, and strives to carry his vision on.

Rivera was an untiring promoter of our literature, quite often crisscrossing the nation to speak, read from his works, and work with other writers and scholars. He did this with great sacrifice of himself, his career, and his family. In his lecturing, as in his writing, Rivera was a poetic and eloquent speaker, but not one of high-sounding rhetoric and recondite vocabulary. In his speaking, as in his writing, he used the language of the common man. A laborer could appreciate what Rivera was saying as well as an academician could. There was no pretense, no elitism, no separation of his role as a writer or speaker from the larger working-class community. This was a powerful example for all of us academics. It was only fitting that Rivera developed his career at public universities, even when those institutions had been perverted by elitist academicians and administrators, who quite often rejected him in his ascent to academic leadership.

Today, many of the dreams and aspirations of Tomás Rivera for his community and for the education system are on their way to realization. Latino literature appears to have won a place for itself in academia, if not in the commercial publishing industry and popular culture. Today, we have a full cadre of Latino professors of literature and creative writing—as well as many Latino professors in varied fields across the curriculum. At the University of Houston, we have the first PhD program in Spanish concentrating on Latino literature, language, and culture of the United States. We also have the first PhD program in creative writing in Spanish in the United States.

Apparently, Latino writers are making their way into mainstream publishing. But wait a minute: Has the teaching of our literature gone beyond explication of the written word to a better understanding of our people and culture in society? Is the confidence that Rivera placed in literature's ability to help the reader discover self and community been misplaced or unrealized today? (Sorry! I'm letting my old warrior-self speak with a message to younger scholars—or maybe not so young. Like Rolando Hinojosa-Smith's character Esteban Echevarría, who speaks "con el pie en el estribo" [with a foot in the stirrup], I cannot help but offer old-timer wisdom.) Have too many of our professors disrespected or forgotten the earlier generations' battles to open up academia, to desegregate these halls and society, to create a space for Latino culture and literature? Have they scoffed at our sacrifices? Have they laughed at and considered as unsophisticated the literature the community produced during the activist and militant phases of the civil rights movements? Are they now embracing writers and a literature that have been approved and filtered through the same corporate enterprises that ultimately disenfranchise and deny our culture? Are Latino teachers, professors, critics, librarians just content to celebrate, prioritize, and promote the products of mainstream publishers and their good Latino boys and girls—who demonstrate the pyrotechnics of what "creative writing departments" call "craftsmanship" and who echo their master's language and ideas, just like the dog listening to his master's voice on the old Victor record labels? (Now, I'm really showing my age, by referring to old Victrolas and 78 RPM records!) Are the scholars, librarians, and gatekeepers choosing these writers' works over works that emanate from and speak directly to our community without the need of approval and investment from the Eurocentric, profit-oriented purveyors of our alienation? Are they just studying and teaching over and over again the works produced only in the last thirty years and thus denying our history, our collective memory here in the United States, which preceded the supposed recent boom in Latino writing?

Are our professors and critics vaingloriously demonstrating the pyrotechnics of jargon-laden, dehumanized theoretical approaches to literature and culture before, I say BEFORE, fully exploring with their students the author's real intentions and meaning? BEFORE treating the works as literature and art and culture, laden with meaning for our practical everyday existence?

If they are doing this, then much of Rivera's and our hopes and aspirations were in vain. If they are doing this—AND I AM NOT ONE TO SAY THEY ARE, HUMMM—then they are just cogs in the gears that grind us up and homogenize us and keep our community from Rivera's triad of remembering, discovering, and creating.

But let me end on a confident note of expectation. Today, we need Rivera, his model, and his writing more than ever. The continued growth of the Latino population of the United States portends many things for us:

1. Our ascendancy to economic and political power.
2. Our serving first as a mediator and later as a unifying force in the hemisphere, precisely because of our bilingualism and biculturalism, but also because of our increasing educational levels and economic and political empowerment.
3. Our future leadership in many areas, but especially on the cultural battlefield, with all its many extensions into academia, the educational system, the museums, ultimately the overall national identity of the United States. The cultural battlefield will be the hardest fought, the most fraught with mines set to explode our concepts about language, culture, and identity.

In Tomás Rivera's literature, I believe, there is an ethic and a rationale for meeting the challenges ahead. Immediately for our literature, I would say that we need to continue to make the Spanish language ours. We need to do the same with the English language. Despite resistance from academia and the other cultural institutions, we need to be the producers and definers of our own culture, and not cede that responsibility to outsiders. We need to expand our vision hemispherically and globally and understand that we are not alone or unique in our circumstances and that peoples around the globe are facing the same challenges. I see all this as presciently implicit in Rivera's writing. If we do not read as a form of empowerment, we are breaking the trust with our author: Tomás Rivera.

CHAPTER 8

Rolando Hinojosa-Smith and the Erasing of Borders

The Klail City Death Trip (KCDT) series (1973–2006), Rolando Hinojosa-Smith's continuing novel, traces generations of inhabitants and their stories in fictional Belken County in the Lower Rio Grande Valley of Texas. Hinojosa's Belken County has often been compared to William Faulkner's Yoknapatawpha County and Gabriel García Márquez's Macondo (see, e.g., Busby; Calderón, *Narratives* 148; Hermans 364; Hernández 86; Martín-Rodríguez, *Life* 30; Saldívar, "Rolando" 48). However, as I hope to prove in this chapter, the organizing structure of generations, even celebrated in one of the novel titles, *Generaciones y semblanzas* (Generations and Portraits), and the geographic determinism of a particular ethnohistoric county are perhaps keys that are too obvious and too easy for understanding Hinojosa's complicated narrative project (see Neate). The facile comparisons between Hinojosa and the two Nobel laureates, whose works emerge from and sustain national canons, are far too limiting—and, needless to say, when Hinojosa's oeuvre is compared on this basis, it comes up short, precisely because he writes not from within the American or the Latin American canon, but outside both and challenging both.[1] He, more than any other writer, draws broadly from *both* these traditions and canons. The comparison with Faulkner and García Márquez is flawed, in addition, because Hinojosa is writing out of hybrid culture.[2] Hybridism characterizes all aspects of his creative project: (1) the use of the two languages, separately and in code-switching; (2) characters who are the product of Mexican and Anglo parents, as is Hinojosa; (3) literary genres and models, as well as references to authors and texts, from both Anglo and Hispanic traditions; (4) and the underlying and constant comparison of two worldviews and their knowledge bases. This last represents a constant challenge to the truth and legitimacy of both, wherein Hinojosa's satire is born.

We who write criticism or publish literature—and I am referring to myself as a publisher, Hinojosa's publisher, in fact—from the margins of dominant societies, and who, like Hinojosa, often serve as translators for both, probably understand best what Hinojosa is doing and where he is going with his ambitious, multiform, multigenerational, multigenre, bilingual, bidialectal project. We find his novels and his project just as worthy as those of the aforementioned Nobel laureates; additionally, we find it more relevant to us in our multicultural and diversely linguistic lives at this juncture in the twenty-first century, after decades of contemporary Latino cultural nationalism.

Rolando Hinojosa (1929–2022) was born and raised in a region that was colonized by Spain in 1749 and later passed from Spanish administration to Mexican governance in 1821, for a period of fifteen or twenty-four years. The ambiguous chronology depends on how you understand Mexican and Texan claims to the area, and which side of the ongoing debate you support: the question of whether the portion of Texas south of the Nueces River was part of the Republic of Texas in 1836 and subsequently part of the United States. The reality is that South Texas remained, at least culturally, part of greater Mexico well beyond 1848, the end of the war with Mexico.

Hinojosa's multivolume narrative project is not a historical novel in the common understanding of the genre. The KCDT series is constructed in a remote time period, evokes and recalls the foundational period of Rio Grande Valley Hispano-Indigenous culture, and updates it in an irrevocable path toward extinction of the original cultural base, at least extinction of the "old ways" on a path toward a new, hybrid culture. Hinojosa's world focuses on the Anglo-Mexican binary and hardly ever considers the original Native American inhabitants, whom Hinojosa sees as "absorbed by the colonial population" ("The Sense" 21), in this chronicling of Hispanic and Anglo-American culture clash and then blending across the generations.

The oldest woman in Hinojosa's valley, Reina Campoy, can trace her lineage back to the settlers of Nuevo Santander in 1749. As to subsequent generations, "Reina's grandmother, Doña Mauricia Puig, was born a Spanish subject in 1814; at age ten she was a Mexican citizen; by the summer of 1836, she was a Texan. Later, in 1845, an American when Texas was annexed. . . . A citizen of the Confederacy in 1860, and an American citizen again after duly being Reconstructed" (*Becky* 107). With such statements uttered by Campoy and other old-timers, Hinojosa seems to indicate that national identity may change while the people themselves persist and endure. But these frequent passages also emphasize that for a little more than a quarter century the area was governed from the far-off capital of Mexico City and, later, as a spoil of war, was added as another star to the American flag. It was so distant geographically and culturally from Washington, D.C., and even from the capital of the new state, Austin, that the Lower Rio Grande Valley only very slowly became incorporated into U.S. society, first only through the U.S. military presence and dominion, followed later by the imposition of new laws and a foreign educational system. However, by and large, the majority of the population, of Hispanic Mexican origin, continued daily life according to the social systems of parentage and *compadrazgo* (coparenthood), which extended beyond the imposed political border of the Rio Grande, and still does today. In this manner, in similar passages, Hinojosa emphasizes that it is the people and their culture, not their "national" identity, that occupies his attention and that is the core concern. Even in his essay "This Writer's Sense of Place," he emphasizes that the inhabitants' worldview, or perspective on life, and the way they interpret particular events are his subject; clearly, it is not the geographic location, per se.[3] He further emphasizes that "my stories are not held together by the *peripeteia* or plot as much as by *what* the people who populate the stories say and *how* they say it, how they look at the world out and the world in; and the works then become studies of perceptions and values and decisions reached by them" (21, original emphasis).

As for geography and politics, represented by the river border that has been imposed to divide two political entities, they too are malleable, subject to change; only the people endure. This is clear when the Buenrostros in *Rites and Witnesses* realign the border by dynamiting the Rio Grande so that it resumes its original, pre-Anglo flow (110). Many KCDT characters may have dreamed of igniting dynamite to alter the borderline, in reality or figuratively. As in life, negating and obviating that border were (are) many cultural systems: familial ties that cross the river, the common Catholic religion ministered by Spanish-speaking priests, and an informal, at times formal, alternative Hispanic educational system, not only in catechism, but also in the type of little Mexican schools that Hinojosa himself attended as a child. Family and experience and culture, and Hinojosa's books themselves, all work to negate that imaginary line that authorities impose to divide people. Of course, in the later installments of KCDT, Mexican immigrants and smugglers continuously negate the border and irrevocably reinforce the Mexican/Hispanic culture of the valley, which will remain predominantly Hispanic, today called Latino, with more than 90 percent of the population, today and into the far-off future.

Born in the small town of Mercedes, Texas, to a Mexican American police officer and an Anglo-American schoolteacher Hinojosa was raised speaking and reading both Spanish and English. The bilingualism and biculturalism of his parents in this majority Hispanic/Mexican social environment nevertheless result from conquest and marginalization; the place is as far to the margin as can be imagined, being a border or frontier region. The bilingual/bicultural environment of Hinojosa's rearing would eventually incline him toward a clear vision of the world, one that would characterize his ideological and narrative stances for the rest of his life. That clarity of vision would allow him to assume the perspective of the observer of the human comedy, always slightly outside and slightly inside the two dominant groups in order to satirize the foibles of both in the Belken County microcosm for which he is so well known. That clarity of mind and vision would allow him to see beyond the constraints of one culture or the other. It would allow him to remove the social masks and criticize the economic and political motivations and structures, the institutions of power in the valley, especially in their imperative to construct and support an official history as a part of the process of integrating the valley residents into a national American culture. Hinojosa's portrayal of the residents in his texts and their linguistic heteroglossia always reveals how successful or not that solidifying and homogenizing of the populace have been. Beginning in the days of the first Spanish-speaking settlers and continuing with the ascendance of the Anglos, the Hispanic background, once declining, later ascends into a reconquest of the valley and its institutions—or at least a hybridization, as in the police department of *Ask a Policeman*, the schools, the bank, and the universities. The end process is most notable in *We Happy Few*, where Mexican Americans are on the path of ascendance and control of a major institution: the university. The linguistic and ethnocultural diversity represented in Hinojosa's texts speaks to what early Chicano critics only saw as resistance.[4] Today, under our examining eyes, we understand this process on the one hand as a synthesis and on the other as a breach between Anglo and Mexican pretensions of nationhood, an interstitial area that speaks and acts for itself and is a cradle of creativity and affirmation beyond national assignations.

After studying Hispanic literature at the University of Texas and the University of Illinois, and after serving in the U.S. Army in Korea, Hinojosa commenced his career as an academic and a writer, producing more than twenty volumes in English, Spanish, or a bilingual format. His first book, *Estampas del Valle y otros relatos* (Sketches of the Valley and Other Works, 1973), won the Premio Quinto Sol in 1973, and along with the first novels by Tomás Rivera and Rudolfo Anaya constituted what the Quinto Sol editors hoped would be the basis for a Chicano literary canon (see Bruce-Novoa, *RetroSpace* 132–45)—a bulwark for the creation of the Chicano cultural nationalism mentioned in the previous chapter. Regardless of the canonicity or not of these marginal, minority-group texts at Quinto Sol, they opened creative pathways and were emulated by literally thousands of writers in an effort to provide a language and literary corpus for what back then was cast as the "sleeping giant" of Mexican American and Latino people in the United States. Hinojosa's mosaic of quirky and picturesque characters were, despite or because of their apparent isolation from a larger world, stubborn and unashamed in their affirmation of place, tradition, dialect, and worldview.

Hinojosa's work even pointed to an apparent golden age, a time of cultural origins prior to the coming of the Anglos, when language was pure, traditions were established, and a sense of identity and place were born. This is particularly evident in *Claros varones de Belken* (*Fair Gentlemen of Belken County*). According to Héctor Calderón, Hinojosa invoked classical models and heroes to be emulated, and this accounts in part for his selected title for this volume, which is derivative of the Spanish Renaissance *Claros varones de Castilla* (Fair Gentlemen of Castile), biographies written by Fernando del Pulgar in 1496.[5] In Hinojosa's volume, the ancient Esteban Echevarría invokes an Edenic past: "I remember, Rafa . . . trees loaded with figs and honey from bees that drank the nectar from the orange blossoms. Sounds from animals that one no longer sees or hears. . . . Dances open to the public and, now, I hear you even have to pay to get in, can you imagine, Rafe? And what about our palm trees? Palm trees that grew as God wanted them to until the Anglos came with those axes o' theirs and then cut them down" (90).[6] This Edenic vision of Chicano origins was a perfect basis for early Chicano critics in their effort to build a cultural nationalism or to fit Hinojosa's works into the internal colonial model popular among academics in the 1970s (see Rodríguez del Pino).

In addition to employing the memory of old-timers such as Echevarría to recall and pass on the old ways and wisdom, Hinojosa himself lent credence to this golden age before borders were imposed and capitalism was introduced, in such essays as "This Writer's Sense of Place": "That river was not yet a jurisdictional barrier and was not to be until almost one hundred years later; but by then, the border had its own history, its own culture, and its own sense of place. . . . The Border wasn't a paradise, and it didn't have to be; but it was more than paradise, it was home. . . . But it also maintained the remains of a social democracy that cried out for independence, for a desire to be left alone and for the continuance of a sense of community" (10–11). Hinojosa's statement is not identical to Echevarría's invocation of a paradise,[7] but it does privilege the culture that existed prior to Anglo immigration and implies that this immigration interrupted or destabilized the original culture/nation. Echevarría's and the other old-timers' function is not just to recall those origins,[8] but also to mourn the loss of native identity and values and bemoan the transformation of life since the coming of the Anglo people:

> Houses without porches, streets without lamp lights. Friends who have died away and the youngsters who no longer speak Spanish, who can't even say, ¿Cómo está? Hah! The Valley's no longer. . . . The Anglos with their landed property, their banks, their legal contracts. . . . What's the use of reaching eighty-three if everything's gone up in smoke? The Vilches. Dead. The Tueros? They're dead, too! The Buenrostros are almost gone and the founding families are drying up like leaves on a dying mesquite. (*Fair Gentlemen* 88–89)[9]

However, as more and more texts in the KCDT series were published, it became more apparent that the voices harking back to a favored, pre-Anglo past existed alongside many other voices and testimonies, from Anglo as well as Mexican residents, that documented opposing views or a sense of synthesis. As Monika Kaup has pointed out, a simultaneity of voices from different generations vie for the reader's attention:

> Significant change has occurred between the traditional, rural pre-Anglo Belken County of the older generation and the present urban,

> Anglo-controlled place, a master difference structuring the pattern of local native Chicano memory. I would suggest that *Hinojosa represents this historical sequence as spatial simultaneity, as separate worlds existing side-by-side in the voices of different generations.* As long as this simultaneous moment lasts (and the voices of the elders are still heard), it softens the impact of one world being shattered by the invasion of another. (64, original emphasis)

The main characters Rafa/Rafe Buenrostro and Jehú Malacara ascend to and transform Anglo institutions on the sociopolitical plane as well as in their personal lives: the former marries Sammie Jo Perkins and becomes part of the ranching-banking power base; the latter weds Becky Escobar, who, by her mestizo Anglo-Mexican heritage, represents the hybrid present and future of the valley. But, as I argue below, their hybridity makes not for a new, synthetic life but for one that is a culture of its own, born of the interstitial space that is the valley; while wedding elements of both nations, it is neither of the two. The mestizo Hinojosa's overriding message, therefore, is neither to resist Anglo culture, as hoped for by Chicano cultural nationalists, nor to create an outpost of "greater Mexico," as Héctor Calderón has theorized (*Narratives* 138–66). Hinojosa himself has stated in his essay "A Voice of One's Own," "All of us live within two cultures—in varying degrees, as I have said, and whatever the degree, the two cultures are inescapable" (3).

The KCDT mosaic formed a firm base from which Hinojosa could focus his skeptical and removed vision, somewhat like the *crónicas*, or local color, satirical columns that were still being published in the valley and San Antonio newspapers during Hinojosa's youth (see Calderón, *Narratives* 140–42). *Estampas del Valle*, we have come to understand, is nothing more than the first chapter of what Hinojosa's narrators call *El cronicón de Belken* or *El cronicón del Valle*: it is an ongoing, open-ended epic that subtly traces the ascension of the Anglo-American population and culture in the valley and the decline of the original Hispanic/Mexican culture there. Of course, today, Hinojosa's latest books chronicle a resurgence of the ethnic Mexican and Mexican American population, just as the old-timer Don Aureliano Mora would envision it in *Klail City*, like the Greeks recuperating their legacy from the Romans who had taken them as slaves (29): "the day will come when we'll see this ground as ours again. As sure as there's a God somewhere around here" (30).

Hinojosa's art is not just a simple chronicling of the ebb and flow of two cultures in contact, of farm and ranch and town real estate (see Karrer), of financial and legal interests (see Gutiérrez-Jones 9–49), or of families and personalities, their conflicts, marriage lines, and separations. Hinojosa's has been a highly literary experiment that not only gives artistic form to a life heretofore never represented adequately in literature and art, but that has also involved, nay demanded, seeing how far he can adapt and mold the literary tools he inherited to capture that life at the crossroads of two cultures and two nations. His experimentation has led him to explore and recapitulate the complete history of literary genres, from oral lore and epic to *nueva narrativa latinoamericana* (new Latin American narrative), from both the Spanish-language and English-language traditions, and from tips of the hat to *El Cid* and the *Quijote* as well as to Ambrose Bierce, Faulkner, and other American writers. Without characterizing each Hinojosa book, I will briefly summarize the trajectory of his conversation with literary genres, which more often than not is a satiric comment on or deconstruction of those same genres.[10] The novel that won the Casa de las Américas Prize in 1976, *Klail City y sus alrededores* (Klail City and Surroundings), in addition to continuing the *crónica* genre, embeds a picaresque novel; Hinojosa would later re-create this work in English as *Klail City*, published much later, in 1987. *Korean Love Songs* (1980), written in verse, may be seen as Hinojosa's *corrido* (ballad) or *epopeya* (epic poem), documenting as a minstrel the Korean battlefield in the epic East-West struggle that would subsequently cool down to a Cold War during much of Hinojosa's adult life. Hinojosa never re-created *Korean Love Songs* in Spanish, but he did weave the war stories and reminiscences into many novels that followed. The war so obsessed him that it erupted into an entire novel, *The Useless Servants* (1993), which takes the form of a war diary. This book found no outlet in Spanish but has come to be the most autobiographical of his works. In *The Useless Servants*, the satirist and distant observer of the human comedy for once, and only once, reveals the depth of his emotions and psychological reaction to pointless horror. Hinojosa's *Mi querido Rafa* (1981) and its re-creation as *Dear Rafe* (1985) are partially epistolary novels in the style of and with the narrative irony of Juan Valera's novel *Pepita Jiménez* (1874), and partially reportage along the lines of García Márquez's *Crónica de una muerte anunciada* (*Chronicle of a Death Foretold*, 1981). However, the novel demands of the reader bilingualism and bi-dialectalism in order to derive the full value of a text that switches back and forth between Spanish and English. It is also the only text that pairs an extensive written document (letters), with monologues resulting from oral interviews. Following on the linguistic experiment of *Rafa*, the novel *Rites and Witnesses* (1982) is transitional, presenting mainly English dialogues and monologues. It continues the dual structure of examining the political and economic machinations in Belken and taking the testimony of the "witnesses" in the form of monologues. *Partners in Crime* (1985) and *Ask a Policeman* (1998) are detective novels, in their police procedural manifestation, and well suited to Hinojosa's search for ultimate truths in a world fragmented by vested interests, politics, and social biases. Hinojosa's *Generaciones y semblanzas* (1986, with a side-by-side translation as *Fair Gentlemen of Belken*) takes us back to Spain's Middle Ages and the early Renaissance lives of noblemen, as cultivated by such authors as Fernando del Pulgar. *Becky y sus amigos*, published simultaneously with its re-creation in English, *Becky and Her Friends* (1990), continues with a type of reportage; however, it has a new narrator, because of the death of Hinojosa's former alter ego P. Galindo (a satiric name meaning something like "on target" or "shoots well," taken from the real newspaper *cronista* Pepe Díaz, read by the young Hinojosa; see Díaz). Hinojosa's last novel, *We Happy Few* (2006), is the only chapter in his *cronicón* situated in the environment that the mature Hinojosa knows best—academia. Its approach is vintage Hinojosa: dry humor and laconic satire, as usual demanding an intelligent reader response.

The continuing novel known as the Klail City Death Trip is obviously of epic proportions, taking us back to the very origins of the novelistic genre. It documents the history, the language, the conflicts, and the aspirations of a fictional community existing at the very point of contact of two nations, two nations in continuous evolution themselves. As Hinojosa compares the national projects of the United States and Mexico—not to mention the nationalistic aspirations of Texans—he questions how history is narrated orally in every form, from gossip to political speech to the tales of old-timers and the *corridos*. He also explores how history is written, from newspaper reports to official depositions, battlefield reports, medical examiner reports, and educational texts, not to mention novelistic representations of history in its relation to nation-building.[11] Frequently, Hinojosa provides three and four versions of an incident in these novels, as well as multiple opinions on the incident by valley residents, and none of these opinions are in total agreement. In the more recent works, he even contrasts television news stories, photos, and videos, as well as detective Rafe Buenrostro's examination of the crime scene. At the heart of Hinojosa's use of multiple, conflicting, and unreliable narrators—even if they are alter egos of himself, such as Rafa, Jehú, P. Galindo, or his unnamed successor, with the former three as the most unreliable—is his belief that perception is never pure or unbiased. Even more so, his ambitious examination of texts, both oral and written, leads Hinojosa to question the empirical base of knowledge, to doubt anything that can be considered ultimate knowledge, to doubt reportage and testimony and written accounts of any sort. In the earlier works, the *corridos* and the tales of the old-timers like Echevarría hold greater sway as alternative history to the official history to be found in books and English-language newspapers (*Rites* 110). And in a more than symbolic act, old-timer Aureliano Mora smashes the historical marker commemorating those Klail soldiers who lost their lives in World War II, two of his family members among them (*Klail City* 37). Thus, the official history, even engraved in metal, can never communicate the oppression and loss felt and expressed orally by Mora. In another iconic comparison of orality and written culture, Brother Tomás Imás in *Klail City* imposes the poorly translated words of an Anglo-Protestant hymn on a well-known popular Spanish song in his effort to convert valley Mexicans (95). This illustrates how the written word is imposed on, attempts to change the meaning of, and supplants original and authentic oral expression and history, in a process that emulates the overlaying of Anglo culture in the Rio Grande Valley. In *Rites and Witnesses*, P. Galindo emphasizes how old-timer Echevarría's handshake and *word* are good as gold (64), amid a novel that details the fraudulent manipulation of contracts, deeds, and laws by the bank and the powers that be in Klail. In the later detective novels, police procedurals, the incisive eyes and ears of detective Buenrostro, lifelong student of the valley, are far more valuable than documentation in legal reports and the media and the fumbling by federal and state agencies (*Partners in Crime* 159).

Despite this great affirmation of oral culture in KCDT, which has been much commented on and, in fact, dominated much of the early criticism of Hinojosa texts,[12] what Hinojosa has produced is a written document, one that recapitulates the history of written culture and consistently transposes and compares written and oral sources. Whether the sources are written or oral, traditional or contemporary, is not important; the importance lies in presenting the multiple resources and perspectives that the readers of his narrative—and, we might add, human beings in society—need to consider in their search for meaning.

The multifaceted and fractured nature of perception imposes on Hinojosa's narrative a heteroglossia as P. Galindo listens to the testimony of scores of characters and, with a wink of the eye, asks his readers to supply what has not been said and to evaluate and complete the narratives.[13] The ultimate truth is beyond our reach, because knowledge is socially constructed, as is history, as is the nation. In *Mi querido Rafa*—which I believe is central to Hinojosa's epistemology—it becomes clear that only through a process of search and research and comparison of all written and oral testimonies, of all the documents and sources, can we begin to construct a history, a truth. But it will never be the ultimate truth, and it will always be a product of culture and not science, *scientia*. This is most clear in the Spanish original of *Mi querido Rafa*, when narrator P. Galindo rejects the apparent motivation for his investigation, the driving force for the plot: finding out what Jehú did and where he is. P. Galindo confesses that this was only tangentially (*tangencialmente*) of interest, in a sentence that Hinojosa did not include in the English rewrite: "Lo que más importaba era tratar de averiguar lo ocurrido y lo que de eso se pensaba en ambos lados de la ciudad" (What was most important was to try to find out what happened and what both sides of town thought about it) (*Dear Rafe* 229). In other words, the crux of the novel relies on attempting to ascertain the truth of a historical event and people's interpretation of it. Interestingly, Hinojosa did not include this sentence in his English-language re-creation of the novel. In this epistemological process in *Dear Rafe* and in *Mi querido Rafa*, the irony is thick, as P. Galindo announces in English and Spanish, respectively,

> As is usually the case, that which was thought to be a simple piece of research turns out not to be that at all. And, in spite of what has been said, by those who would know, and by the rest, those who know less but clamor the more, everything hinders and everything helps that which the wri would like to present and make known. A paradox, but here it is. (103)

> Como siempre, lo sencillo no resultó serlo. A pesar de lo que digan los que deben saber y los otros, los que saben menos y chillan más,

> *todo* impide y *todo* ayuda a esclarecer lo que se quiere traer a luz. Una paradoja, pero es así. (90)

And the Spanish-language testimony of P. Galindo ends with, "El esc. avisa que sigue estando de acuerdo con Roberto Arlt: 'En realidad, uno no sabe qué pensar de la gente'" (91)—(loosely translated) a voiced agreement with Roberto Arlt that, in reality, one never knows what to think of people. Hinojosa does not include the quote from Arlt in the English-language version. The reader has to wait until the end of *Becky and Her Friends* to get the following George Santayana quote from Galindo's successor: "what a strange accident the truth is" (160). In an extraliterary text, an interview entitled "Crossing Literary Borders" with Barbara Strickland, Hinojosa confirms as much:

> "I'm saying that it's very difficult to ascertain what the truth is. I'm not talking about point of view." He sips his iced tea. "People use their imagination more than they use their intellect. And the reason is that the imagination is very active and inventive while the intellect is not. The intellect is very lazy. We prefer, really, not to use our intellect. So you use your imagination. So therefore the search for truth," he says, chuckling, "is ongoing. And you think you've uncovered it and it's like an onion. So I figure, well, the writer shouldn't know everything."

Hinojosa's novels, thus, represent a search for truth, a truth that may be out of reach, complex, and multilayered. When apprehension of the social and historical reality is further complicated by two cultures, or two nations, existing side by side, blending, or competing, truth becomes even more illusive.

At the margins of the national cultures of the United States and Mexico, where even three national anthems are learned—the American, the Mexican, and "Texas, Our Texas" (*Klail City* 76)—Hinojosa's Belken County does not respect linguistic or cultural limits, racial or bloodline purity, geographic or political borders, or official truths. By questioning the official images and histories constructed and reinforced by both societies in contact and often in conflict (but there is also a middle ground of intermarriage, accommodation, and hybridization in Belken), Hinojosa documents another way to be human and independent of the state and its nation construct. However, in so doing, he produces an innovative oeuvre, completely original despite its dialogue with so many genres from literary history and oral tradition. Hinojosa's experimentation, as can be appreciated from the foregoing, is separate and distinct from that of all the other authors with whom the critics have compared him. It is also separate and distinct from the work of Tomás Rivera, in the last chapter, and from that of Gloria Anzaldúa, in the next chapter of this book. Hinojosa's contribution is transitional: whereas Rivera strove to enable a national consciousness for Mexican Americans and Anzaldúa advocates that border dwellers affirm their hybridism and transcend nationalism, Hinojosa negates all national projects as invalid.

In writing outside the canon—nay, destabilizing and undermining the canon by dominating and subverting the canonical genres—Hinojosa in the Klail City Death Trip series operates as a translator and disseminator of texts across cultures. He takes two series of national myths, rewrites them, and generates a new imaginary, one just as fictitious and beautiful and outlandish as the two originals, and, by the way, just as historical or ahistorical in its role as foundation for a people's identity. He creates this history and identity in that interstitial space we call the borderlands, made from both nations but apart from both of them. In this process, he seems to exercise what Homi K. Bhabha described as "a temporality of representation that moves between cultural formations and social processes without a 'centered' logic" (293). Bhabha further explains, "The power of supplementarity is not the negation of the preconstituted social contradictions of the past and the present; its force lies . . . in the renegotiation of those times, terms, and traditions through which we turn our uncertain, passing contemporaneity into the signs of history" (306). What Hinojosa accomplishes in his continuing narrative, to use Bhabha's phraseology once again, is that he

> contests genealogies of "origin" that lead to cultural supremacy and historical priority. Minority discourse acknowledges the status of national culture—and the people—as a contentious, performative space of the perplexity of the living in the midst of the pedagogical representations of fullness of life. Now there is no reason to believe that such marks of difference—the incommensurable time of the subject culture—cannot inscribe "history" of the people or become the gathering points of political solidarity. (308)

Whereas old-timers like Echevarría and Mora may have provided an argument for the historical priority of Hispanic/Mexican culture, and *vendidos* (sellouts) like Ira Escobar may embody a negation of the prior culture in an effort to assimilate and be empowered by the Anglo interlopers, it is the contemporary generation, now mature, of Sammie Jo/Rafa Buenrostro and Becky/Jehú Malacara, that is responsible for generating a new and unique culture that is integrated and powerful and may represent a threat to both nations. I repeat, in deconstructing the literary genres and history of both nations, Hinojosa disassembles the armature of myths that sustain nations. He does not travel the path of cultural nationalism in the process; instead, he posits a different history and literature, complete unto themselves.

Hinojosa not only subverts and replaces the U.S. national myths but also treats the present as past: the United States is no longer an Anglo-European geopolitical-cultural state. Mexico is no longer a Third World backwater reacting to Anglo economic and cultural superiority. That was the past; the Mestizo States of America is the present and future, in praxis, not just in fiction and myth. The cultural transformations at the border represent the future evolution of the United States (and Mexico). The long predestined integration of the Americas is taking place, at least as far north as Canada. Of course, Hinojosa's discourse is directed at readers who are familiar with the conflicting histories, myths, and politics of the two peoples confronting each other at the border. These readers' initial disbelief is assuaged through irony and a subversive humor that allow him to propose what otherwise would be a preposterous mythopoesis; but it is made palatable, even enjoyable, through the technique of reader response. Hinojosa's art has led the reader to greater truths and an insight into not only the reality of, to use Bhabha's words again, the "pagus—colonials, postcolonials, migrants, minorities," but also "the *Heim* of the national culture and its unisonant discourse" (315). He thus erases borders, political and social, and opts for hybridity.

CHAPTER 9

Gloria Anzaldúa

Transcending Nationhood

Much of contemporary Chicano thought has attempted to identify the Chicano nation, whether in whole or in part. As discussed in chapter 7, for example, Tomás Rivera set about delving deep into the culture and worldview of his particular community, Texas agricultural migrant workers, to assert that it had its own history and that its culture was worthy of producing art and literature. In many ways, this was similar to Daniel Venegas's project in the 1920s as he sought to encompass the life and struggles of poor Mexican immigrant workers and draw from their culture to create a history, art, and literature. Neither of these authors' projects was romantic or idealistic. They were both decrying the plight of highly exploited and oppressed workers. Rivera criticized what was impeding his working-class community from liberating itself from a life cycle of oppressive migrant farm labor. Critics almost universally selected Rivera's *. . . y no se lo tragó la tierra / And the Earth Did Not Devour Him* (1971) and his other works as foundational, a canon to be followed in the construction of a Chicano identity, reflective of a people emerging in opposition to both Anglo-American and Mexican national identities. They implicitly situated Chicano nationhood in a cultural space between the United States and Mexico, constructing socio-psychological borders if not geographic ones—although there were calls for establishing a Chicano political nation as separate within the U.S. Southwest, starting with taking back ancestral lands. At first, the critics also sought to fit Rolando Hinojosa-Smith's work into the same mold, that is, within the model of an internal colony of the U.S. empire. But as seen in the last chapter,

Hinojosa wrote the border as a site of hybridity, not a pure Chicano homeland, and he charted that growing hybridity across time through a historical narrative that ran through his entire series of books. Rivera affirmed the existence of his characters and community with an ultimate loving embrace in the last chapter of *Tierra*. Hinojosa, in contrast, never became so intimate as to lovingly embrace his characters; rather, he situated himself above them, and his affect was a sardonic smile as he negated the concepts of nationhood and affirmed the border region as a generator of cultural hybridity. For Hinojosa, all identities were questionable, and ultimate truth was forever illusive. If Rivera's lesson was to liberate oneself by observing, analyzing, and salvaging what is valuable in the psyche and the community, then Hinojosa's message was to cast a critical eye on human and social actions in order to construct an imperfect truth for oneself and the community. In both cases, Rivera's and Hinojosa's, the border was an ever-present locus for creativity, including the generation of new cultural forms. Rivera's border marks the opposition of Anglo and Mexican American cultures, the exploiters and the exploited—and the exploiters can be from within or without Mexican American culture, as it was for Venegas and his *pochos*, *agringados*, and *renegados* (non-Mexicans, the gringoized, and cultural renegades)—whether in Texas or on the road. Hinojosa's border was the very real demarcation between two political states that have at times experienced differentiating events and at other times have grown in similarity and integration. In Hinojosa's world of heteroglossia and hybridity, borders separating the races or ethnicities in the valley were disappearing and social classes were becoming more permeable. But in both Rivera's and Hinojosa's work, the concept of the border remained confined to a place and the people who lived there; even if they migrated away, they took the border with them.

Of all the thinkers and writers covered in this book, the one who today has become most influential and celebrated for fresh ideas and concepts, and who is most studied and cited beyond Latino intellectual circles, is a product of the same border region: the Rio Grande Valley of Texas. She is theorist, poet, and activist Gloria Anzaldúa (1942–2004), and she shares a background in poverty and farmwork with Rivera, and a preoccupation with the border region with Hinojosa. But Anzaldúa went on to expand the theoretical construct of borders to encompass far more than did her two male, straight predecessors in literary history and Latino thought (see Guidotti-Hernández, "Borderlands"). By any measure, Anzaldúa is far more known today *outside* of Latino circles than is either of the previous Chicano foundational writers, although Rivera and Hinojosa both published works for decades, beginning in the late 1960s.[1]

In contrast, too, with Rivera and Hinojosa, neither of whom was ever accorded the celebration of their lives and works with the founding of an academic society dedicated exclusively to them, Anzaldúa was honored in 2007 with the newly created Society for the Study of Gloria Anzaldúa, which has sponsored conferences every eighteen months into the present.[2] Part of the reason for so broad a following for Anzaldúa—even if she did not produce as many books in her short lifetime as Hinojosa or some of the other thinkers studied in these pages—is that her writing has been influential in so many fields: feminist and LGBTQ+ studies, spirituality, literature, pedagogy, and, of course, border studies.[3] What started out as a challenge to white feminism in *This Bridge Called My Back: Writings by Radical Women of Color* (1981) eventually turned into an all-encompassing, inclusive, and unifying vision for progressive social change and self-healing. Thus, while firmly grounded in an empirical analysis of history, especially of colonialism and neocolonialism, Anzaldúa's creative and theoretical writing also encompasses interpretation of myths and dreams, especially from a shamanistic or new age perspective. She combines poetic intuition and Native American spirituality with progressive resistance to racism, imperialist oppression, and patriarchy. Race, class, gender, and the empirical/spiritual are all one piece in her writing and speeches, just as they intersected with one another in her biography.

Anzaldúa was born on her family's ranch in the Rio Grande Valley, where from an early age she worked alongside the hired field hands to pick crops. The ranch had been passed down from the generations of mestizo ancestors who had first settled the area when it was part of New Spain. Because the ranch was not enough to sustain the household, the family was forced into the migrant farmworker stream, toiling for a time in the fields of Arkansas. Anzaldúa's father died when she was fourteen, and she had to work the ranch fields to help the family survive; this she did while continuing her education, until she graduated in 1968 from Pan American College, close to home in Edinburg, Texas ("Gloria Anzaldúa"). After obtaining her degree in English and secondary education, she worked as a teacher. She went on to obtain a master's degree from the University of Texas at Austin in 1972 and began, but never finished, a doctoral degree at the University of California, Santa Cruz. After that, beginning in 1977, she became somewhat of an academic migrant, teaching and lecturing at various universities around the United States, including San Francisco State University and Florida Atlantic University (her specialties were feminist thought and Chicano studies), while also embarking on her writing career. In 1981, she joined as co-editor with Chicana lesbian icon Cherríe Moraga on the groundbreaking *This Bridge Called My Back*, which became a landmark in the movement to identify and proclaim a nonwhite feminism. Anzaldúa went on to become a prolific writer and speaker, contributing essays to various publications, co-editing anthologies, producing bilingual children's literature—*Prietita Has a Friend / Prietita tiene un amigo* (1991), *Friends from the Other Side / Amigos del Otro Lado* (1993), and *Prietita and the Ghost Woman / Prietita y la Llorona* (1995)—and, most importantly, writing her highly influential book *Borderlands/La Frontera: The New Mestiza* (1987). In this last, she mixes and blends the genres of prose and poetry, English and Spanish, and myth and history, and she generally transgresses all borders, including the borders of ethnicity and gender. At each step in her exploration of border-related themes, Anzaldúa uses her own life experiences, dreams, academic studies, and intuition, indirectly creating a lyrical autobiography along the way. Nicole M. Guidotti-Hernández, in her overview of the field of borderland studies and borderlands theory, writes of *Borderlands/La Frontera* as "a hallmark of the field. A strong and unapologetic humanistic theory of the violence embodied in spatial and cultural clashes, Anzaldúa's work addresses intimacy as a shrunken space between two individuals and two nations" ("Borderlands" 23).

Anzaldúa's essay "La Prieta" in *This Bridge Called My Back* announced her quest to resolve the identity issues she faced growing up as a working-class Latina who confronted racism and homophobia in her family and in society at large. In *Borderlands/La Frontera*, she derives the power to create herself from her Indigenous heritage: "My Chicana identity is grounded in the Indian woman's history of resistance" (43). It is because of this powerful history of resistance and survival that she can "stand and claim my space, making a new culture—*una cultura mestiza*—with my own lumber, my own bricks and mortar and my own feminist architecture" (44). But this is not a nationalist affirmation, like Tomás Rivera's, in which one delves deep into everyday experiences and cultural practices; it is a point of departure for an ideology of unity. *Borderlands/La Frontera* provides her mature vision of how *mestizaje* can resist gender, race, and class discrimination while healing the psyche and creating a psychological wholeness in the individual and society. Her extrapolation of the concept of transgressing borders is precisely what makes this possible; it is this concept that has attracted so much attention from within ethnic and feminist studies and beyond. After dealing with the intersectionality of race, class, gender, history, environment, religiosity, and other factors that complicate and often determine identity—that is, European or Indigenous, white skin or brown skin, straight or gay, male or female, the empirical or the spiritual, English or Spanish—Anzaldúa affirms that the individual has many identities specific to varying cultural and social situations. The healing process entails accepting these contradictions and feeling confident in the wholeness of personality; from there, one can then achieve many things and dedicate oneself to social and political change. It is at once an affirmation of being rooted in a specific time-place and an affirmation of going beyond, transgressing social and self-imposed borders. Thus, the borders of language, ethnicity, race, gender, social class, and religion must all be bridged—the bridge is her favorite metaphor for the process—in an all-inclusive outreach to the rest of humanity. Her praxis is to extend *mestizaje* (mixing, miscegenation, hybridity, the negation of binary thinking) to all human activity, to all peoples, as a positive force in human development, not one that should be eschewed, decried, or walled off. Over the span of human evolution, and accelerated in contemporary times, hybridity is normal, and hybridity becomes part of the definition of humanity. In Anzaldúa's evolution as a thinker, hybridity comes to be seen not only as the bridge linking border dwellers, interstitial peoples, and cultures throughout the world, but also as a force to empower them to renovate society into the future.

Borderlands/La Frontera was revolutionary in its espousal of erasure of all types of borders, including the binaries of sexuality. As Sonia Saldívar-Hull states:

> Part of the work of the *mestiza* consciousness is to break down dualities that serve to imprison women. [Anzaldúa's] articulation of Chicana lesbian theory does just that, as she declares herself both male and female. Again, she uses *cuento* and *testimonio* to present theory as she recounts the young neighbor of her youth who was an outsider and labeled "one of the others," half woman, half man. Refusing the condemnation of labels, however, she strategically takes a feminist-nationalist turn to indigenous "tradition" that views alterity as power. The ultimate

> rebellion for Chicanas is through sexuality, and in Anzaldúa's version of queer theory, this is specifically true for lesbians of color. (5)

In her post-*Borderlands/La Frontera* essays, interviews, and speeches, Anzaldúa expanded on and deepened her thoughts on these issues. A collection of these, titled *Light in the Dark / Luz en lo oscuro: Rewriting Identity, Spirituality, Reality,* was published posthumously in 2015. Notably, in this volume, she elevates the cultural geography of the border region into a metaphorical space she calls Nepantla, after the Aztec belief in a place between the Aztec heaven and nether regions:

> *En este lugar entremedio, nepantla,* two or more forces clash and are held teetering on the verge of chaos, a state of *entreguerras.* These tensions between extremes create cracks or tears in the membrane surrounding, protecting, and containing the different cultures and their perspectives. Nepantla is the place where at once we are detached (separated) and attached (connected) to each of our several cultures. . . . Nepantla is the midway point between the conscious and the unconscious, the place where transformations are enacted. Nepantla is a place where we can accept contradiction and paradox. (56)

She goes on to describe Nepantla as a place where presumed heterosexuals can present and voice "their queer, lesbian, gay, bi, or transgendered selves." It is where social class lines can be crossed. Anzaldúa sees the border region as representing the world, the entire planet: "The border, in a constant nepantla state, is an analog of the planet. This is why the borderline is a persistent metaphor in *el arte de la frontera,* an art that expresses such themes as identity, border crossings, and hybrid imaginary" (57). The shifting identities, the border crossings, and the hybridism in this metaphorical space function to decolonize; crossing all types of borders, from the political to the gendered to the cultural, is a strategy for universal decolonization, in Anzaldúa's ideology. Nepantla is the place where *mestizaje* flourishes: "Negotiating with borders results in *mestizaje,* the new hybrid, the new *mestiza,* a new category of identity. *Mestizas* live in between different worlds, in Nepantla. We are forced (or choose) to live in categories that defy binaries of gender, race, class, and sexuality. Living in intersections, in cusps, we must constantly operate in a negotiation mode" (71). Anzaldúa extends this "negotiation mode" beyond our individual thought processes and psychological conflicts. It is also a means of universal outreach to erode the ultimate binaries of us and them, in a type of spirituality that envisions the unity of all humanity: "An identity born of negotiating the cracks between worlds, nos/otras accommodates contradictory identities and social positions, creating a hybrid consciousness that transcends the us versus them mentality of irreconcilable positions, blurring the boundary between us and others. We are both subject and object, conqueror and conquered, oppressor and oppressed. Proximity and intimacy can close the gap between us and them" (79).

In her messianic vision of the *nueva mestiza*, all of us border dwellers (*neplanteras*), regardless of gender, hold the salvation of humanity in our hands. Anzaldúa's is a revolutionary call to action for the dispossessed, the marginalized, the hybrids to reform their national cultures. It is not a call to people from the U.S.-Mexico border or to Latinos and the LGBTQ+ community exclusively; it is for all peoples at the intersections of cultures, political divisions, gender designations, racial divides, and other binaries around the world.[4] And here, she borrows the Buddhist concept that the difference between the self and others is responsible for all evil and sorrow in the world (*Light* 81). There is no self that is separate from the rest of humanity; to pursue the self is the true evil in the world. "Las *neplanteras* know that each of us is linked with everyone and everything in the universe. . . . *Las neplanteras* are spiritual activists engaged in the struggle for social, economic, and political justice, while working on spiritual transformations of selfhoods" (83). "The task of remaking ourselves and our cultures is in our own hands; the task of *las neplanteras* is to point the way" (81). Because *neplanteras* have the "ability to mediate and move between identities and positions," they can cross over all types of borders and build bridges between worlds; they can "shed their toxic values and ways of life" and lead the way in the search for wholeness (93).

Significantly, this ideology and call to action negate nationalism, while still acknowledging cultural grounding as part of identity. Importantly, the type of nationalism they refute is what was first promoted by the Chicano Movement, which was responsible for selecting the works of Rudolfo Anaya, Rivera, and Hinojosa as canonical.[5] In some respects, Anzaldúa's call is reminiscent of Blanca de Moncaleano's anarchist call to arms for women, "Manifiesto a la Mujer" (Manifesto to Women, 1915). This earlier text also negated nationalism, in its quest to re-create society by inspiring women around the world to arise from their oppression at the hands of the state, the church, and capital. But nowhere did Moncaleano base this uprising on the very insights derived from the hybridity or marginality of the oppressed: her radical feminism was firmly rooted in Eurocentric anarchist ideology. In contrast, Anzaldúa's goes beyond those inherited perspectives to embrace Indigenous myths, including shape-shifting, and Eastern religions. And never does Anzaldúa provide us with a clear picture of what society will look like, if and when the *neplanteras* are successful in obliterating borders, whereas we do have a somewhat clear picture of the anarchist's imagined utopia of a type of heaven on Earth. The utopian ideas of the anarchists, indeed, helped make life better for working people. Anzaldúa's ideas may have practical application for the betterment of humanity.

Anzaldúa espoused an internationalist ideology very different from Nemesio García Naranjo's nationalist vision (see chapter 6). Despite his being a border dweller, an insider-outsider, he cemented the binary opposition of Anglo versus Mexican. For him, one had to be Mexican; even for the native-born Mexican American population living in the United States, it was *México de afuera* (a Mexican nation abroad) for all. One had to study and practice Mexican identity, preserve the gender roles as solidified and remembered from the nineteenth century, practice the Catholic religion, and, above all, teach the Spanish language and Mexican values to children in order to preserve the culture in both the Anglo-Protestant United States and Bolshevik Mexico. Anzaldúa did arrive at a similar concept of deterritorialization of Mexican identity, as she states in *Borderlands/La Frontera*: "Deep in our hearts we believe that being Mexican has nothing to do with which country one lives in. Being Mexican is a state of soul—not one mind, not one citizenship. Neither eagle nor serpent, but both. And like the ocean, neither animal respects borders" (84).[6] But in her later essay "Geographies of Selves—Reimagining Identity," in *Light in the Dark / Luz en lo oscuro*, Anzaldúa expresses how immigration gives birth to the type of hybridity that García Naranjo and most immigrant writers fought against:

> The terrain, the planes (and plains) of identity alter when a person moves (immigrates) into another community or social position. One ends up living in a different physical and symbolic environment while retaining the former "home" culture and position. After leaving the home culture's familiar cocoon, you occupy other ideological spaces,

> begin seeing reality in new ways, questioning both the native culture's and the new culture's descriptions of reality. The new culture, like the old one, inculcates you with its values and worldviews. (71)

Simply stated: for García Naranjo identity is static and unchanging; for Anzaldúa it is mutable and leads to hybridity. Whereas Hinojosa looked at hybridity as the natural state of the border region, Anzaldúa universalizes it and makes of it an approach to living in this world. As Martina Koegeler-Abdi states, "These theories of subjectivity are also transformational strategies that start with and transcend individual change, creating new communities and worlds if enough people participate. These individual and collective changes may materialize through the power of language to rename and rewrite identities and personal, mythical, and spiritual histories—for example, with regard to one's location in the conventional ethnic frame of reference or within heteronormativity" (71).

To be sure, there has been criticism of Anzaldúa's "utopianism" and "romanticism," most notably from political scientist David Rieff, who accuses her of an obsession with race and culture and insufficient attention to social class (46). Another critic, Nicole M. Guidotti-Hernández, concedes that

> the Latina/o multi-border perspective can both reorient the narrative history of the Americas and account for the ways in which particular racial or sexual formations such as those of queer, Afro-descendant, or Indigenous populations tend to be erased from the Latina/o United States. The multi-border analytic can guide us to consider comparatively or synchronically, the historic relational and distinct experiences of Spanish colonial spatial organization (the specificities of Spanish empire in the Americas and elsewhere, in relation and conflict with American imperialism), or borderlands as mutually constitutive. ("Borderlands" 24)

However, Guidotti-Hernández and others challenge Anzaldúa's conceptualization of *mestizaje* for having accepted the political use of the term in forging a national identity in Mexico after the revolution of 1910 and negating or brushing over the violence visited on native peoples by the Europeans who engendered the mestizos.[7] As Guidotti-Hernández has stated, Anzaldúa and other scholars "*sometimes* evoke *mestizaje* unproblematically to essentialize Indigeneity as its main component without acknowledging black and Asian peoples or the violence Chicana/os and Mexicans have historically performed against Indigenous people" ("Borderlands Scholarship" 489, original emphasis; see also Saldaña-Portillo).

Other scholars have deconstructed and censured the tenets of Anzaldúa's thought. For instance, they attack her (mis)use of Aztec mythology and her identification with the Aztec past at the neglect of contemporary Amerindian cultures, and they question her application of Chicano/a hybridity to other hybrid cultures across the world; in addition, they fear that Anzaldúa's attempt to transcend race and biology still depends on biological breeding and crossbreeding.

Although Anzaldúa's particular tenets can be subject to these types of queries and challenges, such an expansive vision as hers may seem unrealistic, hopelessly idealistic, especially when considered from the vantage point of our skeptical times. Today, around the world, nationalism has reemerged and borders have been reinforced; quite often, that nationalism, even in such "enlightened" and diverse societies as the European and the American, has been promoted by demagogues who inflame white supremacy groups while deporting racial Others who are political and economic refugees. International institutions, such as the United Nations, the European Union, and the World Health Organization, are under attack, and even founding members, such as the United Kingdom and the United States, consider their exit.

At this point in history, nevertheless, Anzaldúa's call may be more than pertinent; it implicitly calls for reflection on the interrelatedness of people everywhere, the oneness of humanity. Her mobilization of what she calls *neplanteras*, border crossers as mediators, is for agents who can unify the peoples and cultures seen as opposing. This idea may have very practical application and in fact be most needed. Now more than ever, our countries should tap into their natural repositories of bilingual, multilingual, and bicultural people to reach out to other societies. In their recruitment and training, our diplomatic corps should tap into our diversity in order to put forth knowledgeable and intuitive representatives to "foreign" nations. Within Europe itself, this is quite often the rule for diplomatic, corporate, and scientific leaders; they have been educated in the multiethnic, multilingual European Union, a community that diminishes borders and seeks peaceful exchange at all levels. But the United States makes little effort to produce official border crossers, expecting the rest of the world to conduct business in English and to bend to our cultural and economic imperatives. With virtually the complete array of the world languages, ethnicities, and religions within the United States' own geographic borders and populace, it is unfathomable how U.S. institutions waste these human resources by continuing to select and prepare white, monolingual, monocultural, heteronormative men to lead them in imposing neocolonial imperatives within and outside our borders. In the process, they continue to impoverish and marginalize all types of minorities, most of which are potential *neplanteras*. Our schools and universities must prepare bilingual and multilingual diverse people to lead; they should really open the doors of education to our marginalized, racialized, working-class, gender-diverse people. Let us take nationalism, classism, racism, homophobia, and intolerance of all sorts out of education at all levels and, consequently, society.

Anzaldúa's is the ultimate democratic dream; we have to believe it lies within the realm of reality (see Paccacerqua). Let us not nitpick her vision, but work to reform society, as she suggests. If we do not have dreams and aspirations, very little can be achieved.

Conclusion

Latinos in the lands that became the United States struggled to define their identity from the beginning of the nineteenth century, while the concept of nationhood was fluid and still being formed. The ideals and foundational documents that undergirded the former English colonies' separation from the empire served not only as models but also as motivation for early Latino intellectuals to relocate to Philadelphia and other U.S. cities in order to have access to a free press and to learn from the founders and administrators of the nascent American republic. Often exiled from their homelands or abandoning the Spanish parliament (Cortes) in disillusionment, they came to the United States as revolutionists to arm themselves with the sword and with the word, raising funds for armaments and translating and interpreting the United States' founding documents and its thinkers' ideals in the hopes of establishing their own nations. A number of revolutionists returned to their homelands, which became independent nations. But there were many false starts, as seen in chapters 1 and 2. The philosopher-theologian Félix Varela conspired with revolutionaries but would never see his Cuba freed from the Spanish yoke, and, in fact, Cuba and Puerto Rico continued for the entire nineteenth century their struggles for independence and nationhood. Then, too, one of the first and loudest to proclaim Mexican and Cuban nationhood, the scion of Spanish nobility José Alvarez de Toledo y Dubois, went down in defeat in Texas's rebellion and ultimately betrayed the cause and affirmed the power of the Spanish Empire. However, he was the first one to make abundantly clear that Latino identity would have to emerge in the contested physical and ideological space between the empires of Spain, Britain, and France, as well as that of the new American republic on the eve of expansion southward and westward into Indo-Hispanic lands. Alvarez de Toledo, Varela, and many others also firmly established the road to biculturalism and bilingualism for Hispanics within the United States, serving as translators and mediators between the cultures and nations.

By the middle of the nineteenth century, the expansionist, imperial intentions of the United States were confirmed by its filibustering and intervention into Florida and the nascent republics of Central America and, of course, its war to acquire the northern half of Mexico. Chapter 3 documents how a frontier journalist, Francisco Ramírez, precisely because of his biculturalism and bilingualism (even trilingualism) realized that his people were caught on the horns of the bicultural dilemma: their allegiance to the United States and its Constitution offered them certain freedoms, but those freedoms were withheld from them because of their status as a conquered and inferior race not recognized as part of the American nation. In addition, Ramírez realized, as increasingly so many other Latino writers and thinkers of the time were discovering, that their cultural bonds and history tied them irrevocably to the fate of the nations emerging south of the new U.S. border. That is, Latinos' fate as an internal colony was firmly tied to U.S. economic and political expansionism to the south.

Cuba and Puerto Rico became colonies of the United States in 1898, again as result of an unprovoked war of territorial expansion. While the previous chapters dealt at times with the emergence of a New World mestizo (Indo-European) ideology, chapter 4 explores how for the first time the imperialist reach of the United States into Hispanic lands and populations interrupted the process in Cuba and Puerto Rico whereby the descendants of enslaved Africans were exploring their own Afro-Latino identities, which resulted in intellectuals such as Arturo Alfonso Schomburg and Sotero Figueroa influencing the development of Afro-American culture.

Chapters 5 and 6 are to be read in tandem. They explore the tension that has continued to the present between the progressive and conservative traditions, a tension that was heightened as the United States received more and more immigrants from the Spanish-speaking world in the late nineteenth and early twentieth centuries. Chapter 5 recovers the forgotten history of labor activism and anarchism, which solidified worker identity across Latino ethnic identities and even raised their consciousness of their worldwide brethren also exploited by capital, the church, and the state. The movement was highly educational for workers, both in- and outside factories and farms, with schools, study groups, and newspapers arising from coast to coast. Within anarchist ideology there was widespread support, possibly for the first time by organizations led by men, for women intellectuals and activists, to the extent that many women came to prominence not only as leaders but also as editors, publishers, and writers. Anarchism sought to organize workers beyond nationhood and to cross borders, even while some of its activists and ideologues, such as the Flores Magón brothers, fought wars in Mexico and Cuba to establish or reform their nations. Concurrently—and despite attacks on the church by anarchists and the anticlerical tendencies of the newly instituted Mexican revolutionary government—the church's opposition to the revolution, its historical support of the Spanish Empire, and its consequent hold on the masses of Hispanics around the world have cemented to the present a strain of conservatism in the worldview of U.S. Latinos. Chapter 6 briefly documents the evolution of religious thought in Latino communities and analyzes how powerful print media, particularly in the hands of an entrepreneur such as Ignacio E. Lozano, reinforced and invigorated conservative thought and even empowered such conservative Catholic intellectuals as Nemesio García Naranjo in their counterrevolutionary missions. Lozano, García Naranjo, and their cohort furthered an ideology of exile, even among Mexican Americans of many generations back: *México de afuera* (a Mexican nation abroad), where all Mexican-origin peoples had to maintain their Mexican identity, Catholic faith, and Spanish language. While the anarchists negated national assignations to identify Latinos with workers around the world, the conservatives saw only one national identity, Mexican, whether one resided within or outside Mexican national territory. It is ironic that a bilingual border dweller and product of hybridity such as García Naranjo himself would espouse such cultural unilateralism, but Catholic dogma and allegiance to authoritarianism characterized his thought throughout his life. As still the vast majority of Latinos in the United States are working class, these tensions still exist, even while intellectuals, and masses of immigrants and refugees, today are once again transcending borders and nationhood.

Chapters 7, 8, and 9 make a chronological leap to the late 1960s and to the near present to explore how the pursuit of nationhood was articulated by three foundational writers of Chicano literature: Tomás Rivera, Rolando

Hinojosa-Smith, and Gloria Anzaldúa. At the outset, I reveal that I have been intimately involved in the development of this literature since the late 1960s, first as an activist and cultural nationalist and then, from the early 1970s, as an editor and publisher, actually the only editor with fifty years of experience working with leading literary and historical figures of the Chicano Movement.

In summary, these three chapters trace how the cultural nationalism of the first writers and thinkers of the Chicano Movement evolved into a critique and deconstruction of nationalist projects in favor of an internationalism. While Rivera (chapter 7) plumbed the depths of his people's identity in an effort to write them into history and democratize culture in general, his was a bifurcated world, in which Anglos oppressed Mexican-origin peoples and negated their history and culture; his response was to demonstrate how Mexicans should draw from within their own cultural resources to construct themselves as a nation. The bicultural and bilingual Rivera embraced hybridity, in life and in writing, even to the extent of celebrating Texas Mexican dialect; however, hybridity per se was for Rivera only part of the message of constructing nationhood. Chapter 8 documents how Rivera's friend and colleague Rolando Hinojosa-Smith, as a satirist contemptuous of all national projects, erased the U.S.-Mexico border and fully embraced hybridity, crafting novels at times in Spanish, at other times in English, and at still other times in bilingual texts—something that had mostly been the purview of literature more closely tied to community performance, such as poetry and theater. In his project to recapitulate the history of what was once Northern Mexico and was now South Texas, Hinojosa undermined all sources of knowledge, documentary and oral, to affirm at ground level how his people spoke, perceived the world, and represented it, always in conflict and contestation. They were all mestizos, insiders and outsiders at the same time, with their separate and mixing languages, and their separate and mixing ethnicities. Hinojosa, thus, destroyed the binary by depicting—often with satire and humor—the conflicts, synthesis, and hybridity endemic to the border region. Two national histories and national projects made for conflicting truths and worldviews, to be resolved only by the multifaceted perceptions and responses of border dwellers to the illusive nature of ultimate truth.

Finally, in chapter 9 we have Gloria Anzaldúa, who saw the concepts of border, nationhood, indigeneity, gender, and social class as intersected by her development of *mestizaje*, a concept of hybridity that eschewed national, class, and gender binaries to affirm and embrace duality, not only on the border, but throughout the world. The two centuries of Latino pursuit of democracy and liberation, of personhood and civil rights, culminate with the proposition that Latino hybridity is central to resolving the horrific divisiveness of nationalism, bigotry, and homophobia both in the United States and around the world. Latinos, firm in their ethnic identities, are border crossers who must become essential in making democratic principles real in the world. Unlike the calls for revolution to establish separate Hispanic nations in the early nineteenth century and the calls for combat issued by anarchists, such as Blanca de Moncaleano a full century later, or the religio-nationalist preaching of García Naranjo in the mid-twentieth century, Anzaldúa's revolutionary call is for empathy and unity among peoples.

I can only hope that through my scholarship and directorship of Arte Público Press and the Recovering the US Hispanic Literary Heritage program, I have contributed a bit to furthering those principles.

It is ironic that as we Latinos today recognize our relationship to and solidarity with the peoples south of the border and in the Caribbean, whether Indigenes or mestizos or Afro-Latinos, and we accept and embrace immigration, that the political culture across great swaths of the United States has been going in the opposite direction by closing borders and minds in an effort to impose a white nationalism as the bulwark of a Christian nation. The latent forces that empowered U.S. expansionism southward and westward over two centuries and brought within the republic conquered peoples as well as those displaced by U.S. economic imperialism abroad have recently succeeded in electing a white-nationalist president who then proceeded, with the approval of almost half of the body politic, to appoint like-minded Supreme Court justices to bend the law to extend Christian religious beliefs and practices into governmental policy and practice. While Latinos are broadening their perspectives and beginning to tap into the benefits and advantages of bilingualism and biculturalism in all walks of life, the polity—authorized by the very shortsightedness and biases in the Constitution regarding slavery and democratic representation by such institutions as the U.S. Senate and the Electoral College—is closing borders and minds. And this is not just about Anglos versus Latinos or minorities, or Christians versus Muslims; the religiosity and conservatism of Latinos have once again come into play, at times supporting the construction of a Christian nation and even the white nation.

Our modern-day interpretation of *mestizaje* and outreach transcending borders and nations, as articulated by some of our writers and intellectuals, is erased in the popular media and the U.S. national consciousness. We, not only as Latinos but also as border dwellers in a world of innumerable borders, must prevail if we are to survive this white nationalist onslaught.

NOTES

INTRODUCTION

A very short, early version of this overview was written as a report for the National Park Service in 2012; it appears online as "Envisioning and Re-Visioning the Nation: Latino Intellectual Traditions," *National Park Service*, "American Latino Theme Study: Intellectual Traditions," https://www.nps.gov/articles/latinothemeintellectual.htm.

1. It is customary in scholarship to define the terms we call ourselves: in this case, why today we use "Latino" or "Hispanic" when speaking of the peoples who descended from Spanish colonization of the Americas (with its consequent mixing of the heritages of Europe, Africa, and Amerindia), people who have been part of the United States since the beginning of the American republic or have immigrated here since then. Briefly, the terms "Hispanic" and "Latino" owe their genesis to common usage in nineteenth-century communities where there was more than one Hispanic ethnicity present, such as New York, San Francisco, and Tampa, whose residents included immigrants from Spain, Cuba, Mexico, and Puerto Rico, people from as far away as Chile and everywhere else in the Spanish-speaking hemisphere. They referred to their diverse community as *hispano-americanos*, when indicating the Hispanophone group; or *latinoamericanos*, when indicating a mix of Hispanophone, Francophone, and even Lusophone community members. A clear case in point was San Francisco in the early twentieth century, when the newspaper *Hispano América* served a diverse audience of Mexicans, Chileans, Spaniards, Peruvians, "Sonorans," and others. Tampa's Ybor City stands as an outlier; since the nineteenth century, it has considered Italians as part of the "Latino" community. A cursory reading through the lists of periodicals published by Latinos/Hispanos in the United States before World War II will show that there were many more newspapers published in Spanish with a form of *hispano* in their titles, thus defining their market, their community

(Kanellos and Martell, *Hispanic Periodicals in the United States*). Also see Robert McKee Irwin, "Almost-Latino Literature," on the appropriateness of using the term "Latino" to speak about the literature in the nineteenth century, before the term even existed. I, too, have wrestled with the nomenclature. I generally tend toward "Hispanic" when speaking of the greater Spanish-speaking world, and "Latino" when referring to the literature on its continuum of development in the United States.

2. Original: "Diez y seis millones de habitantes que ocupan este delicioso Continente, no se representan jamás á los ojos del Gobierno y Mandatarios de Europa, sino como una horda de esclavos miserables que deben obedecer ciegamente á todo lo que se les mande, y besar en profundo silencio las duras cadenas que arrastran desde los tiempos de Cortés y Pizarro." Except where otherwise noted, all translations in this book are my own.

3. The two revolutionaries later had a falling out, with Alvarez de Toledo and the filibuster William Shaler dissatisfied with Gutiérrez de Lara's constitution and avowed independence from U.S. involvement.

4. Original: "Mujer de corazón, mujer de mentalidad, mujer nueva, la economía es tu problema inminente y tienes que resolverlo. La economía del hogar entra en tu jurisdicción, la economía del mundo es tu herencia."

5. Although Perales died in 1960, no biography was published until Cynthia E. Orozco's *Pioneer of Mexican American Civil Rights*, in 2022.

6. Gutiérrez's publications include his autobiographical *The Making of a Chicano Militant* (1998) and *The Making of a Civil Rights Leader* (2005); his translation of Reies López Tijerina's *They Called Me "King Tiger"* (2000); the guides *A Gringo Manual on How to Handle Mexicans* (1974, 2001) and *Chicano Manual on How to Handle Gringos* (2003); and the biographies *We Won't Back Down* (on Severita Lara, 2005) and *Albert A. Peña Jr.* (2017).

CHAPTER 1

1. Kristin Dykstra rather glibly calls Alvarez de Toledo "the Founding Father Who Wasn't" (267).

2. The report was appended to both the Philadelphia (1811) and the Charleston (1812) editions of his *Manifiesto ó satisfacción pundonorosa*, to be studied later in this chapter.

3. According to Josép María Miquel i Vergés, Monroe counseled Gutiérrez to draft a constitution based on the U.S. Constitution and planned to incorporate a free Texas into the American union, which incensed Gutiérrez and led him to leave Washington without many of the resources he had hoped to garner. This independent attitude of Gutiérrez later led to Alvarez de Toledo and U.S. agent William Shaler plotting against him and deposing him from the leadership of the movement (261–62).

4. Neither the 1811 Philadelphia publication nor the 1812 Charleston reprint identified the printer.

5. Harris Gaylord Warren has slighted this as a "tirade" (25).

6. Original: "Diez y seis millones de habitantes que ocupan este delicioso Continente, no se representan jamás á los ojos del Gobierno y Mandatarios de Europa, sino como una horda de esclavos miserables que deben obedecer ciegamente á todo lo que se les mande, y besar en profundo silencio las duras cadenas que arrastran desde los tiempos de Cortés y Pizarro."

7. Original: "Llegó el momento en que debí separarme de vosotros para evitar la persecución más atroz; y mi ultimo á Dios á ese suelo desgraciado, fue interrumpido por las emociones patéticas de la ternura y del dolor. La memoria de los buenos estará siempre gravada en mi alma con afectuosa estimación y respeto; y la de los malos me servirá en todos tiempos de lección y de escándalo."

8. Carlos M. Trelles credits this document as being the first to call for Cuban independence from Spain. Trelles further declares that the distribution of the *Manifiesto* was widespread in the Americas and that, in fact, the Spanish government declared it subversive and prohibited its entrance into the island, which accounts for its absence from archives in Cuba to this day (16). However, the *Manifiesto* itself was ostensibly addressed to the inhabitants of Santo Domingo, it being the author's desire to render an account to the people he had been elected to represent.

9. Original: "Americanos, los que habitáis las islas y el inmenso continente que sometió a su Imperio la Antigua España: oid mis voces que se exhalan sobre las fecundas y pacíficas riberas del hermoso Delaware, exaltadas por hacer felices a los Pueblos del Nuevo Mundo, y por ser la admiración y la dulce envidia de la orgullosa y tiranizada Europa. . . . Es preciso sacrificarlo todo al bien general; y sobre las bases más puras y sólidas construir la obra que debe hacer inmortal y admirable a la América en las edades venideras. . . . En la Constitución de los Estados Unidos podéis encontrar bellas cosas: elegid lo bueno, y evitado lo que puede ser funesto a la América en algún día."

10. Original: "Americanos: el mundo ha fixado la vista sobre vosotros; después de tres siglos de esclavitud y de ignominia, vais a ocupar un rango sublime entre las naciones cultas, y á sobrepujar la Gloria y el poder magestuoso de la antígua Europa. Mucho tenéis que hacer, mas no se obtienen grandes cosas sin grandes sacrificios, y sin una constancia inalterable, generosa, y superior á los reveses y a los halagos de la fortuna. Corred a donde os llama la Diestra omnipotente y augusta de la Providencia; y acordaos de que la libertad es el mas precioso de todos los bienes; que nunca será mucho lo que se haga por ella."

11. Original: "¡Oh dulces presentimientos de libertad de mi Patria! Si os realizáis, moriré lleno de gozo, aunque sea vertiendo toda mi sangre para defender sus derechos, y aterrar á sus enemigos. Estos son los votos de mi corazón; y oxalá, que sean también los de todos mis hermanos en la Isla de Cuba, y en la vasta extensión del hemisferio Americano."

12. Original: "La España se regocija de la separación del hijo espurio de la Patria; lo considera como un miembro ulcerado y pestífero."

13. Original: "Los que os predican la revolución no llevan otro objeto que el de hacer su fortuna en medio de las convulsiones y el transcurso político de vuestra constitución y gobierno."

14. Here as in his pamphlets, Alvarez de Toledo employed a rhetorical style redolent of oratory and public address, thus confirming what Sandra M. Gustafson sees as the need to lend authority to the written/printed word during these times of emergent nationalism.

15. Original: "Mexicanos: llegado es el tiempo señalado por la Providencia para que sacudáis el yugo bárbaro, y afrentoso, con que por el espacio de casi 300 años os oprimió ignominiosamente el despotismo insolente. Ahora quiere el Gobierno de Cádiz obligaros a que continuéis arrastrando las mismas cadenas, con que is aprisionaron los Reyes de España, los cuales no tenían sobre vosotros más autoridad, que la que vosotros mismos les prestasteis para ser por ella gobernados. . . . Yo os consejo, ilustres hijos de Moctesuma, que no envainéis vuestras espadas hasta no haber reestablecido el orden, y dado entera libertad a vuestro país."

16. In fact, the copy of the manifesto held at the Yale University Library is signed by hand by José Bernardo Gutiérrez; Alvarez de Toledo's initials (J.A.T.), however, are printed at the end of the document, signifying authorship.

17. In fact, a courier was caught in Nacogdoches with copies of the pamphlet (see Garret 295–96).

18. José Servando Teresa de Mier Noriega y Guerra believed it to be a good constitution, as he declared in the first history of the revolution, *Historia de la revolución de Nueva España*, published in London in 1813 (711).

19. This was a far cry from Gutiérrez de Lara's initial appraisal of Alvarez de Toledo: "he is a man of great talents, and passionately devoted to the cause of the liberty of Mexico: up to the present time he has worked much to this end; his merit therein is great and [he is] worthy of recompense and advancement in the cause, at the hands of that nation. The discourses of that gentleman are admirably great and just" (qtd. in Wells 76).

20. These were possibly the same issue with a title change (Gutiérrez-Witt 278). It is noteworthy that the second title of this newspaper appealed to nascent Mexican nationalism, repeating what Alvarez de Toledo had done in his manifesto. With the exception of New Orleans, which had a Spanish government press, Spain did not allow the printing press into its northern provinces in North America, perhaps because of its potential for use by filibusters and revolutionaries. In fact, the press was heavily censored in New Spain. Licenses to publish in the Spanish colonies had to be obtained directly from the Spanish Crown, and materials were subject to review by both state and religious authorities. In 1810, the Spanish Cortes created the Junta Suprema de Censura (Supreme Censorship Commission), and in 1820 the Cortes passed the Ley de Imprenta (Printing Law), which severely restricted printing and publishing. It was not until 1834, under the Mexican Republic, that New Mexico and California received the printing press.

21. Joseph B. Lockey negates the assertion by various historians and commentators that Alvarez de Toledo lost the battle on purpose, countering that intrigues

by officers loyal to Gutiérrez de Lara, desertions, and internal dissension caused his army to arrive too late to effect a winning strategy at the battle of Medina (171).

22. Original: "Nada hay difícil cuando hay dinero, al paso de que cuando éste falta nada se consigue."

23. However, according to Charles H. Bowman Jr., the Scotsman MacGregor was operating on behalf of the Spanish American independence movement (277).

24. In the same issue, there is a letter from Luis Alvarez de Toledo, José's father, beseeching his son to follow through on his offer to the Crown.

25. Nevertheless, accusations of spying and treachery dogged Alvarez de Toledo even in Spain after his reintegration (*Copia de la exposición*). See letters no. 09273 and 09275 in the Regencia de Urgell file for 1822–23 in the Biblioteca Nacional de España (National Library of Spain): "Comunicaciones de Un Buen Español (Balmaseda?) a un Redactor de Prensa refiriendo implicaciones sobre el General Quesada y el Colonel Alvarez de Toledo" (Information from a Good Spaniard [Balmaseda?] to a Newspaper Editor on Implications Regarding General Quesada and Colonel Alvarez de Toledo); and "Copia de la Exposición que los Diputados de la Provincia de Guipúzcoa y encargados de las de Alava y Vizcaya, Miguel María de Aranguren y Manuel de Tellerían, dirigen a S.M. [. . .] la Exposición hecha a la Regencia de España sobre la poca confianza se merecían en el país vascongado, D. Vicente Quesada y D. José Alvarez de Toledo, Tolosa, 28 marzo, 1823 [. . .]" (A Copy of the Exposition Made by the Guipúzcoa Provincial Officials and the Representatives from Alava and Biscayne, Miguel María de Aranguren and Manuel de Tellerían, directed to His Majesty [. . .] the Exposition Made to the Spanish Regency on the Lack of Confidence in the Basque Country in D. Vicente Quesada and D. José Alvarez de Toledo, Tolosa, 28 March, 1823 [. . .]).

26. In fact, it seems that Alvarez de Toledo involved Mina in his Florida plot (Lockey 175–78).

CHAPTER 2

1. Carmen A. Lamas discusses Varela as one of the first Latino (i.e., transnational) figures, a starting point for Latino intellectual culture in the United States, and someone who not only influenced the development of Latino nationalism but also played an important role in the construction of the U.S. nation through his work in education and centering of the Catholic Church (23–56).

2. To this day, the authorship of *Jicoténcal* is disputed. In their 1995 introduction to the novel, Luis Leal and Rodolfo Cortina make a strong case based on style and historical data that Varela was the author, although they state that perhaps there is no definitive answer (for this view, see also Garland). Other scholars have proposed authorship by a number of diverse writers of the period, including the exiled poet José María Heredia (e.g., González Acosta) or a collaboration of authors (e.g., Brickhouse 51). However, Carmen A. Lamas accuses scholars who would deny Varela's authorship of erasing "emerging nineteenth-century Latina/o voices who contributed

to the political dialogues surrounding Spanish American and US American post-independence narratives, and whose perspectives should be counted as foundational for the historiography surrounding the emancipation of the Spanish colonies from the metropolis as well as that of the US from Britain" (33). Even so, Rodrigo Lazo, in *Letters from Filadelfia*, argues against the Varela attribution by highlighting Varela's written word that he was proud to affix his name to everything he wrote and to flaunt it in the face of his enemies (183). Lazo makes the case that anonymity should be respected and argues that to affix author names to anonymous works is to inherently misinterpret them, their purpose, and the intellectual community that produced them.

3. The first Spanish-language newspaper to be published in the United States, *El Mississipi*, was published in New Orleans in 1808, in opposition to the Napoleonic intervention in Spain.

4. The Recovering the U.S. Hispanic Literary Heritage program (a national project to find, preserve, and make accessible the written culture of Latinos in what came to be the United States from the colonial period to 1980), which is centered at the University of Houston and which I direct, has compiled a research bibliography of more than eighteen thousand records of books and pamphlets written or published. On the books from this bibliography that have been located and studied, see my article "Recovering the US Hispanic Literary Heritage."

5. Bailyn discusses at length the pamphlet and the way it provided a firm basis for debate in the public sphere for the ideas that eventually would provide the intellectual underpinning for the Revolution and the U.S. Constitution (4–17).

6. It could be argued that the project to set up a democratic republic in Spanish America, as envisioned by Simón Bolívar and others, was doomed to fail precisely because the sphere of discourse could not extend to the far reaches of the Spanish colonies, and that the link between the development of the bourgeoisie and its access to print was not as advanced or concentrated as in the New England colonies prior to the American Revolution. In the absence of a print revolution, the armed revolution carried the burden, and many of the republics that were set up were destined to be governed by armed *caudillos* rather than the institutions so fervently promoted by the intellectuals in their books and pamphlets—of course, it is much more complicated than this. Michael Warner cites these factors in the rise of print discourse and the democratic public sphere in New England (x–xiii).

7. Anna Brickhouse asserts that a Hispanophone and a Francophone public sphere coexisted with and overlapped the Anglophone one in the Americas beginning in the 1820s and that the rise of nationalism among Hispanic colonials and former colonials accompanied this development of the public sphere in the Americas (23). Brickhouse further asserts that the rise of American nationalism and American literature was inextricably tied to this development among Hispanics, in what she sees as "transamerican and multilingual practices of American arenas" that meant that "the nineteenth-century public sphere itself [was] a plurality of competing and often mutually antagonistic public spheres" (27). In this chapter, I contribute additional

insight into publications that were attempting to create a Hispanic American public sphere and provide a basis for emergent nationalism in the two decades before Brickhouse's 1820s timeline.

8. Kathryn Garrett, among others, attributes *El amigo de los hombres* to José Alvarez de Toledo (295–96).

9. In *Letters from Filadelfia,* Lazo distinguishes these revolutionist writers as a "trans-American elite" because they had the financial resources to obtain an advanced, often international, education, to easily travel internationally, and to pay for the publication of their tracts (22, 74–80).

10. Thomas Jefferson had a complete collection of all twenty of Foronda's *cartas* in his personal library, which he later donated to the Library of Congress (see Fernández López).

11. The genre of *cartas,* or epistolary writing, was commonly used among revolutionary intellectuals to signify that their ideal readers were located in their homelands, often thousands of miles away. Lazo discusses the evolution and prominence of the genre at this time, asserting that this meant that "a community of intellectuals was being formed across the Americas" (*Letters* 10).

12. The Spaniard (Mallorcan) Picornell had led a rebellion against the throne in Spain in an attempt to establish a republic there. Later, in exile, he became involved in the movements for Spanish American independence, particularly in Venezuela, and published translations of Paine's *The Rights of Man* and the U.S. Constitution (Riva Palacio López et al. 490–91).

13. It has been noted that Spanish American revolutionaries sometimes published their tracts abroad in Spanish America but claimed on the title page that their volumes were published in Philadelphia, thus not only giving them protection from persecution but also implying that their books were related to the intellectual ferment associated with "Filadelfia," the birthplace of the American republic and a known community of expatriate Spanish American intellectuals. Some scholars include this Rocafuerte title among those "false" Philadelphia imprints (see Leal and Cortina xvi).

14. "Al final Varela aceptó dirigir el movimiento independentista siempre que no tuviese que someterse a la tiranía de las logias o sociedades" (In the end, Varela accepted leadership of the independence movement as long as he did not have to submit to the tyranny of lodges and secret societies) ("Félix Varela y Morales").

15. The Library Company of Philadelphia has in its holdings two letters penned by Varela to Joel R. Poinsett, who was a member of the House of Representatives, President Madison's expert on Spanish America, and a known filibuster (with the president's covert approval). A proven abolitionist, Varela was against the annexation of Cuba to the United States, which would have entailed continuing slavery on the island. Rather, he sought U.S. support for Cuban independence and U.S. protection thereafter, under the usual terms of favored trade concessions and political agreements offered to filibusters: "como nación protectora y estableciendo pactos políticos y mercantiles ventajas a ambas partes" (as a protector nation and establishing political and commercial pacts advantageous to both parties) (28 Jan. 1825). In closing,

Varela beseeched Poinsett, "Agregue usted amigo mío a sus fructuosos trabajos en favor de la libertad americana, este último golpe, que dará nuevo luster a su carrera política, y le dará un nuevo título al aprecio de los pueblos americanos" (Add to your fruitful endeavors, my friend, the freedom of the Americas, a last blow that will add luster to your political career and will provide a new reason of appreciation from the people of the Americas). The letters, held in Poinsett's correspondence file, are dated January 27 and 28, 1825, shortly before Poinsett was appointed U.S. envoy to Mexico. Unfortunately, it was the unstated policy of the United States to refrain from supporting Cuban independence or Latin American revolutionary activity on the island, in hopes of buying Cuba from Spain at a later, more opportune moment. Thirteen years before Varela penned these letters, José Bernardo Gutiérrez de Lara maintained similar correspondence with Poinsett; a letter dated November 25, 1812, in the same collection petitions Poinsett for men and supplies during his war of Texas liberation.

CHAPTER 3

A much earlier version of this chapter was published as "*El Clamor Público*: Resisting the American Empire," *California History*, vol. 84, no. 2, 2006–7, pp. 10–18, 69–70.

1. On December 6, 1856, the *Los Angeles Star* (a Democratic organ and supporter of slavery) quoted the *San Francisco Herald* in calling *El Clamor Público* the most rabid of the "Free Nigger organs" in the state of California. The *Star* claimed that *El Clamor Público* had obtained its monopoly on city printing from the city council because it was Republican and abolitionist (see Rice 152–53, 155–56).

2. Actually, California's first newspaper, the *Californian*, founded in Monterey in 1846, was a bilingual newspaper, with a section published in Spanish. The first independent Spanish-language newspaper in the state was San Francisco's *La Crónica*, started in 1854 (see Kanellos and Martell, geographical and chronological indexes). *El Clamor Público* was actually founded as a transfer of the Spanish-language page from the *Los Angeles Star*. Notably, *El Clamor Público* would sometimes include entire sections in English or French. For instance, from September to November 1856, it ran an English-language section corresponding to the duration of the electoral campaign; the *Star* (15 May 1858) identified John O. Wheeler, a Republican Party operative, as the actual editor of this section (on Ramírez and Wheeler, see Rice 131–33).

3. The term *raza* in the Spanish of the time, and still today throughout much of the Spanish-speaking world, refers more precisely to culture or heritage than to skin color or other physiological manifestations of blood lineage. Tomás Almaguer explores the concepts of *raza* and race, as well as the racialization of Latinos by Anglos.

4. Original: "la defensa de los intereses morales y materiales del Sur de California . . . al servicio de mis compatriotas nativos de California, generalmente de todos los hispano-americanos."

5. Ramírez's title is the same as a contemporary Madrid newspaper, published from 1844 to 1864, that was known as a progressive, liberal organ. Ramírez may

have been inspired by this title from the newspaper or from any of the books that the newspaper's imprint published as freestanding volumes.

6. Original: "El pueblo gime bajo el peso de los magistrados, y tan efectivas han sido las injusticias cometidas por ellos. . . . ¿De qué sirve que un hombre posea algo estando expuesto a perderlo todo por medio de las tecnicalidades de la ley, o la malicia de los jueces y demás prosélitos?"

7. Original: "¡Hé aquí el desenfreno y la inmoralidad, que desde siete años asola y destroza los intereses de familias honradas, sancionado ahora por una ley del Estado! ¡Hasta dónde puede llegar la arbitrariedad del fuerte contra el débil, del conquistador contra el conquistado!"

8. Original: "Una legislatura tan hambrienta como injusta, ha decretado que todos los terrenos serán considerados como propiedad pública. . . . ¡Podía hacerse una injusticia mayor! ¡Podía hacerse un insulto más descarado a los solemnes tratados de Hidalgo!"

9. Original: "Muchos de los viejos Californios que ahora seis años se veían gozando tranquilamente la posesión de los terrenos que les legaron sus padres, se ven ahora en la miseria e indigencia más lamentable por causa de los litigios a que han sido sujetos para obtener la aprobación de sus títulos."

10. Original: "¡Mexicanos! Ya ha llegado el tiempo para mostrarnos ante el mundo entero que somos dignos del suelo en que vimos la luz primera. Más que nadie, tenemos nosotros ciertos derechos indisputables en la nación en que ahora vivimos. El Tratado de Guadalupe Hidalgo nos ha concedido amplios privilegios para gozar libremente de nuestra vida y propiedad."

11. Along these lines, his "Expedición de Walker" editorial bears examination. Here he sustains an argument that Anglo-Saxons have piracy in their blood, "el instinto pirático," and that it continues to manifest itself in the numerous American filibustering forays into Spanish America and the expansion of the British Empire to as far away as India (28 Aug. 1856).

12. Original: "Principalmente hemos puesto nuestro mayor conato en servir como órgano del sentimiento general de la raza española para manifestar las injurias atroces de que han sido víctimas en este país en donde nacieron y en el cual ahora se ven en un estado inferior al más infeliz de sus perseguidores."

13. Original: "Desde que apareció el Know-Nothingism en el elemento político de los Estados Unidos la emigración extranjera ha sufrido una disminución considerable." See also a series of editorials from 1855 (3 July, 10 July, 31 July, 14 Aug., and 16 Oct.).

14. Original: "Nuestros lectores comprenderán que hacernos estas observaciones hablando del modo como se organizan las expediciones filibusteras en los Estados Unidos de América. Primeramente iban a enajenar el Canadá—después Texas, y otras partes de México—y por fin Cuba. Ahora Nicaragua es el núcleo de su apariencia y ambición."

15. Original: "Al fin México desaparecería del catálogo de las naciones, o acabaría como un tercio de zarzas, vendido al menudeo por piezas y por yardas, o como el

queso a rebanadas." The rhetorical stance of the letter writer is ambiguous, and it may be Ramírez himself writing or Ramírez paraphrasing a letter he was privy to. Either way, the letter represents the first time in the newspaper that the "raza latina" is placed in opposition to the "raza anglo-sajona." Ramírez speaks of "Latin America" and "la raza latina" precisely because he includes in his inventory Brazil and the French Caribbean, as well as the Native American populations and territories.

16. Original: "Desde el cobarde tratado de Guadalupe Hidalgo, y desde el innecesario de la Mesilla, se ha envanecido e infatuado Norte América, al extremo de considerarse llamada a dominar el continente de América."

17. Original: "En la tierra de Washington y Franklin, donde se ven a cada instante violados los derechos de la humanidad, la forma natural y viviente de cada pueblo, o invadida la soberanía de las naciones. Las conquistas efectuadas recientemente en México, desmembrando la mitad del territorio nacional, los escandalosos sucesos de la América Central, las pretensiones injustas sobre los naturales de Panamá en Nueva Granada, las reclamaciones de la Isla de las Aves en Venezuela, Galápagos en el Ecuador y Lobris en el Perú, las pretensiones sobre las Antillas, sea por la fuerza de las armas o por razón de la enajenación, que en el lenguaje de la moral de las naciones es la última expresión de la ignominia, etc. etc. . . . Aquí en compendio el mapa delineado en la imaginación desmesurada de la gran República Federal, que se extenderá hasta Buenos Aires si no se la detiene en la carrera de las conquistas. ¿Será factible esa fusión de razas y de lenguas, de costumbres y religiones, para fundar un pueblo único de cien naciones diferentes absorbiendo los estados latinos y ensanchando la democracia continental con detrimento de los intereses vecinos? No, mil veces, no, es el grito de la opinión popular y no, mil veces, no es el eco que repiten todos los miembros descendientes de la raza de Gonzalo de Córdoba y del Cid contra esta tendencia perniciosa que protegen sus leyes y principios: cada hispano-americano cual otro Aníbal en todas partes enemigos sempiternos que venguen las rapiñas y usurpaciones de su patria."

18. Original: "California ha caído en las manos de los ambiciosos hijos de América del Norte que no la abandonarán hasta haber saciado sus pasiones, ultrajado a los primeros ocupantes del suelo de este país, vilipendiado su religión, y afeado sus costumbres. Las injusticias que cada día se repiten son una causa más para que los desgraciados ciudadanos de México, que en todo tiempo han dado muestras de su acendrado patriotismo y se han sacrificado para salvar a la patria de una ruina inevitable consintiendo a ser enajenados con sus propiedades a la República de los Estados Unidos, se vayan a otra parte para gozar tranquilamente el fruto de sus trabajos."

19. Original: "Los mexicanos residentes en California están resueltos a emigrar a Sonora, para huir de un país inhospitalario en que tanto han tenido que padecer. Esta emigración será un borón en la historia de los Estados Unidos."

20. Original: "Han estado sujetos todos los hispano-americanos a un tratamiento que no tiene ejemplo en la historia de ninguna nación conquistada por salvajes o por gentes civilizadas. Todos están convencidos de que *California está perdido para todos los hispano-americanos.*"

21. According to the January 7, 1860, issue of the *Los Angeles Star*, what forced *El Clamor Público* to fold were its overwhelming financial problems.

CHAPTER 4

An earlier version of this chapter was published as "Sotero Figueroa: Writing Afro-Caribbeans into History in the Late Nineteenth Century," *The Latino Nineteenth Century*, edited by Rodrigo Lazo and Jesse Alemán, New York UP, 2016, pp. 323–40.

1. In fact, within the last ten years, a scholarly debate has developed about Schomburg's contribution to African American studies and culture, and about the influences on him, whether they were Puerto Rican, Afro-Caribbean, Masonic, or even matrilineal (see, e.g., Laó-Montes).

2. Original: "Lo que puede la fuerza creadora del genio, aún no auxiliada por la educación."

3. Original: "Como tantos hijos de este país á quienes faltan alas de oro para volar á otras regiones donde saciar el ansia de saber, que es tanto más vehemente cuanto mayores son los obstáculos que se oponen a ello."

4. Original: "Pobre hijo del pueblo, marcado con el sello de la degradación (que así se decía en épocas de lamentable atraso del que tenía la piel negra)."

5. Original: "Que se levanta del nivel común, sobrepuja en consideración de sus paisanos, *y por su propio y exclusivo esfuerzo* escribe su nombre en el templo inmortal de nuestros benefactores."

6. Interestingly, among the numerous paintings of aristocrats and landed gentry effected by José Campeche, there is a painting of a very dark Cordero, teaching students of various hues of skin color.

7. Original: "¡Perfeccionad al negro, filántropos que os creeis de raza privilegiada!"

8. Original: "La iniquidad de los siglos." The "formerly" enslaved were required to work for three additional years and could not participate in the political process for five years. The reaction among plantation owners was to round up the abolitionists, including Belvis and the mulatto lawyer-abolitionist Ramón Emeterio Betances, and send them into exile in Spain.

9. Original: "Máquinas de carne que se movían continuamente en el fondo de las plantaciones y establecimientos agrícolas, accelerando la fatigosa faena al sentir el chasquido del látigo sobre su extenuado cuerpo."

10. Original: "¡Libres! ¡Con cuánta emoción no lanzarían los esclavos por primera vez esta palabra! Es decir, que ya amparados por la ley, eran *hombres* y no *cosas*. Ya podían andar los lazos de la familia, sin pensar en que sus hijos fueran arrancados del seno materno, y vendidos para otras poblaciones. . . . Ya podían ilustrar su razón, tener creencias, fundar familias sin temor á que las brutas caricias del *capataz* ó del *amo* violaran, con su dignidad, la honra de sus esposas, la inocencia de sus hijas."

11. Original: "Como un ejemplo admirable de lo que puede la voluntad auxiliada por la inteligencia."

12. There is no documented evidence that Figueroa was persecuted or sent into exile because of his criticism of Spanish rule in Puerto Rico, but one can imagine that it would have been uncomfortable for him to remain on the island as his biography was circulated and commented on. In fact, he went into hiding in 1887, when Spanish authorities pursued political dissidents without quarter, so much so that it became known as "the terrible year" that resulted in many patriots going into exile; it is thought that while hiding in 1887, Figueroa was able to write his *Ensayo biográfico* (Toledo 34).

13. Original: "Toussaint, que surge de las lobregueces de la esclavitud y derrota las mejores huestes de la Francia napoleónica; su amor para los infelices subyugados, su magnaminidad para los vencidos."

14. Original: "No reconoce categorías ni colores, sino hermanos en la patria y la libertad."

15. Original: "Será igualmente justa la revolución en que han caído, sin mirarse los colores, todos los cubanos . . . (donde no) se distinguiera un hombre de otro por el calor del corazón ó por el fuego de la frente."

16. Original: "Dar la vida por la redención de su pueblo, se lanza pobre y oscuro, solo é indefenso, a través de la Judea, a levantar en los corazones el imperio de la justicia, abolir la ley de casta, predicando el dogma iluminador de las conciencias y dignificador de la humanidad, que se encierra en estas tres sublimes palabras: Libertad, Igualdad, Fraternidad. . . . Los que se excluyan de la revolución por arrogancia de señorío ó por reparos sociales." The ambiguous use of *oscuro* (dark) may mean that Jesus emerged from obscurity or, even more interesting, that Jesus was dark complected.

17. Original: "Los dominadores de la colonia . . . apenas si se detenían a pensar que el esclavo podía ser libre, y que el criollo debía administrar sus propios intereses."

18. Original: "La clase obrera para que marche conscientemente a la conquista de sus derechos"; "El hombre modesto, que se prodiga sin ostentación."

19. Flor Piñero de Rivera (19) constructs a complete educational history for Schomburg, extending through college in the Virgin Islands, based on the 1977 report "The Spirit That Moves Us," published by the Schomburg Collection. But many of Schomburg's biographical references have been contradictory and given little credence by scholars.

20. His friend Bernardo Vega attested to Schomburg's self-education, although Vega states that he possibly attended some primary education classes and learned from the equally self-educated tobacco workers, who were among the most enlightened of the working classes (195).

21. Jesse Hoffnung-Garskof clarifies that "Martí's idea of a Cuba with no Blacks or Whites could also hide persistent racism and racial inequality behind a mask of race blindness" ("The World" 79).

22. In an in-depth study comparing Schomburg's and Martí's ideas on race in the Americas, Kevin Meehan concludes that Martí's pronouncements of African heritage were largely impressionistic, if not paternalistic, while Schomburg was intent on

transforming the image of Afro-Latinos from passive to powerful and, in the process, decolonizing them intellectually (see, e.g., p. 78).

23. Thabiti Asukile sees this dedication to self-education as a mainstay contribution of African-descended people to the Americas: "a long tradition of non-academic intellectuals who were committed to the life of the mind" (70).

CHAPTER 5

A brief, early version of this chapter was published as "Spanish-Language Anarchist Periodicals in Early Twentieth-Century United States," *Dissent on the Page*, edited by James Danky and Caroline F. Sloat, U of Wisconsin P, 2015, pp. 59–84.

1. Avrich lists *Aurora, Cultura Obrera, Cultura Proletaria, El Despertar*, and *Regeneración* (529–33). Conversely, while Helvetia Martell and I do not index newspapers by such terms as *anarchist* in our *Hispanic Periodicals in the United States*, our geographic index of extant and missing newspapers includes numerous titles that typify anarchist publications (278–308).

2. Christopher J. Castañeda, for example, discusses the interethnic Cuban-Spanish expatriate conflict that came about among anarchists during the Cuban war for independence from Spain.

3. The article went on to accuse Esteve of advocating assassination and of training men "in the business of assassination and . . . the gospel of hate."

4. According to Marcelino García, Esteve had been touring Spain in 1891 with Errico Malatesta, the famed Italian anarchist leader, when authorities associated him with an anarchist uprising in Jerez, and he had to flee to Portugal, then England, and finally the United States (qtd. in Avrich 391).

5. *Cultura Obrera* (19 Sept. 1926) has him arriving in New York in 1890. This seems to contradict the other sources mentioned in my text, which have him arriving in the New York/New Jersey area later.

6. Francisco Ferrer i Guàrdia (1859–1909) was a Catalonian martyr of the anarchist cause whose extensive writings on education and ideology were reprinted in most Spanish-language anarchist newspapers. As a freethinker, he developed a program for education that allowed children to follow their curiosity and thirst for knowledge at their own pace, free of religious or political orientation and free of competition or coercion. In 1901, he founded his own Escuela Moderna (Modern School) in Barcelona to implement these ideas and wrote a book about it. Authorities claimed that he was involved in a plot to kill the king of Spain, and he was executed by firing squad. His two published and translated books were widely influential, and "modern schools" were established in many European and U.S. cities in the early twentieth century. In New York, one such school became a cultural center and gathering place for Spanish and other anarchists (see Martínez-Salanova Sánchez). Spanish-language anarchists used various titles symbolizing the light of knowledge for their organizations and publications. Included among these favorite metaphors were *antorcha* (torchlight), *aurora* (dawn), *nuevo día* (new day), and, of course, *luz* (light).

7. According to Alberto Martin et al., *El Despertar* was originally published and edited by the group El Despertar a la Vida (Awakening to Life), but Esteve took it over at some point (31).

8. Sueiro Seoane states that Esteve had actually written some inflammatory articles for the union paper *El Internacional,* which he was editing, during a violent strike in 1910 (not 1911), and that was the cause for his arrest and departure from Tampa. He also states that authorities back in Spain had identified Esteve as a conspirator in a plot to assassinate the king of Spain and Francisco I. Madero in Mexico ("El asesinato" 175).

9. Esteve was a delegate to the International Anarchist Conference, delivering "Notes on the Spanish Situation" (Apuntes sobre la Situación Española) (see Bou). *Socialismo anarquista,* which had a second edition in 1927, after Esteve died, was a compilation of essays that Esteve had published in newspapers. So too was the short (eighty-eight-page) book *Reformismo, dictadura, federalismo* (New York, c. 1922).

10. Original: "El libro sí, como él decía, es hermoso, es grande, pero ¿es posible su divulgación? ¿Podrá llegar a aquellos cerebros que después de una ruda tarea en el trabajo buscan descanso?"

11. Jacinto Barrera Bassols states that Pedro Esteve, Jaime Vidal, and José Pujal were the central figures linking Spanish anarchism to Flores Magón and the Mexican Liberal Party (PLM). He states that Esteve organized the Grupo Pro-Revolución Mexicana de Tampa (Pro–Mexican Revolution Group of Tampa), and collected money from the tobacco workers to support the PLM (6n23).

12. Barrera Bassols lists other pamphlets that Esteve published: *A los anarquistas de España y Cuba* (1893), *Reflexiones sobre el movimiento obrero en México* (1911), *Socialismo anarquista, La ley* (date unk.), *La violencia* (date unk.), *El anarquismo* (date unk.), and *La revolución social* (1902) (8).

13. There is some discrepancy among survivors and scholars as to whether García or the Argentine Roberto Muller took over the editorship during those last two years following Esteve's death (see Avrich 173).

14. Alberico Pirani stated in an interview that during the 1920s and 1930s the Spanish anarchist group that met at the Centro Internacional in New York was the largest anarchist group in the city, numbering around two hundred (Avrich 148). This was reportedly a Ferrer Center.

15. In Barcelona, Valle also employed the pseudonyms "Forastero" (Stranger or Outlander), "Fructidor" (Bearer of Fruit), and "Hindus Fakir." His nonjournalistic publications in New York included *Narraciones rápidas. Marta* (1894) and *Fin de fiesta. Cuadro dramático* (1898), and he published numerous texts in Cuba (Esenwein 130; "Valle, Adrián del"). Notably, Joan Casanovas i Codina states that "Adrián del Valle," too, was a pseudonym, chosen for initiation into the Free Masons, and that his real name was probably Abdó Terrades (11n2).

16. The newspaper was originally titled *Frente Popular,* but the confederation changed the title to *España Libre* in November 1939 in order to distance itself from

radical elements. Montse Feu-López explains their reasoning: "the working class was better served with moderate democratic parties than with communists" (*España Libre* 114, and see 188–92 for a list of the confederation's 110 participating organizations).

17. The other major reasons included avoiding U.S. tariffs, getting closer to the cigar industry's major market, and escaping the disruptions brought about by the Cuban independence movement (Kanellos and Martell 61).

18. Paul Avrich interviewed Marcelo Salinas, a native of Cuba who helped organize an IWW chapter among cigar workers in Tampa, but was deported by authorities. The level of militancy may be inferred from the fact that his roommate in Tampa, Manuel Pardiñas, assassinated the Spanish prime minister, José Canalejas, in 1912. Salinas was deported twice from the United States and once from Spain; he was declared persona non grata by the United States after being accused of participating in a plot to assassinate President Woodrow Wilson (397–98).

19. In 1894, *El Esclavo* was using the term *slave* as synonymous with proletarian. Pedro Esteve's son told Paul Avrich in an interview that *El Esclavo*'s press was smashed by vigilantes, but the 1894 issues of the newspaper say that it was printed by the *Tampa Tribune*. Whether this arrangement was a stopgap after losing the press is not known.

20. These pamphlets were *La ley y la autoridad, Entre campesinos, El tiempo de elecciones, La política parlamentaria, El crimen de Chicago, El mensaje del gobernador de Chicago, Consideraciones sobre el hecho y la muerte de Pallás, La anarquía,* and *Diálogo entre un burgués y su hijo.*

21. R. Miqueli may have been either Roy Miqueli, described as a Puerto Rican actor and director active in Tampa and New York during the period, or, given the family-oriented nature of this periodical, Violeta Miqueli's brother, in which case he would have been Cuban American. See *España Libre* (3 May 1940) and *Traducción Prensa* (Translation Press, 27 Sept. 1945); in both cases R. Miqueli seems to have a relationship with anarchists, as with the *España Libre* group and the Centro Obrero (Worker Center) in Ybor City. *Ecos* (11 Apr. 1954) also has R. Miqueli performing at New York's Teatro Hispano.

22. The January 15, 1915, issue of San Francisco's *Fuerza Consciente* published Capetillo's address in Tampa for those wishing to purchase her books directly from her. That issue includes excerpts from one of her essays on free love. Capetillo's essays were published in many periodicals and seem to have been well known, even to the extent that there was opposition to her thought, as evidenced by an attack published in the Los Angeles IWW newspaper *Huelga General* on March 7, 1914.

23. I am indebted to my student Rosario Casillas for much of the information in this paragraph.

24. From U.S. soil, the PLM administered forty-four guerrilla groups and liberal clubs throughout Mexico and coordinated their political activities in bringing about the revolution of 1910 (Hart 92). But John M. Hart states that most PLM members (in Mexico) were not anarchists: "Some were socialists, but a majority simply wanted

democracy in Mexico. The majority abandoned the anarchist-dominated PLM Junta and supported Francisco I. Madero once the revolution against Díaz began" (88).

25. It seems that Gutiérrez de Lara had repeated confrontations with the authorities. The newspaper *Revolución* (7 Dec. 1907) reported that he was incarcerated in Los Angeles because his writings attacked President Porfirio Díaz of Mexico. This was followed by a long, front-page story on his incarceration (18 Jan. 1908). The *Dallas Morning News* (19 Oct. 1909) documented his arrest in Los Angeles on October 9 for "disturbing the peace," charges levied as a precautionary measure to safeguard President Taft on his arrival in the city. The arresting officer was quoted as stating, "He is accused of uttering words against the United States—against all governments, in fact. He is accused of being undesirable. He has not been in this country three years and he may be deported if found guilty." He was also arrested in El Paso in 1911 for trying to organize a parade of Mexican revolutionaries (see *A Walking Tour*). He was arrested by Mexican authorities in Matamoros and incarcerated in a Monterrey penitentiary in 1912, according to San Antonio's *El Regidor* (Register) (9 Aug. 1912), for insulting the federal army. This periodical and others document his socialist organizing and speechmaking on the border and in the San Antonio area for months.

26. The *Los Angeles Herald* (9 Oct. 1909) quoted him as saying, "I am not an anarchist, never have been one and never will be one. I am not in sympathy with anything that savors of disorder. I am a Socialist who believes in the brotherhood of man. My arrest is the result of persecution by the Mexican government, and it is largely due to the information I furnished John K. Turner for his series of articles in the *American Magazine* entitled 'Barbarous Mexico.' If I am deported I believe firmly that I will no sooner be on Mexican soil than I will be done away with. I may be placed in some prison or I may be shot."

27. *El pueblo mexicano* was published by F. H. Arizméndez on the presses of Los Angeles's *El Mosquito* newspaper.

28. Guerrero (1882–1910) was an anarchist journalist in Mexico who, after immigrating to the United States and working as a miner in Arizona, edited *Alba Roja* (Red Dawn) in San Francisco and contributed to other anarchist periodicals including Los Angeles's *Regeneración* and *Revolución*, as well as *Evolución Social* (Social Evolution) of Bridgeport, Texas. In El Paso, he founded and directed *Punto Rojo* (Red Point). In fact, when Flores Magón and his group were jailed in Los Angeles in 1907, Guerrero took the helm of *Revolución*, where his writing became more well known and celebrated. Guerrero's militancy was not limited to writing; he raised an army in El Paso and led it into battle in Northern Mexico, where he lost his life. Flores Magón, in *Regeneración* (30 Dec. 1911), baptized him the first anarchist to spill his blood in battle in Mexico and effectively proclaimed him a martyr to the cause, a claim that numerous historians have repeated (see Albro; Vargas Valdéz).

29. Emilio Zamora, in the 1975 article "Chicano Socialist Labor Activity in Texas, 1900–1920," was the first scholar to discover and study Ramírez, and he

continued to research her writings and those of other female anarchists in subsequent articles and his 1986 book *El movimiento obrero mexicano en el sur de Texas, 1900–1920*.

30. Original: "Hoy el dilema es otro: tomar lo que se necesita, ¡libertad! ¡Hay que ser rebeldes! Primero morir, antes que consentir que nuestros hijos lleven el estigma de la esclavitud. A nosotras, madres y esposas, hermanas o hijas, nos toca encausar este dilema."

31. Published in Mexico City, the *Mexican Herald* (13 Sept. 1912) provided seemingly erroneous biographical information about the Colombia-born Juan Francisco Moncaleano, stating that he was born in the Canary Islands and was a pupil of Ferrer's: "Authorities Deport Subject of Spain. A Pupil of Ferrer Sent from Country on Account of Rabid Doctrines. . . . He is accused of propagating pernicious doctrines and of attempting to found a school of anarchy in this country." On his activities in Mexico City, see Rojas; "La Expulsión."

32. According to *Regeneración* (8 Feb. 1913), the Moncaleanos and Carmona signed a lease for $100 per month with an option to buy the building, situated in the Italian quarter of Los Angeles, for $50,000; if they could not purchase the building by March 1, 1914, then the rent would increase to $150. When the rift with the Flores Magón group—represented by editor Araujo while Flores Magón was in prison—occurred, the loss of the house soon ensued. Also lost were the plans to set up a Modern School, following the Ferrer model, and to serve as well as a meeting hall for unions and a refuge for immigrant families (for the building plans, see *Regeneración*, 22 Feb. 1913). John M. Hart provides a detailed account of the structure and operation of, as well as the anarchist classes taught at, the Casa del Obrero Mundial and Escuela Racionalista they founded in Mexico City (114–15). Juan Francisco and A. Ferrés had edited a newspaper in Mexico City that corresponded with *Regeneración* before the Moncaleanos arrived in Los Angeles, and Flores Magón on a number of occasions praised the paper's content (see *Regeneración*, 31 Aug. 1912).

33. The distribution of her articles was extensive enough to reach *Fraternidad* newspaper in Boston, where her essays "Amancipémonos" (Emancipate Ourselves) and "Manifiesto a la Mujer" (Manifesto to Women) were published. For a collection of her articles and essays published in Colombia, Mexico, Cuba, and the United States, including those from *Pluma Roja* and *Fraternidad*, see Moncaleano, *Blanca de Moncaleano*.

34. I am not including the original Spanish for Moncaleano's "Manifiesto" here. For the complete Spanish-language text, see Kanellos, "An Early Feminist."

35. Original: "Engolfados los hombres en su supuesta superioridad, fatuos por su ignorancia, han creído que sin la ayuda de la mujer pueden llegar a la meta de la emancipación humana."

36. The split was portrayed as acrimonious by Araujo in an account in *Regeneración* published on May 10, 1913. In subsequent issues of *Regeneración*, however, Araujo published notices and articles attacking Juan Francisco Moncaleano, Car-

mona, and Martínez, and warning readers in Texas, where the three had relocated, to ostracize them (see, esp., 21 June 1913). The campaign was so effective against the trio—Araujo was claiming that the trio wanted to take over *Regeneración*—that the newspaper printed letters in solidarity from anarchists located as far away as New York, Cuba, and Argentina.

37. Juan Francisco Moncaleano was also a pamphleteer, issuing such works as *Alma en rebelión* (Rebellious Soul), published in Los Angeles by La Biblioteca Roja (Red Library), probably an imprint of Carmona. Martínez was involved in a plot to repatriate Mexican workers, occupy land in Northern Mexico, and work together as communists, according to Flores Magón in *Regeneración* (15 Jan. 1916).

38. Lina DeVito, one of my students, discovered a trove of Moncaleano/Lawson papers in California, which she organized and which are now part of the archives of Recovering the US Hispanic Literary Heritage collection at the University of Houston. DeVito also provided information on the change of name to Lawson and the next generation of formerly Moncaleanos.

39. Constant Leroy also provides evidence that Vidal and Esteve were involved in a plot to assassinate authority figures in Spain. In fact, he records testimony that Vidal boasted that what the revolutionaries in Europe could not accomplish, those in the United States would do (6–7).

40. Original: "Para abrir paso al progreso y dar oportunidad a las ideas sociales para desenvolverse entre los esclavos."

41. It does not seem that the IWW in Tampa—whether its organizing efforts or its newspapers, such as the short-lived *El Obrero Industrial* (Industrial Worker, 1914)—fared well among Latinos, given the competition from so many already well-established unions among the tobacco workers.

CHAPTER 6

1. Lozano, from a successful business family in Northern Mexico, relocated to San Antonio in 1908 in search of business opportunities; there he opened a bookstore and gradually learned the newspaper business through on-the-job experiences while working first for San Antonio's *El Noticiero* and later for *El Imparcial de Texas* (Stefano 99–103).

2. Included among the conservative ideas that García Naranjo espoused were opposition to agrarian reform, to universal and female suffrage, and to compulsory education; he supported Catholic mission schools instead of public education.

3. Original: "Población sigue siendo nuestra, porque sigue rezando a la Virgen de Guadalupe y aclamando al cura Hidalgo."

4. Original: "Nos proponemos levantar el crédito de nuestro pueblo; desvanecer las calumnias propaladas en contra de nuestra raza . . . contribuir al mejoramiento de aquellos compatriotas que desde hace medio siglo viven en este país." (*Raza* in Spanish refers to culture, not race.)

5. Original: "Uno de los puntos de la política internacional de los Estados Unidos, consiste precisamente en humillar a la raza latina, disolver sus instituciones, pulverizar sus tradiciones, convertirla en algo inferior, despreciable y ruin."

6. Original: "En vez de pelear se procura invilecer; en lugar de herir con 'mausseres' se va limando poco a poco la dignidad y el orgullo; y al través de dos generaciones, se logran dos objetos: conquistar las tierras anheladas y preparar la servidumbre que se empleará en su explotación."

7. Original: "Todo quedó esterilizado, todo quedó destruído y hoy parece campo de muerte lo que hace una década era asiento venturoso de trabajo y de bonanza." Like many of his speeches, this one was reprinted in newspapers throughout the Southwest, from Laredo's *Evolución* (6 July 1919) to Los Angeles's *El Heraldo de México* (9 July 1919).

8. Original: "La Patria espiritual que es más bella que la Patria geográfica."

9. Original: "Y no hemos muerto en las tierras segregadas de la Patria, hace tres cuartos de siglo. El espíritu mexicano sigue alentando al norte del río Bravo, entre los mexicanos expatriados, como también en extraña tierra lo protegiese el cielo incomparable de Anáhuac. Y no solamente los que han venido de Méxco, piensan en la Patria ausente: también los que aquí nacieron y se criaron siguen siendo irreductiblemente mexicanos. Todos llevan el nombre de México como un diamante incrustado en el corazón."

10. Original: "Quiso Iturbide representar en él la religión católica, y ella sigue imperando de un extremo al otro de la República."

11. Original: "La unidad espiritual del país. . . . México vivie bajo la Cruz de Cristo y abrasado en el fuego purificador de los Evangelios."

12. Original: "Y es más triste mirar como se desbarata la configuración física de un país . . . es mucho más impresionante ver la fe de un pueblo convertida en añicos, las tradiciones heroicas calcinadas por vergüenzas evidentes, el carácter nacional sepultado bajo lavas de odio y cien años de trabajo noble y fecundo, disueltos en renconores criminales y en estériles venganzas."

13. Original: "¡Magnífico! Lo malo fue que Mr. Wilson quería 'salvar' a los mexicanos. También Napoleón III hace sesenta años quiso salvar a nuestro país. Eso es la lacra de nuestra historia: las gentes de afuera que se han propuesto salvarnos."

14. A typed manuscript of the series, dated September 1930, New York, is held in the Nemesio García Naranjo collection in the Recovering the US Hispanic Literary Heritage archives, University of Houston. I have not been able to find where and when these English-language articles were published, if at all, although he did publish the series in Spanish in San Antonio's *La Prensa* (22–25 Sept. 1930). Actually, García Naranjo developed this theme in many of his Spanish-language articles and speeches, just not with such polite language. In a *La Prensa* article entitled "Los Perros de Wall Street" (The Dogs of Wall Street, 29 Nov. 1927), for example, he spoke of the hero of the masses President Plutarco Elías Calles and his relationship with J. P. Morgan: "¿Qué van a decir los apologistas cuando vean a su campeón protegido

por el banquero Morgan, encadenado a Wall Street, convertido en un perro mudo del imperialismo, que tanto ha anunciado combatir?" (What will the apologists say when they see their champion protected by banker Morgan, chained to Wall Street, transformed into a mute dog of the imperialism that he had claimed to combat?).

15. Despite his stated resolve not to return to Mexico, *El Heraldo de México* reported on June 10, 1921, that García Naranjo had attempted to enter Mexico to start a job as editor of *El Porvenir* newspaper in Monterrey, but was turned back by Mexican immigration officers.

16. Original: "Durante el último año, oh, patriotas que vivís desterrados en El Paso, vosotros habéis sido los principales sostenedores de la bandera."

17. Characteristically, this insider-outsider from his perch in New York justified the Cristero War and at the same time satirized the U.S. practice of religious tolerance; it was practically inconceivable to him that the heads of the Catholic, Protestant, and Jewish religious institutions in New York City would form a committee—he calls it a "trust"—to avoid friction among the sects (*La Prensa*, 27 Apr. 1927).

18. García Naranjo frequently published excerpts of his books in his *La Prensa* column, while publisher Lozano printed almost-daily advertisements for the excerpted books.

19. García Naranjo had published this story earlier in *La Prensa* under the title of "El entierro de Cristo" (The Burial of Christ, 14 Apr. 1922), which was one of a series of religious articles he published in April, during the Easter season that year.

CHAPTER 7

1. Ríos joined the staff as literary editor in 1970 (on Quinto Sol, see Kanellos, *Greenwood*, 1: 374).

2. This symposium was organized by Professor Luis Dávila and held on April 6 and 7, 1972, under the title of Tomás Rivera and Chicano Literature: A Symposium (see Olivares 193).

3. One early reviewer to perceive this distinction was Seymour Menton, who stated in 1972, "The fact that the words Chicano, Mexican-American or Anglo never appear in the book is only one indication that Rivera is totally immersed in the world he creates and is concerned with human beings, not prototypes" (112).

4. Reviewing *Tierra* in 1973, William H. González stressed that this is the novel of "Mexican Americans": "The Mexican-American is observed from within by an author who reflects the feelings, the experiences and the frustrated hopes of a society which has been excluded from a dominant culture because of its different approach to life" (229).

5. I served on the advisory committee for the National Endowment for the Humanities–sponsored film adaptation of *Tierra*, titled . . . *and the Earth Did Not Swallow Him* (1995), written and directed by Severo Pérez. It was a battle to prevail on the screenwriter to refrain from naming the main character "Tomás"; like some professors, he was interpreting the novel as an autobiography.

6. Original: "Fue mi empeño que una voz colectiva expresara."

7. Manuel Martín-Rodríguez has stated that Rivera felt an ethical obligation to "[tell] those stories that the official discourse had silenced, and [tell] them in a manner that is both meaningful to his audience and respectful of his audience's ways" ("Reading" 28). I wholeheartedly agree.

8. Latinos need this confident and heralding message now more than ever, on the eve of our numerical ascendance in U.S. society.

9. The English version of the essay is titled "Remembering, Discovery and Volition in the Literary Imaginative Process." The Spanish version reads: "Creo que en la literatura todo se unta de lo específico. Entre más esté el hombre en su ambiente, mejor se comprende por todos. Entre más nacional sea, más internacional se vuelve. . . . Es decir, cuanto más se revela el hombre específico en su elemento dialectal y natural, más se revela su universalidad humana" (*Tomás Rivera* 297–98).

10. The Quinto Sol and Editorial Justa editions were translated by Herminio Ríos, the Arte Público Press edition by Evangelina Vigil. Rolando Hinojosa also published a very loose translation and reorganization of *Tierra* as *This Migrant Earth* (1986).

11. The Spanish version reads: "El niño se inventa . . . es pura fuerza volitiva" (*Tomás Rivera* 300).

12. While Rivera deserves much credit for institutionalizing Chicano literature, he has also been censured for his traditionalist and at times stereotypical representation of women in his works; Quinto Sol in its canon formation efforts and the Chicano Movement leadership have likewise been censured for their phallocentrism (see Fuente; Lizárraga).

CHAPTER 8

1. Hinojosa himself recognized this and, as he saw it, suffered from the marginalization of his work. He blamed canonizing institutions such as the Modern Language Association, the *New York Times Book Review*, and major publishing houses for pigeonholing his work as minority, regional, and ethnic, like they do with most Chicano and Latino writers (see Hinojosa, "The Other").

2. Virtually the only critic to challenge this commonplace comparison with García Márquez has been José Limón, who refutes José David Saldívar's thesis in *The Dialectics of Our America* with the following: "[Saldívar] largely overlooks Hinojosa's rendering of the complex Mexican Anglo hybridity of the area and of the internal class divisions and exploitations within the Mexican-origin community" (163).

3. Hinojosa writes, "A place is merely that until it is populated, and once populated, the histories of the place and its people begin" ("The Sense" 19).

4. Even today, some critics continue to see resistance as the predominant thrust of the KCDT, especially in its use of oral cultural authority (e.g., Kaup 56–58), rather than seeing an irreversible evolution toward hybridism, as I emphasize later in this chapter. For example, Rolando Calderón Guerra sees the main characters Rafa Buenrostro and Jehú Malacara as "Mexican," and does not recognize their hybridity and or its function

in the KCDT series: "ellos seguían siendo mexicanos" (they continued being Mexicans) (42). Likewise, Rosemary A. King, while not studying Hinojosa per se, sees much of the literature produced by Native Americans and Chicanos as reconquering at least a metaphoric space, "carving out and reclaiming sacred Chicano/a and Indian homelands in the U.S.-Mexico borderlands" (98). In José David Saldívar's *The Dialectics of Our America*, this resistance theory graduates to a new level, the global, as this critic seeks to integrate Chicano and borderland literature within the context of Caribbean and Latin American literatures through resistance or opposition to the American empire. I, of course, do not agree with this. Rather, I support Monika Kaup's observation that the testimony of such old-timers as Esteban Echevarría, Manuel Guzmán, Aureliano Mora, and Braulio Tapia represents their effort to "salvage the memory of a disappearing local chronotope"; like the *corrido* as a historical document in Hinojosa, their testimonies are presented as "one among many unrelated stories in the unending talk that composes Hinojosa's dialogic universe of Texas Mexican cultural conversation" (57).

5. Calderón states, "there is a sense of looking back at the turn of the century, and prior to the coming of Anglo settlers, as a classic period with Mexican models to emulate, claros varones, hombres rectos y cabales, 'complete gentlemen, just and real men.' As in Guzmán and Pulgar, Hinojosa's *claros varones* are dead" (*Narratives* 159).

6. The English is quoted from Hinojosa's rewrite in *Fair Gentlemen*. Original: "Me acuerdo, Rafa . . . árboles llenos de higos y de miel de abejas que chupaban la flor de naranjos . . . ruidos de animales que ya no se oyen ni se ven . . . bailes con gente invitada y ahora me cuentan que se tiene que pagar la entrada, pero ¿te das cuenta, Rafa? Y allí están las palmeras. . . . Las palmeras que se daban en el Valle y que crecían como Dios quería hasta que la bolillada vino con sus hachas y las cortaron" (191–92).

7. But Hinojosa's words are close to another statement by Echevarría in *Claros varones de Belken*: "Tiempos malos fueron aquéllos también con sus rinches, la ley aprovechada, los terratenientes, las sequías y el engruesamiento de la vida misma . . . pero . . . al fin y al cabo era mi tiempo, mi gente, mi Valle querido . . . antes que hubiera tal cosa como el condado de Belken y Klail City y todo lo demás . . . había gente, Rafa, gente. . . . Labores y rancherías, y ese Río Grande que era para beber y no pa' detener gente los de un lado contra el otro . . . no . . . eso vino después con la bolillada y sus ingenieros y el papelaje todo en inglés" (*Fair Gentlemen* 191). Hinojosa's rewrite in *Fair Gentlemen*: "Bad times, too; bad times with the rangers; *upholding the law!* Ha! And the big landholders who brought the rangers in. And the droughts, the pure hell of life. But! But those were my times, my people, my Valley. Yeah, before there was such a thing as Belken County or a Klail City and the rest of it, there were people, Rafe, people. Fields and small towns and the Rio Grande, which was for drinking, not for keeping those on one side away from the others on the other side. No, that came later: with the Anglos and their civil engineers and all those papers in English" (89).

8. Klaus Zilles states that Echevarría incarnates the collective oral culture of the valley, with its pastoral heritage. He further states, "Esteban Echevarría, el más anciano de los cronistas, pertenece a la primera generación de tejanos que nacieron como ciudadanos estadounidenses después de la anexión de Tejas en 1845. En cierta

manera, su nacimiento marca el nacimiento de una minoría, el comienzo de la paulatina extinción de una sociedad ranchera, la pérdida de sus tierras y la inminente anulación de su cultura y lengua. La muerte de Echevarría, que se narra en *Varones*, significaría . . . la muerte de la cultura chicana, si no fuera por las nuevas generaciones de cronistas como Rafa y Jehú" (Esteban Echevarría, the oldest of the *cronistas*, belongs to the first generation of *tejanos* born as U.S. citizens after the annexation of Texas in 1845. In a certain way, his birth marks the birth of a minority, the slow extinction of a ranching society, the loss of their lands, and the imminent demise of their language and culture. The death of Echavarría as narrated in *Varones* means . . . the death of Chicano culture, if it were not for the new generations of *cronistas* like Rafa and Jehú) (8).

9. The English is quoted from Hinojosa's rewrite in *Fair Gentlemen*. Original: "Casas sin corredores, calles sin faroles, amigos que mueren, jóvenes que ya no hablan español ni saben saludar. . . . ¡Heh! Desaparece el Valle. . . . Los bolillos con sus propiedades, sus bancos y contratos. . . . ¿Pa' qué le sirve a uno vivir ochenta y tres años si todo lo que uno vio nacer está enterrado? ¿Los Vilches? Muertos. ¿Los Tuero? ¡También! Los Buenrostro se acaban y las familias fundadoras se secan como las hojas del mesquite doliente" (190–91).

10. Manuel Martín-Rodríguez identifies this process as "coherent deformation" and states that this is the means that Hinojosa uses to involve the reader "as major player" in the narration to "(re)construct reality from a literary point of view" (*Life* 31).

11. Many critics, such as Manuel Martín-Rodríguez (*Life* 28), believe that Hinojosa is writing an alternative history, one that supplements and contests official history, as written for example by such historians of the West as Walter Prescott Webb. I believe, conversely, that Hinojosa's mission goes far beyond writing an alternative history.

12. I, myself, have studied the oral culture in KCDT (see my "Orality"). Nevertheless, I believe that critics who only interpret Hinojosa's texts as recovering, sustaining, and making oral culture available to the reader are only partially correct; they also need to consider the written resources and perspectives in Hinojosa's tool kit and purpose. Thus I cannot accept such essentialist statements, for example, as the following from Guillermo E. Hernández: "Hinojosa does not aspire merely to transpose an oral into a writing mode but to attain an artistic re-elaboration of traditional culture" (104).

13. Klaus Zilles refutes the idea that Hinojosa is presenting the fragmented nature of an oral culture in which the truth is not apprehensible, as in many postmodern texts; rather, he emphasizes that readers complete the texts and arrive at their own conclusions: ". . . en lugar de una visión posmoderna de una cultura frontera fragmentada. El propósito sea una representación mimética de una cultura oral mediante la inclusión del lector como jugador en un juego de descodificar las múltiples y enredadas interlocuciones" (. . . in place of a postmodern version of a fragmented border culture. The purpose must be a mimetic representation of an oral culture by including the reader as gambler in a game to decode the multiple, intertwined in-

terlocutions) (14). In my opinion, Zilles overemphasizes the importance of oral text at the expense of the written documents that Hinojosa includes and counterposes throughout the KCDT.

CHAPTER 9

1. At the end of the twenty-fifth-anniversary edition (2012) of Anzaldúa's groundbreaking book *Borderlands/La Frontera*, the editors included a fourteen-page bibliography on her works. Today, I dare calculate that such a bibliography would be ten times longer. As for Anzaldúa's international impact, see, e.g., Akila; and Zaccaria. These are just two indications of the many conferences, papers, and publications in Europe.

2. It can be correctly argued that the Cuban thinker, poet, and revolutionary José Martí has had more influence in the Hispanic world than has Anzaldúa. Martí is treated, and rightly so, in Latin America as a giant, above most other canonized figures of Latin American nations. I, too, have singled out his works produced in the United States during his ten years of exile as important for the construction of a U.S. Latino literary history. But academics *in the United States* are by and large significantly more familiar with and sympathetic to Anzaldúa's works than they are Martí's, and today, the evolution of Latino letters and serious thought in this country has forever been enriched by Anzaldúa's contributions.

3. In the realm of spirituality, Anthony Lioi sees her as a Catholic essayist, not in terms of Catholic orthodoxy but in the broadest sense as well as in the specific use of Catholic symbology (see also Partridge). In literature, Macarena García-Avello studies the way that Anzaldúa's writing has influenced Latina writers of the twenty-first century. I would add that her works have also influenced the writing of Latino men and have actually gone beyond ethnicity to influence a wide spectrum of writers from all backgrounds. In pedagogy, Cinthya M. Saavedra and Ellen D. Nymark have developed a teaching method based on Anzaldúa's writing (see also Klotz and Whithaus; Giglioli.)

4. As Emma Pérez states, "Germans, Españoles, Mexicanas/os, the Dutch, southeast Asians, and so many more across the globe have read and studied Gloria's inspirational words. It's astounding when you stop to think that a *chicanita, prietita, jotita del valle de tejas* has made an indelible mark upon the global community" ("Gloria Anzaldúa" 8).

5. Martina Koegeler-Abdi states, "I have argued here against the perception that mestiza consciousness is bound by and to Chicana ethnicity, even if Anzaldúa's approach is grounded in a specific Chicana context. I believe Anzaldúa was aware that easy identification with any one ethnicity could not escape the imperial logic of divide and conquer, manifest in internal hierarchies and the marketability of certain hip multiculturalisms at the expense of others" (84).

6. In her essay "Geographies of Selves—Reimagining Identity," Anzaldúa explores how immigration gives birth to the type of hybridity that García Naranjo and most

immigrant writers fought against: "The terrain, the planes (and plains) of identity alter when a person moves (immigrates) into another community or social position. One ends up living in a different physical and symbolic environment while retaining the former 'home' culture and position. After leaving the home culture's familiar cocoon, you occupy other ideological spaces, begin seeing reality in new ways, questioning both the native culture's and the new culture's descriptions of reality. The new culture, like the old one, inculcates you with its values and worldviews" (*Light* 71).

7. Adriana Novoa, while still positive about Anzaldúa's contribution to systematic thought and her centering of women and hybridity, suggests substituting the concept of *amasijo* (kneading, as in bread dough) for *mestizaje*. To sustain what I believe is an untimely and impractical suggestion, she develops a long essay on the history of time and space in Spanish American thinkers, especially José Vasconcelos and Octavio Paz (see also Medina). Also see Trace Hedrick, who discusses Anzaldúa as continuing Mexican and Latin American modernist conceptions of *mestizaje*, ultimately questioning her innovations.

BIBLIOGRAPHY

Acuña, Rodolfo. *Occupied America: A History of Chicanos*. 4th ed., Longman, 2000.

Akila, Kizzi, editor. Colloque International Anzaldua Paris programme definitif. Université de Paris, May 2019, posted to Academia.edu, https://www.academia.edu/39057278.

Albizu Campos, Pedro. "Concept of Race." *The Intellectual Roots of Independence: An Anthology of Puerto Rican Political Essays*, edited by Iris M. Zavala and Rafael Rodríguez, Monthly Review Press, 1980, pp. 181–82.

Albizu Campos, Pedro. "Observations on the Brookings Institute Report." *The Intellectual Roots of Independence: An Anthology of Puerto Rican Political Essays*, edited by Iris M. Zavala and Rafael Rodríguez, Monthly Review Press, 1980, pp. 173–80.

Albizu Campos, Pedro. "Pedro Albizu Campos Speech in Lares (September 23, 1950)." *Write to Fight*, 22 Sept. 2011, https://writetofight.wordpress.com/2011/09/22/pedro-albizu-campos-speech-in-lares-september-23-1950/.

Albro, Ward. *To Die on Your Feet: The Life, Times and Writing of Práxedis Guerrero*. Texas Christian UP, 1996.

Almaguer, Tomás. *Racial Fault Lines: The Historical Origins of White Supremacy in California*. U of California P, 1994.

Alvarez de Toledo y Dubois, José. *Contestación á la carta del Indio Patriota, con algunas reflexiones sobre el diálogo entre el Entusiasta Liberal, y el Filósofo Rancio—y sobre las notas anonymas con que ha salido reimpreso el Manifiesto de dn. José Alvarez de Toledo*. Imprenta de Blocquerst, 1812.

Alvarez de Toledo y Dubois, José. "José Alvarez de Toledo to the Council of the City of Santo Domingo, October 2, 1811." *Aurora*, 17 Dec. 1811.

Alvarez de Toledo y Dubois, José. *Manifiesto ó satisfacción pundonorosa, a todos los buenos españoles europeos y todos los pueblos de América, por un diputado de las cortes reunidas en Cádiz*. Philadelphia, 1811; Charleston, 1812. [Philadelphia publication is cited except where indicated.]

Alvarez de Toledo y Dubois, José. *Mexicanos, llegado es el tiempo señalado por la Providencia para que sacudáis el yugo bárbaro [. . .]*. Philadelphia, 1811.

Anderson, Benedict. *Imagined Communities: Reflections on the Origins and Spread of Nationalism*. Verso Books, 1991.

Anzaldúa, Gloria. *Borderlands/La Frontera: The New Mestiza*. 2nd ed., Aunt Lute Books, 1999.

Anzaldúa, Gloria. "La Prieta." *This Bridge Called My Back: Writings by Radical Women of Color*, 3rd ed., edited by Cherríe Moraga and Gloria Anzaldúa, Third Woman Press, 2002, pp. 220–33.

Anzaldúa, Gloria. *Light in the Dark / Luz en lo oscuro: Rewriting Identity, Spirituality, Reality*. Edited by Ana Louise Keating, Duke UP, 2015.

Arroyo, Sossianna. "Technologies: Transculturations of Race, Gender & Ethnicity in Arturo A. Schomburg's Masonic Writings." *Centro Journal*, vol. 12, no. 2, 2005, pp. 5–19.

Asukile, Thabiti. "Arthur Alfonso Schomburg (1874–1938): Embracing the Black Motherhood Experience in Love of Black People." *Afro-Americans in New York Life and History*, vol. 30, no. 2, 2006, pp. 69–97.

Avrich, Paul. *Anarchist Voices: An Oral History of Anarchism in America*. Princeton UP, 1995.

Bailyn, Bernard. *Pamphlets of the American Revolution, 1750–1776*. Vol. 1, *1750–1765*. Harvard UP, 1965.

Barrera Bassols, Jacinto. "La biblioteca Sociológica de 'Regeneración' y la red internacional anarquista." Paper presented at the Encuentro Cultura y Práctica del Anarquismo, desde sus orígenes hasta la Primera Guerra Mundial, 23–24 Mar. 2011, Cátedra México-España de El Colegio de México.

Barton, Paul. *Hispanic Methodists, Presbyterians, and Baptists in Texas*. U of Texas P, 2006.

Benavides, José Luis. "'Californios! Whom Do You Support?': *El Clamor Público*'s Contradictory Role in the Racial Formation Process in Early California." *California History*, vol. 14, no. 2, 2006–7, pp. 40–53.

Benavides Lucas, Manuel, and Cristina Rollán Carvajal. *Valentín Foronda: los sueños de la razón*. Editora Nacional, 1984.

Ben-Ur, Aviva. *Sephardic Jews in America: A Diasporic History*. New York UP, 2012.

Bhabha, Homi K. "DissemiNation: Time, Narrative, and the Margins of the Modern Nation." *Nation and Narration*, edited by Homi K. Bhabha, Routledge, 1990, pp. 291–322.

Bookchin, Murray. *The Spanish Anarchists: The Heroic Years, 1868–1936*. AK Press, 2001.

Bou, Xavier. "Pere Esteve, nuestro anarquista más internacional." *Historias del poblenou*, 14 June 2019, http://historiasdelpoblenou.blogspot.com/2012/07/pere-esteve-nuestro-anarquista-mas.html.

Bowman, Charles H., Jr. "Vicente Pazos and the Amelia Island Affair, 1817." *Florida Historical Quarterly*, vol. 53, no. 3, 1975, pp. 273–95.

Brackenridge, R. Douglas, and Francisco García-Treto. *Iglesia Presbiteriana: A History of Presbyterians and Mexican Americans in the Southwest.* 2nd ed., Trinity UP, 1987.

Brickhouse, Anna. *Transamerican Literary Relations and the Nineteenth-Century Public Sphere.* Cambridge UP, 2004.

Bruce-Novoa, Juan. "*La Prensa* and the Chicano Community." *Américas Review*, vol. 17, nos. 3–4, 1989, pp. 150–56.

Bruce-Novoa, Juan. *RetroSpace: Collected Essays on Chicano Literature.* Arte Público Press, 1990.

Busby, Mark. "Faulknerian Elements in Rolando Hinojosa's *The Valley*." *MELUS*, vol. 11, no. 4, 1984, pp. 103–9.

Calderón, Héctor. "At the Crossroads of History, on the Borders of Change: Chicano Literary Studies Past, Present and Future." *Left Politics and the Literary Profession*, edited by Lennard J. Davis and M. Bella Mirabella, Colombia UP, 1990, pp. 211–35.

Calderón, Héctor. *Narratives of Greater Mexico: Essays on Chicano Literary History, Genre, and Borders.* U of Texas P, 2004.

Calderón Guerra, Rolando. "Literatura fronteriza tejana: El compromiso con la historia en Américo Paredes, Rolando Hinojosa y Gloria Anzaldúa." *Mester*, vol. 23, no. 1, 1993, pp. 41–61.

Camp, Roderic A. *Mexican Political Biographies, 1884–1935.* U of Texas P, 1991.

Casanovas i Codina, Joan. "Introduction for Pedro Esteve's *Socialismo anarquista: La ley, la violencia, el anarquismo, la revolución social*." *Catalan Review*, vol. 3, no. 2, 1989, pp. 9–44.

Castañeda, Christopher J. "Anarchism and the End of Empire: José Cayetano Campos, Labor, and Cuba Libre." *Writing Revolution: Hispanic Anarchism in the United States*, edited by Christopher Castañeda and Montse Feu-López, U of Illinois P, 2019, pp. 53–66.

Chipman, Donald E. *Spanish Texas, 1519–1821.* U of Texas P, 1992.

Cleaves, W. S. "The Political Life of Lorenzo de Zavala." U of Texas, MA thesis, 1931.

Copia de la exposición que los Diputados de la provincia de Guipúzcoa y encargados de las de Alava y Vizcaya Manuel María de Araguren y Manuel de Tellería, dirigen a S. M. Cma. enviándole, con su decreto marginal, la Exposición hecha a la Regencia de España sobre la poca confianza que merecían en el país vascongado, D. Vicente Quesada y D. José Alvarez de Toledo. Tolosa, 28 marzo 1823; oficio de remisión a Balmaseda. Tolosa, 29 marzo 1823, y dos minutas casi iguales, dirigidas por Balmaseda al Ministro y Secretario de Estado. Biblioteca Nacional de España, microfilm 09275, section 7, no. 14.

Diálogo sobre la independencia de la América Española entre un entusiasta liberal y un filósofo rancio. Palmer, 1812.

Díaz, José. *P. Galindo: Obras (In)completes de José Diaz.* Edited by Manuel M. Martín-Rodríguez, Arte Público Press, 2016.

Dolan, J. P., and Allan Figueroa Deck. *Hispanic Catholic Culture in the U. S.: Issues and Concerns.* U of Notre Dame P, 1994–97. 3 vols.

Dykstra, Kristin. "On the Betrayal of Nations: José Alvarez de Toledo's Philadelphia Manifesto (1811) and Justification (1816)." *New Centennial Review*, vol. 4, no. 1, 2004, pp. 267–305.

Espinoza, Dionne. "Rethinking Cultural Nationalism and La Familia Through Women's Communities: Enriqueta Vásquez and Chicana Feminist Thought." *Enriqueta Vásquez and the Chicano Movement: Writings from El Grito del Norte*, edited by Lorena Oropeza and Dionne Espinoza, Arte Público Press, 2006, pp. 205–31.

Esenwein, George Richard. *Anarchist Ideology and the Working-Class Movement in Spain, 1868–1898.* U of California P, 1989.

"Félix Varela y Morales." *Guije.com*, http://www.guije.com/public/bohemia/4708/varela/index.htm. Accessed 5 Nov. 2022.

Fernández López, Manuel. "*Cartas* de Foronda: Su Influencia en el Pensamiento Económico Argentino." Paper presented at the XLI Reunión Anual de la Asociación Argentina de Economía Política, Nov. 2006, Salta, Argentina.

Feu-López, Montse. *España Libre (1939–1977) and the Spanish Exile Community in New York.* U of Houston, PhD dissertation, 2011.

Feu-López, Montse. "Transnational Working-Class Women's Activism in New York's Confederated Hispanic Societies (1939–1977)." *Feminism and Migration: Cross-Cultural Engagements*, edited by Glenda Tibe Bonifacio, Springer, 2012, pp. 187–207.

Figueroa, Sotero. "Discursos en la confirmación de la proclamación del Partido Revolucionario Cubano." *WWNorton.com*, http://www.wwnorton.com/college/english/latino-literature/pdfs/2_Annexations/Figueroa_Discursos.pdf. Accessed 5 Nov. 2022.

Figueroa, Sotero. *Ensayo biográfico de los que más han contribuído al progreso de Puerto Rico.* Editorial Coquí, 1973.

Flores Magón, Ricardo. *Land and Liberty! Anarchist Influences in the Mexican Revolution.* Edited by Dave Poole, Cienfuegos Press, 1977.

Fornet, Ambrosio. *El libro en Cuba.* Editorial Letras Cubanas, 1994.

"Free Pedro Albizu Campos!" *Saudade Brothers*, http://saudadebrothers.com/2011/06/30/free-pedro-albizu-campos/. Accessed 5 Nov. 2022.

Fuchs, Maura L. *Revista Mexicana: Constituting the Conservative Mexican Nation in Exile.* U of Houston, PhD dissertation, 2006.

Fuente, Patricia de la. "Invisible Women in the Narrative of Tomás Rivera." *International Studies in Honor of Tomás Rivera*, edited by Julián Olivares, Arte Público Press, 1986, pp. 81–89.

García, Richard A. *Rise of the Mexican American Middle Class: San Antonio, 1929–1941.* Texas A&M UP, 1991.

García-Avello, Macarena. "Beyond the Latina Boom: New Directions Within the Field of US Latina Literature." *Atlantis*, vol. 41, no. 1, 2019, pp. 69–88.

García Naranjo, Nemesio. *Discursos.* Casa Editorial Lozano, 1923.

García Naranjo, Nemesio. *El quinto evangelio*. Casa Editorial Lozano, 1929.

García Naranjo, Nemesio. *Memorias*. Talleres del Porvenir, 1956–63. 10 vols.

Garland, Marissa L. "The Authorship of *Jicoténcal*." *Hispania*, vol. 8, no. 3, 2005, pp. 445–55.

Garrett, Kathryn. "The First Constitution of Texas, April 17, 1813." *Southwestern Historical Quarterly*, vol. 40, no. 4, 1937, pp. 290–308.

Giglioli, Ilaria. "A World of Walls? Unmaking Borders Through Comparative Pedagogies." *Critical Ethnic Studies*, vol. 6, no. 2, 2020, https://www.jstor.org/stable/48629284.

"Gloria Anzaldúa." *Voices from the Gaps*, University of Minnesota, 2009, https://conservancy.umn.edu/bitstream/handle/11299/167856/Anzaldua,%20Gloria.pdf. Accessed 5 Nov. 2022.

Goldman, Emma. "Anarchism: What It Really Stands For." *Anarchism and Other Essays*, by Emma Goldman, Mother Earth, 1911, *Anarchist Library*, 15 Feb. 2009, http://theanarchistlibrary.org/library/emma-goldman-anarchism-and-other-essays#toc3.

Gonzáles-Berry, Erlinda, and Tey Diana Rebolledo. "Growing Up Chicano: Tomás Rivera and Sandra Cisneros." *International Studies in Honor of Tomás Rivera*, edited by Julián Olivares, Arte Público Press, 1986, pp. 109–20.

González, William H. Review of *. . . y no se lo tragó la tierra*, by Tomás Rivera. *Modern Language Journal*, vol. 57, no. 4, 1973, p. 229.

González Acosta, Alejandro. *El enigma de Jicoténcal: Dos estudios sobre el héroe de Tlaxcala*. Instituto Tlaxcalteca de Cultura, 1997.

Grijalva, Joshua. *A History of Mexican Baptists in Texas, 1881–1891*. Baptist General Convention of Texas, 1982.

Guidotti-Hernández, Nicole M. "Borderlands." *Keywords for Latina/o Studies Book*, edited by Deborah R. Vargas, Nancy Raquel Mirabal, and Lawrence La Fountain-Stokes, New York UP, pp. 21–24.

Guidotti-Hernández, Nicole M. "Borderlands Scholarship for the Twenty-First Century." *American Quarterly*, vol. 68, no. 2, 2016, pp. 487–98.

Gustafson, Sandra M. *Eloquence Is Power: Oratory and Performance in Early America*. U of North Carolina P, 2000.

Gutiérrez, José Angel. *Albert A. Peña Jr.: Dean of Chicano Politics*. Michigan State UP, 2017.

Gutiérrez, José Angel. *A Chicano Manual on How to Handle Gringos*. Arte Público Press, 2003.

Gutiérrez, José Angel. *A Gringo Manual on How to Handle Mexicans*. 1974. Rev. and exp. ed., Arte Público Press, 2001.

Gutiérrez, José Angel. *The Making of a Chicano Militant: Lessons from Cristal*. U of Wisconsin P, 1998.

Gutiérrez, José Angel. *The Making of a Civil Rights Leader*. Arte Público Press, 2005.

Gutiérrez, José Angel, translator and editor. *They Called Me "King Tiger": My Struggle for the Land and Our Rights*. By Reies López Tijerina, Arte Público Press, 2000.

Gutiérrez, José Angel. *We Won't Back Down: Severita Lara's Rise from Student Leader to Mayor*. Arte Público Press, 2005.

Gutiérrez-Jones, Carl. *Rethinking the Borderlands: Between Chicano Culture and Legal Discourse*. U of California P, 1995.

Gutiérrez-Witt, Laura. "Cultural Continuity in the Face of Change: Hispanic Printers." *Recovering the U. S. Hispanic Literary Heritage*, vol. 11, edited by Erlinda Gonzáles-Berry and Chuck Tatum, Arte Público Press, 1996, pp. 260–78.

Habermas, Jürgen. *The Structural Transformation of the Public Sphere*. MIT P, 1991.

Harrison, George. *The I.W.W. Trial: Story of the Greatest Trial in Labor's History by One of the Defendants*. Arno Press, 1969.

Hart, John M. *Anarchism and the Mexican Working Class, 1860–1931*. U of Texas P, 1978.

Hedrick, Trace. "Of Indians and Modernity." *Review of International American Studies/Revue d'Études Américaines Internationales*, vol. 5, nos. 3–4, 2011–12, pp. 101–28.

Hermans, Hub. "Hacia una Lectura Deconstructivista de la Narrativa de Rolando Hinojosa." *Actas Irvine 92: Asociación Internacional de Hispanistas*, vol. 5, edited by Juan Villegas, University of California, Irvine, 1994, pp. 363–69.

Hernández, Guillermo E. *Chicano Satire: A Study in Literary Culture*. U of Texas P, 1991.

Hinojosa-Smith, Rolando. *Becky and Her Friends*. Arte Público Press, 1990.

Hinojosa-Smith, Rolando. *Dear Rafe / Mi querido Rafa*. Arte Público Press, 2005.

Hinojosa-Smith, Rolando. *Fair Gentlemen of Belken County / Claros varones de Belken*. Arte Público Press, 2015.

Hinojosa-Smith, Rolando. *Klail City*. Arte Público Press, 1987.

Hinojosa-Smith, Rolando. "The Other American Literatures." *Old Southwest / New Southwest: Essays on a Region and Its Literature*, edited by Judy Nolte Lensink, Tucson Public Library, 1987, pp. 17–24.

Hinojosa-Smith, Rolando. *Partners in Crime*. Arte Público Press, 2011.

Hinojosa-Smith, Rolando. *Rites and Witnesses*. Arte Público Press, 1982.

Hinojosa-Smith, Rolando. "This Writer's Sense of Place." *A Voice of My Own: Essays and Stories*, by Rolando Hinojosa-Smith, Arte Público Press, 2011, pp. 9–16.

Hinojosa-Smith, Rolando. "A Voice of One's Own." *A Voice of My Own: Essays and Stories*, by Rolando Hinojosa-Smith, Arte Público Press, 2011, pp. 1–8.

Hoffnung-Garskof, Jesse. "The Migrations of Arturo Schomburg: On Being Antillano, Negro, and Puerto Rican in New York, 1891–1938." *Journal of American Ethnic History*, vol. 21, no. 1, 2001, pp. 3–49.

Hoffnung-Garskof, Jesse. *Racial Migrations: New York City and the Revolutionary Politics of the Spanish Caribbean*. Princeton UP, 2019.

Hoffnung-Garskof, Jesse. "To Abolish the Law of Castes: Merit, Manhood and the Problem of Colour in the Puerto Rican Liberal Movement, 1873–92." *Social History*, vol. 36, no. 3, 2011, pp. 312–42.

Hoffnung-Garskof, Jesse. "The World of Arturo Alfonso Schomburg." *The Afro-Latin@ Reader*, edited by Miriam Jiménez-Román and Juan Flores, Duke UP, 2010, pp. 70–91.

Irwin, Robert McKee. "Almost-Latino Literature: Approaching Truncated Latinidades." *The Latino Nineteenth Century*, edited by Rodrigo Lazo and Jesse Alemán, New York UP, 2016, pp. 110–23.

I.W.W. Prisoners Just Before Surrendering at Federal Penitentiary, Leavenworth, Kan. Photograph, c. 1920–25, negative no. UW11383, Industrial Workers of the World photograph collection (PH Coll 922), University of Washington Libraries, Special Collections, https://digitalcollections.lib.washington.edu/digital/collection/social/id/485/.

Jamieson, Stuart. *Labor Unionism in American Agriculture*. Arno Press, 1976.

Kanellos, Nicolás. "An Early Feminist Call to Action: 'Manifiesto a la Mujer,' by Blanca de Moncaleano." *Latino Studies*, vol. 11, no. 4, 2013, pp. 587–97.

Kanellos, Nicolás. "*El Clamor Público*: Resisting the American Empire." *California History*, vol. 84, no. 2, 2006–7, pp. 10–18, 69–70.

Kanellos, Nicolás. "Envisioning and Re-Visioning the Nation: Latino Intellectual Traditions." *National Park Service*, "American Latino Theme Study: Intellectual Traditions," https://www.nps.gov/articles/latinothemeintellectual.htm. Accessed 5 Nov. 2022.

Kanellos, Nicolás, editor. *Greenwood Encyclopedia of Latino Literature*. Greenwood Press, 2008. 3 vols.

Kanellos, Nicolás. *Hispanic Firsts: 500 Years of Extraordinary Achievement*. Gale, 1997.

Kanellos, Nicolás. "Hispanic Intellectuals Publishing in the Nineteenth-Century United Status: From Political Tracts in Support of Independence to Commercial Publishing Ventures." *Hispania*, vol. 88, no. 4, 2005, pp. 687–92.

Kanellos, Nicolás. "Orality and Hispanic Literature of the United States." *Redefining American Literary History*, edited by A. LaVonne Brown Ruoff and Jerry W. Ward, Modern Language Association, 1991, pp. 115–23.

Kanellos, Nicolás. "Recovering the US Hispanic Literary Heritage." *PMLA*, vol. 127, no. 2, 2012, pp. 371–74.

Kanellos, Nicolás. "Sotero Figueroa: Writing Afro-Caribbeans into History in the Late Nineteenth Century." *The Latino Nineteenth Century*, edited by Rodrigo Lazo and Jesse Alemán, New York UP, 2016, pp. 323–40.

Kanellos, Nicolás. "Spanish-Language Anarchist Periodicals in Early Twentieth-Century United States." *Dissent on the Page*, edited by James Danky and Caroline F. Sloat, U of Wisconsin P, 2015, pp. 59–84.

Kanellos, Nicolás, and Helvetia Martell. *Hispanic Periodicals in the United States: A Brief History and Comprehensive Bibliography*. Arte Público Press, 2000.

Karrer, Wolfgang. "Realism and Real Estate in Rolando Hinojosa's Klail City Death Trip Series." *Perspectivas transatlánticas en la literatura chicana: Ensayos y cre-*

atividad, edited by María Herrera-Sobek, Francisco Lomelí, and Juan Antonio Perles Rochel, Universidad de Málaga, 2002, pp. 167–80.

Kaup, Monika. *Rewriting North American Borders in Chicano and Chicana Narrative*. Peter Lang, 2001.

King, Rosemary A. *Border Confluences: Borderland Narratives from the Mexican War to the Present*. U of Arizona P, 2004.

Klotz, Sarah, and Carl Whithaus. "Gloria Anzaldúa's Rhetoric of Ambiguity and Antiracist Teaching." *Composition Studies*, vol. 43, no. 2, 2015, pp. 72–91.

Koegeler-Abdi, Martina. "Shifting Subjectivities: Mestizas, Nepantleras, and Gloria Anzaldúa's Legacy." *MELUS*, vol. 38, no. 2, 2013, pp. 71–88.

Kushner, Sam. *Long Road to Delano: A Century of Farmworkers' Struggle*. International, 1975.

"La Expulsión de Moncaleano." *Regeneración*, 5 Oct. 1912.

Lamas, Carmen A. *The Latino Continuum and the Nineteenth-Century Americas: Literature, Translation, and Historiography*. Oxford UP, 2021.

Laó-Montes, Agustín. "Afro-Latinidades and the Diasporic Imaginary." *Iberoamericana*, vol. 5, no. 17, 2005, pp. 117–30.

Lazo, Rodrigo. *Letters from Filadelfia: Early Latino Literature and the Trans-American Elite*. U of Virginia P, 2020.

Lazo, Rodrigo. *Writing to Cuba: Filibustering and Cuban Exiles in the United States*. U of North Carolina P, 2005.

Leal, Luis, and Rodolfo Cortina. "Introducción." *Jicoténcal*, by Félix Varela, edited by Luis Leal and Rodolfo Cortina, Arte Público Press, 1995, pp. vii–xlvii.

Lemoine Villicaña, Ernesto. *Morelos: su vida revolucionaria a través de sus escritos y de otros testimonios de la época*. Universidad Nacional Autónoma de México, 1965.

Leroy, Constant. *Los misterios del anarquismo. El asesinato de Ferrer*. Uploaded by Kclibertaria, *Issuu*, 11 Dec. 2014, https://issuu.com/kclibertaria/docs/los_misterios_del_anarquismo_-_cons.

Limón, José. "Border Literary Histories, Globalization, and Critical Regionalism." *American Literary History*, vol. 20, nos. 1–2, 2008, pp. 160–82.

Lioi, Anthony. "The Best-Loved Bones: Spirit and History in Anzaldua's 'Entering into the Serpent.'" *Feminist Studies*, vol. 34, nos. 1–2, 2008, pp. 73–98.

Lizárraga, Sylvia. "The Patriarchal Ideology in 'La noche que se que se apagaron las luces.'" *International Studies in Honor of Tomás Rivera*, edited by Julián Olivares, Arte Público Press, 1986, pp. 90–95.

Lockey, Joseph B. "The Florida Intrigues of José Alvarez de Toledo." *Florida Historical Society Quarterly*, vol. 12, 1934, pp. 145–78.

Lomas, Clara. "The Articulation of Gender in the Mexican Borderlands, 1900–1915." *Recovering the US Hispanic Literary Heritage*, edited by Ramón Gutiérrez and Genaro Padilla, Arte Público Press, 1993, pp. 293–308.

Lomas, Laura. "On the 'Shock' of Diaspora: Lourdes Casal's Critical Interdisciplinarity and Intersectional Feminism." *Cuban Studies*, vol. 46, 2019, pp. 10–38.

López, Dennis. "Good-Bye Revolution—Hello Cultural Mystique: Quinto Sol Publications and Chicano Literary Nationalism." *MELUS*, vol. 35, no. 3, 2010, pp. 183–210.

López Portillo Tostado, Felícitas. *Tres intelectuales de la derecho hispanoamericana: Alberto María Carreño, Nemesio García Naranjo, Jesús Guisa y Azevedo*. Universidad Nacional Autónoma de México Centro de Investigaciones sobre América Latina y el Caribe, 2012.

"Luigi Galleani." *Sources Select Resources*, http://www.sources.com/SSR/Docs/SSRW-Galleani_Luigi.htm. Accessed 5 Nov. 2022.

Martí, José. *Obras completas*. Editorial Nacional de Cuba, 1975. 29 vols.

Martin, Alberto, Vladimiro Muñoz, and Federica Montseny. *Breve historia del movimiento anarquista en Estados Unidos de América del Norte*. Ediciones Cultura Obrera, c. 1973.

Martínez-Salanova Sánchez, Enrique. "Francisco Ferrer i Guardia: Una Educación Libre, Solidaria, que Lucha contra la Injusticia." *Portal de la educomunicación*, http://www.uhu.es/cine.educacion/figuraspedagogia/0_ferrerguardia.htm. Accessed 5 Nov. 2022.

Martín-Rodríguez, Manuel. *Life in Search of Readers: Reading (in) Chicano/a Literature*. U of New Mexico P, 2003.

Martín-Rodríguez, Manuel. "Reading, from *Don Quijote de La Mancha* to *The House on Mango Street*: Chicano/a Literature, Mimesis, and the Reader." *Spanish Perspectives on Chicano Literature: Literary and Cultural Essays*, edited by Jesús Rosales and Vanessa Fonseca, Ohio State UP, 2017, pp. 19–34.

Matos, Félix V. "Introduction." *A Nation of Women: An Early Feminist Speaks Out / Mi opinión sobre las libertades, derechos y deberes de la mujer*, by Luisa Capetillo, Arte Público Press, 2004, vii–li.

Matovina, Tim M., and Gerald E. Poyo, editors. *Presente! US Latino Catholics from Colonial Origins to the Present*. Orbis Books, 2000.

McKnight, Joseph. *The Spanish Elements in Modern Texas Law*. J. W. McKnight, 1979.

McWilliams, Carey. *North from Mexico: The Spanish-Speaking People of the United States*. Lippincott, 1949.

Medina, Rubén. "El mestizaje a través de la frontera: Vasconcelos y Anzaldúa." *Estudios Mexicanos / Mexican Studies*, vol. 5, no. 1, 2009, pp. 101–23.

Meehan, Kevin. "Martí, Schomburg y la cuestión racial en las Américas." *Afro-Hispanic Review*, vol. 25, no. 2, 2006, pp. 73–88.

Meléndez, Gabriel. *So All Is Not Lost: The Poetics of Print in Nuevomexicano Communities, 1834–1958*. U of New Mexico P, 1997.

Menton, Seymour. Review of . . . *y no se lo tragó la tierra*, by Tomás Rivera. *Latin American Literary Review*, vol. 1, no. 1, 1972, pp. 111–15.

Meyer, Doris. *Speaking for Themselves: Neomexicano Cultural Identity and the Spanish-Language Press, 1880–1920*. U of New Mexico P, 1996.

Mier Noriega y Guerra, José Servando Teresa de. *Historia de la revolución de Nueva España*. London, 1813.

Miquel I Vergés, Josép María. *Diccionario de insurgentes*. Editorial Porrúa, 1969.

Moncaleano, Blanca de. *Blanca de Moncaleano y el triunfo de la anarquía*. La Valija del Fuego Editorial, 2022.

Moncaleano, Blanca de. "Manifiesto a la Mujer." *Fraternidad*, Sept. 1915.

Mormino, Gary A., and George E. Pozzetta. "Spanish Anarchists in Tampa, Florida, 1886–1931." *"Struggle a Hard Battle": Essays on Working-Class Immigrants*, edited by Dirk Hoerder, Northern Illinois UP, 1986, pp. 170–98.

Neate, Wilson. "The Function of Belken County in the Fiction of Rolando Hinojosa: The Voicing of the Chicano Experience." *Americas Review*, vol. 18, no. 1, 1990, pp. 92–102.

Novoa, Adriana. "Places of Resistance, Bodies of Assimilation: Spanish American History in Gloria Anzaldúa's Thought." *Interamerican Journal of Philosophy*, vol. 5, no. 1, 2014, pp. 101–25.

Olivares, Julián, editor. *International Studies in Honor of Tomás Rivera*. Arte Público Press, 1986.

Oropeza, Lorena. "*Viviendo y luchando*: The Life and Times of Enriqueta Vásquez." *Enriqueta Vásquez and the Chicano Movement: Writings from El Grito del Norte*, edited by Lorena Oropeza and Dionne Espinoza, Arte Público Press, 2006, xix–liii.

Orozco, Cynthia E. *Pioneer of Mexican American Civil Rights: Alonso S. Perales*. Arte Público Press, 2022.

Paccacerqua, Cynthia M. "Gloria Anzaldúa's Affective Logic of *Volverse Una*." *Hypatia*, vol. 31, no. 2, 2016, pp. 334–51.

Park, Robert E. *The Immigrant Press and Its Control*. Harper and Brothers, 1922.

Partridge, Cameron. "'Scotch-Taped Together': Anti-'Androgyny' Rhetoric, Transmisogyny, and the Transing of Religious Studies." *Journal of Feminist Studies in Religion*, vol. 34, no. 1, 2018, pp. 68–75.

Perales, Alonso S. "Alonso S. Perales on the Ideals of Mexican Americans." *Testimonio: A Documentary History of the Mexican American Civil Rights Struggle*, edited by F. Arturo Rosales, Arte Público Press, 2000, p. 167.

Pérez, Emma. *The Decolonial Imaginary: Writing Chicanas into History*. Indiana UP, 1999.

Pérez, Emma. "Gloria Anzaldúa: La Gran Nueva Mestiza Theorist, Writer, Activist-Scholar." *NWSA Journal*, vol. 17, no. 2, 2005, pp. 1–10.

Pernicoe, Nunzio. "Luigi Galleani and Italian Anarchist Terrorism in the United States." *Terrorism: Critical Concepts in Political Science*, vol. 1, edited by David C. Rapoport, Routledge, 2006, pp. 189–210.

Pineda-Madrid, Nancy. "Celebrating Our Latina Feminist Foremothers: A Response to Elisabeth Schüüssler Fiorenza." *Journal of Feminist Studies in Religion*, vol. 27, no. 1, 2011, pp. 110–14.

Piñero de Rivera, Flor, editor. *Arturo Schomburg: Un puertorriqueño descubre el legado histórico del negro, sus escritos anotados y apéndices*. Centro de Estudios de Puerto Rico y el Caribe, 1989.

Regencia de Urgell. File, 1822–23, Biblioteca Nacional de España.

Rice, William B. *The Los Angeles Star, 1851–1864*. Greenwood Press, 1947.

Rieff, David. "Professional Aztecs and Popular Culture." *New Perspectives Quarterly*, vol. 8, no. 1, 1991, pp. 42–46.

Rieu-Millán, Marie-Laure. "Fray Servando de Mier en Londres y Miguel Ramos de Arispe en Cádiz (su actividad política y propagandística según una carta inédita de Mier, 1812)." *Anuario de Estudios Americanos*, vol. 46, no. 2, 1989, pp. 55–73.

Riva Palacio López, Antonio, Estela Guadalupe Jiménez Codinach, and Ma. Teresa Franco González Salas, *Pliegos de la diplomacia insurgente*. Senado de la República, 1987.

Rivera, John Michael. "Introduction." *Journey to the United States of North America*, by Lorenzo de Zavala, Arte Público Press, 2005, pp. vii–xxix.

Rivera, Tomás. *This Migrant Earth*. Translated by Rolando Hinojosa, Arte Público Press, 1986.

Rivera, Tomás. *Tomás Rivera: The Complete Works*. Edited by Julián Olivares, Arte Público Press, 1992.

Rodríguez del Pino, Salvador. *La novela chicana escrita en español*. Bilingual Press, 1982.

Rodríguez O., Jaime E. *The Emergence of Spanish America: Vicente Rocafuerte and Spanish Americanism, 1808–1832*. U of California P, 1975.

Rojas, Antonio. "Un Hombre de Carácter." *Regeneración*, 28 Sept. 1912.

Romo, Ricardo. *East Los Angeles: History of a Barrio*. U of Texas P, 1983.

Rosales, F. Arturo. *Chicano! The History of the Mexican American Civil Rights Movement*. Arte Público Press, 1997.

Rosales, F. Arturo. *Dictionary of Latino Civil Rights History*. Arte Público Press, 2006.

Ruiz de Burton, María Amparo. *Who Would Have Thought It?* 1872. Edited by Amelia Maria de la L. Montes, Penguin Classics, 2009.

Saavedra, Cinthya M., and Ellen D. Nymark. "Borderland-*Mestizaje* Feminism: The New Tribalism." *Handbook of Critical and Indigenous Methodologies*, edited by Norma K. Denzin, Yvonna S. Lincoln, and Linda Tuhiwai Smith, Gage, 2008, pp. 255–76.

Saldaña-Portillo, María Josefina. *Indian Given: Racial Geographies Across Mexico and the United States*. Duke UP, 2016.

Saldívar, José David. *The Dialectics of Our America: Genealogy, Cultural Critique, and Literary History*. Duke UP, 1991.

Saldívar, José David. "Rolando Hinojosa's Klail City Death Trip: A Critical Introduction." *The Rolando Hinojosa Reader: Essays Historical and Critical*, edited by José David Saldívar, Arte Público Press, 1985, pp. 44–63.

Saldívar-Hull, Sonia. "Introduction to the Second Edition." *Borderlands/La Frontera*, by Gloria Anzaldúa, Aunt Lute Books, 1999, pp. 1–15.

Sánchez, Rosaura. "Dismantling the Colossus: Martí and Ruiz de Burton on the Formulation of Anglo America." *José Martí's "Our América": From National to Hemispheric Cultural Studies*, edited by Jeffrey Belnap and Raúl Fernández, Duke UP, 1998, 115–28.

Sandoval, Moisés, editor. *Fronteras: A History of the Latin American Church in the USA Since 1513*. Mexican American Cultural Center, 1983.

Schomburg, Arthur A. "The Economic Contribution by the Negro to America." *Papers of the American Negro Academy*, 1915, *Project Gutenberg*, 21 Feb. 2011, https://www.gutenberg.org/files/35352/35352-h/35352-h.html.

Schomburg, Arthur A. "The Negro Digs Up His Past." *The Norton Anthology of Latino Literature*, edited by Ilan Stavans, Norton, 2011, pp. 372–77.

Schomburg, Arthur A. "Racial Integrity." *The Afro-Latin@ Reader: History and Culture in the United States*, edited by Miriam Jiménez Román and Juan Flores, Duke UP, 2010, pp. 67–69.

Shaffer, Kirwin R. *Black Flag Boricuas: Anarchism, Antiauthoritarianism, and the Left in Puerto Rico, 1897–1921*. U of Illinois P, 2013.

Sinnette, Elinor Des Verney. *Arthur Alfonso Schomburg, Black Bibliophile and Collector: A Biography*. New York Public Library, 1989.

Sommers, Joseph. "From the Critical Premise to the Product: Critical Modes and Their Applications to a Chicano Literary Text." *New Scholar*, vol. 6, 1977, pp. 67–75.

Spell, Jefferson Rea. "An Illustrious Spaniard in Philadelphia, Valentín de Foronda." *Hispanic Review*, vol. 4, no. 2, 1936, pp. 136–40.

Spell, Lota M. *Pioneer Printer: Samuel Bangs in Mexico and Texas*. U of Texas P, 1963.

"'The Spirit That Moves Us': A Profile of Arthur A. Schomburg." *Journal—Schomburg Center for Research in Black Culture*, vol. 1, no. 2, 1977, pp. 1–19.

Stefano, Onofre di. "*Venimos a Luchar*: Brief History of *La Prensa*'s Founding." *Aztlán*, vol. 16, nos. 1–2, 1985, pp. 95–118.

Stevens-Arroyo, Anthony M., and Ana María Díaz-Stevens. "Religious Faith and Institutions in the Forging of Latino Identities." *Handbook of Hispanic Culture in the United States: Sociology*, edited by Félix Padilla, Arte Público Press, 1994, pp. 257–92.

Strickland, Barbara. "Crossing Literary Borders." *Austin Chronicle*, 29 Aug. 1997.

Sueiro Seoane, Susana. "El asesinato de Canalejas y los anarquistas españoles en Estados Unidos." *El nacimiento del terrorismo en Occidente: Anarquía, nihilismo y violencia revolucionaria*, edited by Juan Avilés Farré and Angel Herrerín López, Siglo XX, 2008, pp. 159–88.

Sueiro Seoane, Susana. "Spanish-Speaking Anarchists in the United States: The Newspaper *Cultura Obrera* and Its Transnational Networks (1911–1927)." *Writing Revolution: Hispanic Anarchism in the United States*, U of Illinois P, 2019, pp. 86–102.

Toledo, Josefina. *Sotero Figueroa, Editor de Patria*. Editorial Letras Cubanas, 1985.

Tovar, Inés Hernández. *Sara Estela Ramírez: The Early Twentieth-Century Mexican Poet*. U of Houston, PhD dissertation, 1984.

Trejo, Arnulfo D. "As We See Ourselves in Chicano Literature." *The Chicanos: As We See Ourselves*, edited by Arnulfo D. Trejo, Arizona UP, 1979, pp. 187–211.

Trelles, Carlos M. *Un precursor de la independencia de Cuba: Don José Alvarez de Toledo*. Academia de la Historia de Cuba, 1926.

"Valle, Adrián del." *Diccionario de la Literatura Cubana, Biblioteca Virtual Miguel de Cervantes*, https://www.cervantesvirtual.com/obra-visor/diccionario-de-la-literatura-cubana--0/html/. Accessed 5 Nov. 2022.

Valle-Ferrer, Norma. *Luisa Capetillo: Pioneer Puerto Rican Feminist (Nuestra Voz)*. Peter Lang, 2006.

Varela, Félix. *Jicoténcal*. Edited by Luis Leal and Rodolfo Cortina, Arte Público Press, 1995.

Varela, Félix. *Letters to Elpidio*. Edited by Felipe J. Estévez, Paulist Press, 1989.

Vargas Valdéz, Jesús. "La Fragua de los Tiempos." Paper presented 20 June 2010, Chihuahua, Mexico.

Vásquez, Enriqueta. *Enriqueta Vásquez and the Chicano Movement: Writings from El Grito del Norte*. Edited by Dionne Espinoza and Lorena Oropeza, Arte Público Press, 2006.

Vega, Bernardo. *Memoirs of Bernardo Vega: A Contribution to the History of the Puerto Rican Community in New York*. Edited by César Andreu Iglesias, Monthly Review Press, 1984.

Vera-Rojas, María Teresa. "Betances Jaeger, Clotilde." *Greenwood Encyclopedia of Latino Literature*, vol. 1, edited by Nicolás Kanellos, Greenwood Press, 2008, p. 48.

Vogeley, Nancy. *The Bookrunner: A History of Inter-American Relations—Print, Politics, and Commerce in the United States and Mexico*. American Philosophical Society, 2011.

A Walking Tour: Mexican Revolution Sites in El Paso and Juarez. Uploaded by faculty.utep.edu, *Yumpu*, 2 Nov. 2013, https://www.yumpu.com/en/document/view/9648775/.

Warner, Michael. *The Letters of the Republic: Publication and the Public Sphere in Eighteenth-Century America*. Harvard UP, 1992.

Warren, Harris Gaylord. *The Sword Was Their Passport: A History of American Filibustering in the Mexican Revolution*. Louisiana State UP, 1943.

Wells, Elizabeth H. "Diary of José Gutiérrez de Lara." *American Historical Review*, vol. 34, no. 1, 1928, pp. 55–77; vol. 34, no. 2, 1929, pp. 281–94.

Zaccaria, Paola. "Impact of Anzaldua's Border Poetics and Thinking on Mediterranean Areas Crossed by Migration." *Signs*, vol. 37, no. 1, 2011, pp. 10–18.

Zamora, Emilio. "Chicano Socialist Labor Activity in Texas, 1900–1920." *Aztlán: Chicano Journal of the Social Sciences and the Arts*, vol. 6, no. 2, 1975, pp. 221–38.

Zamora, Emilio. *El movimiento obrero mexicano en el sur de Texas, 1900–1920*. Secretaría de Educación Pública, 1986.

Zavala, Lorenzo de. *Journey to the United States of North America / Viaje a los Estados Unidos del Norte América*. Edited by John Michael Rivera, Arte Público Press, 2005.

Zilles, Klaus. "Cultura y memoria oral en la comunidad chicana de Rolando Hinojosa." *Revista Aleph*, 10 Aug. 2008. https://revistaaleph.com.co/index.php/component/k2/item/200-cultura-y-memoria-oral-en-la-comunidad-chicana-de-rolando-hinojosa.

Zimmer, Kenyon. *"The Whole World Is Our Country": Immigration and Anarchism in the United States, 1885–1940*. University of Pittsburgh, PhD dissertation, 2010.

INDEX

ABOUT THE AUTHOR

Nicolás Kanellos is Brown Foundation Professor of Hispanic Literature at the University of Houston, where he directs Arte Público Press and the Recovering the US Hispanic Literary Heritage project. His *A History of Hispanic Theatre in the United States: Origins to 1940* (1990) received two book awards. Other books include *Hispanic Literature of the United States: A Comprehensive Reference* (2003), which was named an Outstanding Academic Book by *Choice*, and *Hispanic Immigrant Literature: El Sueño del Retorno* (2011), winner of the PEN Southwest Award for Nonfiction.